CAMBRIDGE LIBRAR

Books of enduring scho

Philosophy

This series contains both philosophical texts and critical essays about philosophy, concentrating especially on works originally published in the eighteenth and nineteenth centuries. It covers a broad range of topics including ethics, logic, metaphysics, aesthetics, utilitarianism, positivism, scientific method and political thought. It also includes biographies and accounts of the history of philosophy, as well as collections of papers by leading figures. In addition to this series, primary texts by ancient philosophers, and works with particular relevance to philosophy of science, politics or theology, may be found elsewhere in the Cambridge Library Collection.

Conversations of Goethe with Eckermann and Soret

Originally published by Goethe's friend and personal secretary, Johann Peter Eckermann (1792–1854), in German in 1836, this work comprises Eckermann's recollections of his conversations with the German writer and philosopher during the last nine years of his life. Eckermann published a further volume in 1848 using both his own memories and material from the journals of Swiss scientist Frédéric Soret, who was also a close acquaintance of Goethe. The work initially sold poorly in Germany, but quickly became popular internationally, and contributed to the rehabilitation of Goethe's scholarly reputation both within Germany and throughout the world. This edition, translated by British playwright and translator John Oxenford (1812–77) was published in two volumes in London in 1850. Oxenford combined the original three volumes, putting the conversations in chronological order. The topics discussed include religion, politics, literature, poetry and natural sciences. Volume 1 covers the years 1822 to 1827.

Cambridge University Press has long been a pioneer in the reissuing of out-of-print titles from its own backlist, producing digital reprints of books that are still sought after by scholars and students but could not be reprinted economically using traditional technology. The Cambridge Library Collection extends this activity to a wider range of books which are still of importance to researchers and professionals, either for the source material they contain, or as landmarks in the history of their academic discipline.

Drawing from the world-renowned collections in the Cambridge University Library, and guided by the advice of experts in each subject area, Cambridge University Press is using state-of-the-art scanning machines in its own Printing House to capture the content of each book selected for inclusion. The files are processed to give a consistently clear, crisp image, and the books finished to the high quality standard for which the Press is recognised around the world. The latest print-on-demand technology ensures that the books will remain available indefinitely, and that orders for single or multiple copies can quickly be supplied.

The Cambridge Library Collection will bring back to life books of enduring scholarly value (including out-of-copyright works originally issued by other publishers) across a wide range of disciplines in the humanities and social sciences and in science and technology.

Conversations of Goethe with Eckermann and Soret

VOLUME 1

JOHANN PETER ECKERMANN
TRANSLATED BY JOHN OXENFORD

CAMBRIDGE
UNIVERSITY PRESS

CAMBRIDGE UNIVERSITY PRESS

Cambridge, New York, Melbourne, Madrid, Cape Town,
Singapore, São Paolo, Delhi, Tokyo, Mexico City

Published in the United States of America by Cambridge University Press, New York

www.cambridge.org
Information on this title: www.cambridge.org/9781108040914

© in this compilation Cambridge University Press 2012

This edition first published 1850
This digitally printed version 2012

ISBN 978-1-108-04091-4 Paperback

This book reproduces the text of the original edition. The content and language reflect
the beliefs, practices and terminology of their time, and have not been updated.

Cambridge University Press wishes to make clear that the book, unless originally published
by Cambridge, is not being republished by, in association or collaboration with, or
with the endorsement or approval of, the original publisher or its successors in title.

CONVERSATIONS OF GOETHE

WITH

ECKERMANN AND SORET.

TRANSLATED FROM THE GERMAN

By JOHN OXENFORD.

IN TWO VOLUMES.

VOL. I.

LONDON:
SMITH, ELDER & CO., 65, CORNHILL.

1850.

London:
Printed by Stewart and Murray,
Old Bailey.

TRANSLATOR'S PREFACE.

ANY introduction referring to the subject of this book would be superfluous. It records the opinions, on the most varied topics, of one of the greatest literary geniuses of the present century, during the last ten years of a very long life. Goethe was born in August 1749, and died in March 1832, so that his age is seventy-three when the Conversations begin, and eighty-two when they terminate.

However, the form in which this translation is presented to the English public requires a short explanation.

In 1836, John Peter Eckermann, who gives a full account of himself in the "Introduction" (vol. i. p. 13), published, in two volumes, his "Conversations with Goethe." In 1848, he published a third volume, containing additional Conversations, which he compiled from his own notes, and from that of another friend of Goethe's, M. Soret, of whom there is a short account in the "Preface to the Third or Supplemental volume" (vol. i. p. 6). Both these works are dedicated to Her Imperial Highness Maria Paulouna, Grand-Duchess of Saxe-Weimar and Eisenach.

Had I followed the order of German publication, I should have placed the whole of the Supplementary volume after the contents of the first two; however, as the Conversations in that volume are not of a later date than the others (which, indeed, terminate with the death of Goethe), but merely supply gaps, I deemed it more conducive to the reader's convenience to re-arrange in chronological order the whole of the Conversations, as if the Supplement had not been published separately.

Still, to preserve a distinction between the Conversations of the First Book and those of the Supplement, I have marked the latter with the abbreviation " Sup.", adding an asterisk (thus, Sup.*) when a Conversation has been furnished, not by Eckermann, but by Soret.

I feel bound to state that, while translating the First Book, I have had before me the translation by Mrs. Fuller, published in America. The great merit of this version I willingly acknowledge, though the frequent omissions render it almost an abridgment. The contents of the Supplementary volume are now, I believe, published for the first time in the English language.

J. O.

CONVERSATIONS OF GOETHE

WITH

ECKERMANN.

AUTHOR'S PREFACE.

THIS collection of Conversations with Goethe took its rise chiefly from an impulse, natural to my mind, to appropriate to myself by writing any part of my experience which strikes me as valuable or remarkable.

Moreover, I felt constantly the need of instruction, not only when I first met with that extraordinary man, but also after I had lived with him for years; and I loved to seize on the import of his words, and to note it down, that I might possess them for the rest of my life.

When I think how rich and full were the communications by which he made me so happy for a period of nine years, and now observe how small a part I have retained in writing, I seem to myself like a child who, endeavouring to catch the refreshing spring shower with open hands, finds that the greater part of it runs through his fingers.

AUTHOR'S PREFACE.

But, as the saying is, that books have their destiny, and as this applies no less to the origin of a book than to its subsequent appearance in the broad, wide world, so may we use it with regard to the origin of this present book. Whole months often passed away, while the stars were unpropitious, and ill health, business, or various toils needful to daily existence, prevented me from writing a single line; but then again kindly stars arose, and health, leisure, and the desire to write, combined to help me a good step forwards. And then, where persons are long domesticated together, where will there not be intervals of indifference; and where is he who knows always how to prize the present at its due rate?

I mention these things to excuse the frequent and important gaps which the reader will find, if he is inclined to read the book in chronological order. To such gaps belong much that is good, but is now lost, especially many favourable words spoken by Goethe of his widely scattered friends, as well as of the works of various living German authors, while other remarks of a similar kind have been noted down. But, as I said before, books have their destinies even at the time of their origin.

For the rest, I consider that which I have succeeded in making my own in these two volumes, and which I have some title to regard as the ornament of my own existence, with deep-felt gratitude as the gift of Providence, and I have a certain confidence that the world with which I share it will also feel gratitude towards me.

I think that these conversations not only contain

AUTHOR'S PREFACE.

many valuable explanations and instructions on science, art, and practical life, but that these sketches of Goethe, taken directly from life, will be especially serviceable in completing the portrait which each reader may have formed of Goethe from his manifold works.

Still, I am far from imagining that the whole internal Goethe is here adequately portrayed. We may, with propriety, compare this extraordinary mind and man to a many-sided diamond, which in each direction shines with a different hue. And as, under different circumstances and with different persons, he became another being, so I, too, can only say, in a very modest sense, this is *my* Goethe.

And this applies not merely to his manner of presenting himself to me, but to my capacity for apprehending and reproducing him. In such cases a reflection* takes place, as in a mirror; and it is very seldom that, in passing through another individuality, nothing of the original is lost, and nothing foreign is blended. The representations of the person of Goethe by Rauch, Dawe, Stieler, and David, have all a high degree of truth, and yet each bears more or less the stamp of the individuality which produced it. If this can be said of bodily things, how much more does it apply to the fleeting, intangible objects of the mind! However it may be in my case, I trust that all those who, from mental power or personal acquaintance with Goethe, are fitted to judge, will not misinterpret my exertions to attain the greatest possible fidelity.

Having given these explanations as to the manner

* In the German "Spiegelung," but "refraction" furnishes a more adequate image.—*Trans.*

of apprehending my subject, I have still something to add as to the import of the work.

That which we call the True, even in relation to a single object, is by no means something small, narrow, limited; rather is it, even if something simple, at the same time something comprehensive, which, like the various manifestations of a deep and widely reaching natural law, cannot easily be expressed. It cannot be disposed of by a sentence, or by sentence upon sentence, or by sentence opposed to sentence, but, through all these, one attains just an approximation, not the goal itself. So, to give a single instance, Goethe's detached remarks on poetry often have an appearance of one-sidedness, and indeed often of manifest contradiction. Sometimes he lays all the stress on the material which the world affords; sometimes upon the internal nature of the poet; sometimes the only important point is the subject; sometimes the mode of treating it; sometimes all is made to depend on perfection of form; sometimes upon the spirit, with a neglect of all form.

But all these contradictions are single sides of the True, and, taken together, denote the essence of truth itself, and lead to an approximation to it. I have, therefore, been careful, in these and similar cases, not to omit these seeming contradictions, as they were elicited by different occasions, in the course of dissimilar years and hours. I rely on the insight and comprehensive spirit of the cultivated reader, who will not be led astray by any isolated part, but will keep his eye on the whole, and properly arrange and combine each particular.

Perhaps, too, the reader will find much here which at first sight seems unimportant. But if, on looking deeper, he perceive that such trifles often lead to something important, or serve as a foundation to something which comes afterwards, or contribute some slight touch to a delineation of character, these may be, if not sanctified, at least excused, as a sort of necessity.

And now I bid a loving farewell to my so long cherished book on its entrance into the world, wishing it the fortune of being agreeable, and of exciting and propagating much that is good.

WEIMAR, 31*st October* 1835.

PREFACE

TO

THIRD OR SUPPLEMENTAL VOLUME.

Now, I at last see before me this long promised third part of my Conversations with Goethe : I enjoy the pleasant sensation of having overcome great obstacles.

My case was very difficult; it was like that of a mariner who cannot sail with the wind that blows to-day, but must often patiently wait whole weeks and months for a favourable gale, such as has blown years ago. When I was so happy as to write my first two parts, I could sail with a fair wind, because the freshly-spoken words were then still ringing in my ears, and the living intercourse with that wonderful man sustained me in an element of inspiration, through which I felt borne, as if on wings, to my goal.

But now when that voice has been hushed for many years, and the happiness of those personal interviews lies so far behind me, I could attain the needful inspiration only in those hours in which it was granted me to enter into my own interior, and, in undisturbed reverie, to give a fresh colouring to the past, where it began to revive within me, and I saw great thoughts, and great characteristic traits before me, like mountains; distant indeed, but, nevertheless, plainly discernible, and illumined as by the sun of the actual day.

Thus did my inspiration arise from my delight in that great man; the details of thought and of oral expression were again fresh, as if I had experienced them yesterday. The living Goethe was again there: I again heard the peculiarly charming sound of his voice, to which no other can compare. I saw him again in the evening, with his black frock and star, jesting, laughing, and cheerfully conversing amid the social circle in his well-lighted room. Another day, when the weather was fine, he was with me in the carriage in his brown surtout, and blue cloth cap, with his light gray cloak laid over his knees; there he was, with his countenance brown and healthy as the fresh air; his words freely flowing forth, and sounding above the noise of the wheels. Or I saw myself in the evening by the quiet taper light again transported into his study, where he sat opposite to me at his table, in his white flannel dressing-gown, mild as the impression of a well spent day. We talked about things good and great: he set before me the noblest part of his own nature, and his mind kindled my own—the most perfect harmony existed between us. He extended his hand to me across the table, and I pressed it: I then took a full glass which stood by me, and which I drank to him without uttering a word, my glances being directed into his eyes across the wine.

Thus was I again associated with him as in actual life, and his words again sounded to me as of old.

But as it is generally the case in life, that, although we can think of a dear departed one, our thoughts for weeks and months can be but transient, on account of the claims of the actual day; and that the quiet moments of such a reverie, in which we believe that we once more possess, in all its living freshness, a beloved object that we have lost, belong to a few happy hours—so was it with me with respect to Goethe.

Months often passed when my soul, engrossed by the contact of ordinary life, was dead to Goethe, and he uttered not a word to my mind. And again came other weeks and months, during which I was in a barren mood, so that nothing would bud or blossom within me. I was forced, with great patience, to let these periods of inanity pass unemployed, for anything written under such circumstances would have been worthless. I was compelled to wait for my good fortune to bestow a return of those hours when the past would stand before me in all its liveliness, and my soul would be elevated to such a degree of mental strength and sensible ease, as to be a worthy receptacle for the thoughts and feelings of Goethe; for I had to do with a hero whom I must not allow to sink. To be truly delineated he must appear in all the mildness of his disposition; in the full clearness and power of his mind; and in the accustomed dignity of his august personality—and this was no trifling requisition.

My relation to him was peculiar, and of a very intimate kind: it was that of the scholar to the master; of the son to the father; of the poor in culture to the rich in culture. He drew me into his own circle, and let me participate in the mental and bodily enjoyments of a higher state of existence. Sometimes I saw him but once a week, when I visited him in the evening; sometimes every day, when I had the happiness to dine with him either alone or in company. His conversation was as varied as his works. He was always the same, and always different. Now he was occupied by some great idea, and his words flowed forth rich and inexhaustible; they were often like a garden in spring where all is in blossom, and where one is so dazzled by the general brilliancy that one does not think of gathering a nosegay. At other times, on the contrary, he was taciturn and laconic, as if a cloud pressed upon his soul; nay, there were days when it seemed as if he were filled with icy coldness, and a keen wind was sweeping over plains of frost and snow. When one saw him again he was again like a smiling summer's day, when all the warblers of the wood joyously greet us from hedges and bushes, when the cuckoo's voice resounds through the blue sky, and the brook ripples through flowery meadows. Then it was a pleasure to hear him; his presence then had a beneficial influence, and the heart expanded at his words.

Winter and summer, age and youth, seemed with him to be engaged in a perpetual strife and change; nevertheless, it was admirable in him, when from seventy to eighty years old, that youth always recovered the ascendancy; those autumnal and wintry days I have indicated were only rare exceptions.

His self-control was great—nay, it formed a prominent peculiarity in his character. It was akin to that lofty deliberation (*Besonnenheit*) through which he always succeeded in mastering his material, and giving his single works that artistical finish which we admire in them. Through the same quality he was often concise and circumspect, not only in many of his writings, but also in his oral expressions. When, however, in happy moments, a more powerful demon* was active within him, and that self-control abandoned him, his discourse rolled forth with youthful impetuosity, like a mountain cataract. In such moments he expressed what was best and greatest in his abundant nature, and such moments are to be understood when his earlier friends say of him, that his spoken words were better than those which he wrote and printed. Thus, Marmontel said of Diderot, that whoever knew him from his writings only knew him but half; but that as soon as he became animated in actual conversation he was incomparable, and irresistibly carried his hearers along.

If, on the one hand, I may now hope that I have succeeded in preserving in these conversations much that belonged to those happy moments, it is perhaps, on the other hand, no less advantage to this book that it contains two reflections of Goethe's personality, one towards myself, the other towards a young friend.

M. Soret, of Geneva, a liberal republican, called to Weimar in the year 1822, to superintend the education of the hereditary grand-duke, remained, from that year to Goethe's death, in very close connection with him. He was a constant guest at Goethe's table, and a frequent and welcome visitor at his evening parties; moreover, his attainments in natural science offered

---

* It is almost needless to observe that the word " demon " is here used in reference to its Greek origin, and implies nothing evil.—*Trans.*

many points of contact on which to base a lasting intercourse. As a profound mineralogist he arranged Goethe's crystals, while his knowledge of botany enabled him to translate Goethe's " Metamorphosis of the Plants" into French, and thus to give a wider circulation to that important work. His position at court likewise brought him frequently into Goethe's presence, as he sometimes accompanied the prince to Goethe's house, while sometimes commissions to Goethe, from his royal highness the archduke, and her imperial highness the archduchess, gave him occasion for visits.

These personal interviews were often recorded by M. Soret in his journals ; and some years ago he was kind enough to give me a small manuscript compiled from this source, in order that I might, if I pleased, take what was best and most interesting, and introduce it into my third volume in chronological order.

These notes, which were written in French, were sometimes complete, but sometimes cursory and defective, accordingly as the author found time to make them in his hurried and often greatly occupied days. Since, however, no subject appears in his manuscript which was not repeatedly and thoroughly discussed by Goethe and myself, my own journals were perfectly adapted to complete the notes of Soret, to supply his deficiencies, and to develop sufficiently what he often had only indicated. All the conversations which are based on Soret's manuscript, or for which that manuscript has been much used, as is particularly the case in the first two years, are marked with an asterisk (*) placed against the date, to distinguish them from those which are by me alone, and which, with a few exceptions, make up the years from 1824 to 1829 (inclusive), and a great part of 1830, 1831, and 1832.

I have now nothing further to add, but the wish that this third volume, which I have so long and so fondly kept by me, will meet with that kind reception which was so abundantly accorded to the first two.

WEIMAR, 21*st December* 1847.

INTRODUCTION.

THE AUTHOR GIVES AN ACCOUNT OF HIMSELF AND HIS PARENTS, AND OF THE ORIGIN OF HIS CONNECTION WITH GOETHE.

AT Winsen on the Luhe, a little town between Lüneburg and Hamburg, on the border of the marsh and heath-lands, I was born at the beginning of the nineties, in nothing better than a hut, as we may well call a small house which had only one room capable of being heated, and no stairs, and in which they mounted at once to the hayloft by a ladder, which reached to the house-door.

As the youngest born of a second marriage, I, properly speaking, did not know my parents till they had reached an advanced age; and, to a certain extent, I grew up with them alone. Two sons of my father's first marriage were still alive. One of them, after several voyages as a sailor, had been taken prisoner in foreign parts, and had not since been heard of; while the other, after being several times engaged in the whale and seal fisheries in Greenland, had returned to Hamburg, and there lived in moderate circumstances. Two sisters of my father's second marriage had grown up before me. When I had attained my twelfth year, they had already left the parental hut, and were in service in our town and in Hamburg.

The principal means of supporting our little family was a cow, which not only supplied us with milk for our daily wants, but gave us every year a calf for fattening, and sometimes milk enough to sell for a few groschen. We had besides a piece of land, which supplied us with vegetables for the wants of the year. Corn for bread, and flour for the kitchen, we were, however, obliged to buy.

My mother was particularly expert at spinning wool; she also gave much satisfaction by the caps she made for the women of the village, and in both ways earned some money.

My father's business consisted of a small traffic, which varied according to the seasons, and obliged him to be often absent from home, and to travel on foot about the country. In summer, he was seen with a light wooden box on his back, going in the heath-country from village to village, hawking ribbons, thread, and silk. At the same time he purchased here woollen stockings and *Beyderwand** (a cloth woven out of the wool of the sheep on the heaths, and linen yarn), which he again disposed of in the *Vierlande* on the other side the Elbe, where he likewise went hawking. In the winter, he carried on a trade in rough quills and unbleached linen, which he bought up in the villages of the hut and marsh country, and took to Hamburg when a ship offered. But in all cases his gains must have been very small, as we always lived in some degree of poverty.

* *Anglice*, Linsey-woolsey.—*Trans.*

If now I am to speak of *my* employments in childhood, these varied according to the season. When spring commenced, and the waters of the Elbe had receded after their customary overflow, I went daily to collect the sedges which had been thrown upon the dykes and other places, and to heap them up as litter for our cow. But when the first green was springing over the broad meadows, I, with other boys, passed long days in watching the cows. In summer, I was actively employed on our field, and brought dry wood from the thickets scarce a mile (German) off, to serve for firing throughout the year. In harvest time, I passed weeks in the fields as a gleaner, and when the autumn winds shook the trees I gathered acorns, which I sold by the peck to persons of opulence, to feed their geese. When I was old enough, I went with my father on his travels from hamlet to hamlet, and helped to carry his bundle. This time affords some of the fairest remembrances of my youth.

Under such influences, and busied in such employments, during which, at certain periods, I attended a school, and barely learned to read and write, I reached my fourteenth year; and every one will confess, that from this situation to an intimate connection with Goethe there was a great step, and one that seemed scarcely probable. I knew not that there were in the world such things as Poetry or the Fine Arts; and, fortunately, there was not within me even so much as a blind longing and striving after them.

It has been said that animals are instructed by their very organization; and so may it be said of man, that, by something which he does quite accidentally, he is often taught the higher powers which slumber within him. Something of the sort happened to me, which, though insignificant in itself, gave a new turn to my life, and is therefore stamped indelibly on my memory.

I sat one evening with both my parents at table by the light of a lamp. My father had just returned from Hamburg, and was talking about his business there. As he loved smoking, he had brought back with him a packet of tobacco, which lay before him on the table, and had for the crest a horse. This horse seemed to me a very good picture, and, as I had by me pen, ink, and a piece of paper, I was seized with an irresistible inclination to copy it. My father continued talking about Hamburg, and I, being quite unobserved, became wholly engaged in drawing the horse. When finished, it seemed to me a perfect likeness of the original, and I experienced a delight before unknown. I showed my parents what I had done, and they could not avoid praising me and expressing admiration. I passed the night in happy excitement, and almost sleepless; I though constantly of the horse I had drawn, and longed impatiently for morning, that I might have it again before my eyes, and delight myself with beholding it.

From this time the once-excited propensity for visible imitation was never forgotten. And as I found no other help of any sort in our place, I deemed myself most happy when our neighbour, who was a potter, lent me some outlines, which served him as models for painting his plates and dishes.

These outlines I copied very carefully with pen and

ink, and thus arose two books of drawings, which soon passed from hand to hand, and at last came under the eye of the upper Bailiff (Oberamtmann), Meyer, the first man of the place. He sent for me, made me a present, and praised me in the kindest manner. He asked me if I should like to become a painter, for if so, he would, when I was confirmed, send me to a proper master at Hamburg. I said that I should like it very much, and would talk of it with my parents. They, however, who belonged to the peasant class, and lived in a place where scarce any occupations were followed except tilling and grazing, thought of a painter only as one who paints doors and houses. They, therefore, advised me earnestly against it, saying it was not only a very dirty, but a very dangerous trade, at which one might break one's legs or neck, as was indeed often the case, especially in Hamburg, where the houses are seven stories high. As my own ideas of a painter were not more elevated, I abandoned my fancy for this trade, and put quite out of my head the offer of the good Bailiff.

However, the attention of higher persons having been once bestowed on me, I was kept in sight, and efforts were made to aid me in various ways. I was permitted to take private lessons with the few children of that rank; I learned French, and a little Latin and music: I was also provided with better clothing, and the worthy superintendent, Parisius, did not disdain to give me a seat at his own table.

Henceforth, I loved school very much. I sought to make this pleasant state of things last as long as possible, and my parents readily consented that I should not be confirmed before my sixteenth year.

But now arose the question, what was to be done with me. Could I have followed my wishes, I should have been sent to pursue learned studies at a gymnasium; but this was out of the question, as I was not only destitute of means, but felt myself imperiously called upon by my circumstances to get into some situation as soon as possible, where I could not only take care of myself, but in some measure help my poor old parents.

Such a situation presented itself immediately after my confirmation, for a judicial functionary (Justizbeamter) of the place offered to take me to do copying and other little services for him, and I joyfully consented. I had, during the last year and a half of my schooling, acquired not only a good hand, but practised a great deal in composition, so that I might consider myself very well qualified for such a post. I also carried on some of the minor parts of an advocate's business, frequently drawing up both judgment and petition, according to prescribed forms: this lasted two years, viz. till 1810, when the Hanoverian office, at Winsen on the Luhe, was broken up, and the place being taken into the department of Lower Elbe, was incorporated with the French empire.

I then received an appointment in the office of direct taxes at Lüneberg, and when this also was broken up in the following year, I entered the office of the under prefect in Uelzen. Here I worked till near the end of the year 1812, when the prefect, Herr von Düring, patronized me, and made me secretary of the mayoralty at Bevensen. This post I held till the spring of 1813, when the approach of the Cossacks gave us hopes of being freed from the French yoke. I now took my leave and returned home, with no other intention than that of joining the ranks of those patriotic warriors who began secretly to form themselves in various places. This plan I carried out. Towards the end of the summer I joined as a volunteer, with rifle and holster, the Kielmannsegge Jäger corps, and in Captain Knop's company made the campaign of the winter of 1813-14, through Mecklenburg, Holstein, and before Hamburg, against Marshal Davoust. Afterwards we crossed the Rhine against General Maison, and in the summer marched about a great deal in the fertile provinces of Flanders and Brabant.

Here, at the sight of the great pictures of the Netherlands, a new world opened to me; I passed whole days in churches and museums. These were, in fact, the first pictures I ever saw in my life. I understood now what was meant by being a painter. I saw the honoured happy progress of the scholars, and I could have wept that I was not permitted to pursue a similar path. However, I took my resolution at once. I made the acquaintance of a young artist at Tournay; I obtained black crayons and a sheet of drawing-paper of the largest size, and sat down at once before a picture to copy it. My enthusiasm somewhat supplied my deficiencies in practice and instruction, and thus I succeeded in the outlines of the figures. I had also begun to shade the whole from the left side, when marching orders broke up my happy employment. I hastened to indicate the gradations of light and shade in the still unfinished parts with single letters, hoping that thus I might yet complete my work in some tranquil hour. I then rolled up my picture, and put it in a case, which I carried hanging at my back with my gun, all the long march from Tournay to Hameln.

Here, in the autumn of 1814, the Jäger corps was disbanded. I went home; my father was dead; my mother was still alive, and resided with my elder sister, who had married, and had taken possession of the paternal house. I began now to continue my drawing. I completed first the picture I had brought from Brabant; and then, as I had no proper models, I stuck to some little engravings of Ramberg's, of which I made enlarged copies in black chalk. But here I felt the want of proper knowledge and preparation. I had no idea of the anatomy either of men or animals; I knew as little how to treat properly the various kinds of trees and grounds; and it cost me unspeakable toil to make anything look decently well by my own mode of proceeding.

Thus I soon saw that, if I wished to become an artist, I must set to work in a way somewhat different, and that more of this groping about in my own way would only be lost labour. Now my plan was to find a suitable master, and begin from the very beginning.

The master whom I had in my eye was no other than Ramberg, of Hanover, and it seemed to me the more possible to stop in that city, as a beloved friend of my earlier days lived there in easy circumstances. On his friendship I could rely for my support, and he was constantly inviting me.

Without further delay, therefore, I tied up my bundle, and took, in the midst of the winter of 1815, a walk of almost forty leagues, quite alone, over the heath and through the deep snow. I arrived at Hanover in a few days, without accident.

I went immediately to Ramberg, and told him my wishes. After looking at what I laid before him, he seemed not to doubt my talent, yet he remarked that I must have bread first; that the mastery of the technical part of art demanded much time, and that the prospect of earning a subsistence by art lay at a great distance. Meanwhile, he showed himself willing to help me as much as he could; he looked up immediately, from the mass of his drawings, some suitable sheets with parts of the human body, and gave them to me to copy.

So I lived with my friend, and drew after Ramberg. I made good progress, for the drawings which he gave me were more and more advanced. I drew the whole anatomy of the human frame, and was never weary of repeating difficult hands and feet. So passed some happy months. When we came to May, however, my health began to give way; and on the approach of June my hands trembled so much that I could no longer hold a pencil.

We consulted a skilful physician, and he found my situation dangerous. He said that in consequence of the campaign, perspiration was checked, that my internals were attacked by a consuming heat, and that, if I continued a fortnight in this condition, I should inevitably be a corpse. He prescribed warm baths, and similar remedies to restore the action of the skin; cheering signs of improvement very soon appeared, but the continuation of my artistic studies was not to be thought of.

My friend had hitherto paid me the kindest care and attention; there was not the least thought or hint that I was, or could afterwards become, a burden to him. I, however, thought of it, and as the uneasiness which I had long harboured on this head had probably hastened the breaking out of my dormant illness, so did it now come forward in all its force, as I saw heavy expenses before me on account of my recovery.

At such a time of external and internal embarrassment, the prospect opened to me of an appointment, with a commission, which had for its object the clothing of the Hanoverian army, and hence it was not surprising that, renouncing the artistical path, I yielded to the pressure of circumstances, solicited the appointment, and was delighted to obtain it.

My recovery was soon complete, and a state of health and cheerfulness returned which I had not enjoyed for a long time. I found myself able, in some measure, to requite the kindness my friend had generously shown me. The novelty of the services into which I was now to be initiated gave occupation to my mind. My superiors seemed to me men of the noblest views, and with my colleagues, some of whom had made the campaign in the same corps with me, I was soon on a footing of cordial intimacy.

Being now fairly settled, I began with some freedom to look about the city, which contained much that was worth observation, and, in leisure hours, I was never weary of rambling, over and over again, about its beautiful environs. With a pupil of Ramberg's, a promising young artist, I had formed a close intimacy, and he was my constant companion in my rambles. And since I was forced to give up the practice of Art on account of my health and other circumstances, it was a great solace that I could, at least, daily converse about it with him. I took interest in his compositions, which he showed me in sketches, and about which we conversed. He introduced me to many instructive works: I read Winckelmann and Mengs; but, never having had before me the objects which they discuss, I could only imbibe generalities from their works, and received, indeed, but little benefit.

My friend, who had been born and brought up in the city, was in advance of me in every kind of mental culture, and had, what I entirely wanted, considerable acquaintance with the *belles lettres*. At that time, Theodore Körner was the venerated hero of the day. My friend brought me the "Lyre and Sword," which did not fail to make a deep impression on me, as well as others, and to excite my admiration.

Much has been said of the artistical effect of poems, and many have ranked it very high; but it seems to me that the subject-matter is, after all, the chief point. Unconsciously, I made this experience in reading the "Lyre and Sword." For that I, like Körner, had fostered in my bosom an abhorrence of those who had been our oppressors for so many years; that I, like him, had fought for our freedom, and, like him, had been familiar with all those circumstances of tedious marches, nightly bivouacs, outpost service, and skirmishes, and amid them all had been filled with thoughts and feelings similar to his: this it was which gave to these poems so deep and powerful an echo in my heart.

Since nothing of import could have an effect upon me without moving me deeply and rendering me productive, so it was with these poems of Theodore Körner. I bethought me that I too had, in childhood and the years immediately following, written little poems from time to time, without caring any more about them, because at the time I attached no great value to things so easily produced, and because a certain mental ripeness is required for appreciation of poetical talent. This talent now in Körner appeared to me as something enviable and noble, and I felt a great desire to try if I could succeed, by following him in some degree..

The return of our patriotic warriors from France afforded me a good opportunity, and, as I had fresh in my memory all the unspeakable hardships which the soldier must undergo in the field, while often no inconvenience is endured by the citizen in his comfortable home, I thought it would be good to set forth this contrast in a poem, and, by working on the feelings, to prepare for the returning troops a more cordial reception.

I had several hundred copies of this poem printed at my own expense, and distributed through the town. The effect produced was favourable beyond my expectations. It procured me a throng of very pleasant acquaintances; people sympathized with the views and feelings I had uttered, encouraged me to make similar attempts, and were generally of opinion that I had given proof of a talent which deserved further cultivation. The poem was copied into periodicals, printed, and sold separately in various places; I even had the pleasure of seeing it set to music by a very favourite composer, though, in fact, it was ill adapted for singing, on account of its length and rhetorical style.

Not a week passed now in which I was not happy enough to produce some new poem. I was now in my four-and-twentieth year: within me, a world of feelings, impulses, and good-will, was in full action; but I was entirely deficient in information and mental culture. The study of our great poets was recommended to me, especially of Schiller and Klopstock. I procured their works—I read, I admired them, without receiving much assistance from them; the path of these geniuses, though I was not aware of it at the time, being too far from the natural tendency of my own mind.

At this time, I first heard the name of Goethe, and obtained a volume of his poems. I read his songs again and again, and enjoyed a happiness which no words can express. I seemed as if I had not till now begun to wake, and attain real consciousness; it appeared to me that my own inmost soul, till then unknown even to myself, was reflected in these songs. Nowhere did I meet any learned or foreign matter beyond the reach of my own uncultivated thoughts and feelings; nowhere any names of outlandish and obsolete divinities, which to me said nothing; but, on the contrary, I found the human heart, with its desires, joys, and sorrows—I found a German nature, clear as the bright actual day—pure reality in the light of a mild glorification.

I lived whole weeks and months absorbed in these songs. Then I succeeded in obtaining "Wilhelm Meister," then "Goethe's Life," then his dramas. "Faust," from whose abysses of human nature and perdition I at first, shuddering, drew back, but whose profound enigmatical character ever attracted me again, I read always in holidays. My admiration and love increased daily; for a long time I completely lived in these works, and thought and talked of nothing but Goethe.

The advantage which we derive from studying the works of a great author may be of different kinds; but the chief benefit probably consists in this, that we become more clearly conscious, not only of our own internal nature, but also of the varied world without us. Such an effect was produced on me by the works of Goethe. I was also impelled by them to a better observation and apprehension of sensible objects and characters; I came gradually to understand the unity or internal harmony of an individual with itself, and thus the enigma of the great variety in phenomena, both of nature and art, was solved to me more and more.

After I had in some measure grounded myself in Goethe's writings, and had also made many practical attempts in poetry, I turned to some of the best writers of other countries and earlier times, and read in the best translations, not only the principal pieces of Shakspeare, but also Sophocles and Homer.

Here, however, I soon perceived that in these sublime works I could only appreciate the *generally Human* (das Allgemein-menschliche), and that the understanding of the details, both of language and history, presupposed an amount of knowledge and an education that is commonly acquired only in schools and universities.

Moreover, it was shown to me, from many sides, that I was toiling in vain by thus following my own way, and that, without what is called a classical education, a poet can never succeed either in writing his own language with elegance and expression, or, indeed, performing anything excellent even as to its import. When, too, I read many biographies of distinguished men to see what educational path they had adopted to attain to anything good, and perceived how they all went through the routine of schools and colleges, I resolved, in spite of my advanced age and the many obstacles which surrounded me, to do the same.

I forthwith applied to an eminent philologian, who had been appointed teacher in the gymnasium at Hanover, and took private instruction, not only in Latin, but also in Greek, on which studies I spent all the time which the hours (at least six a day) claimed from me by my office would afford me.

Thus I passed a year. I made good progress, but with my excessive ardour it seemed to me that I went on too slowly, and must devise some other plan. I thought that if I could pass four or five hours daily in the gymnasium, and thus live altogether in a learned atmosphere, I should progress in quite another fashion, and attain my end infinitely sooner.

In this opinion I was confirmed by the advice of competent persons; I therefore resolved to carry out my scheme, and easily obtained the consent of my superiors; for the hours of the gymnasium chiefly fell in a part of the day when I was disengaged.

I therefore applied for admission; and, accompanied by my teacher, went on a Sunday forenoon to the worthy director to go through the requisite probation. He examined me with all possible kindness; but as I was not prepared for the traditional school questions, and with all my industry lacked the proper routine, I did not stand so well as I really ought to have done. However, on the assurance of my teacher that I knew more than appeared from my examination, and, in consideration of my uncommon ardour, the director placed me in the second class.

I need hardly say that a man of nearly twenty-five, and one already employed in the king's service, made but an odd figure among scholars who were, for the most part, mere boys, and that my situation was at first rather strange and unpleasant; but my great thirst for knowledge enabled me to overlook and endure everything. And, on the whole, I had no cause for complaint. The tutors esteemed me; the elder and better scholars of the class treated me in the most friendly manner, and even the most mischievous had forbearance enough not to play their tricks on me.

I was thus, on the whole, very happy in the attainment of my object, and proceeded with great zeal in this new path. I woke at five in the morning, and soon set about preparing my lessons. About eight I went to the school, and staid till ten. Thence I hastened to my office, where my attendance was required till one. I then flew home, swallowed a little dinner, and was again at school soon after one. The hours then lasted till four, after which I was occupied in my office till seven, and devoted the remainder of the evening to preparation and private instruction.

Thus I lived some months; but my strength was unequal to such exertion, and the ancient saying, "No man can serve two masters," was confirmed. Want of free air and exercise, and of time and quiet for eating, drinking, and sleep, gradually reduced me to an unhealthy state; I found myself paralyzed both in body and mind, and saw that I must, as a matter of necessity, give up either the school or my office. As my subsistence depended on the latter, I had only the former alternative, and again left the school in the beginning of the spring of 1817. As I saw it was my destiny to make many trials, I did not repent that I had also made trial of a learned school.

Indeed, I had advanced a good step; and as I still had the university in view, there was no course left me but to go on with my private instruction, which I did with the greatest ardour.

After getting rid of the burden of the winter, I the more cheerfully enjoyed the spring and summer. I was much in the open country, which this year spoke with peculiar sympathy to my heart, and many poems were produced; Goethe's juvenile songs were floating as a high example before my eyes.

On the commencement of winter, I began seriously to think how it would be possible to enter the university, at least within a year. I was so far advanced in Latin as to write metrical translations of such parts as especially struck me in Horace's Odes, Virgil's

Eclogues, and Ovid's Metamorphoses, and could read with some facility Cicero's Orations and Cæsar's Commentaries. With this I could by no means look upon myself as suitably prepared for academical studies, but I thought that I might advance considerably within a year, and then make good all deficiencies in the university itself.

Among the higher persons in the city, I had gained many patrons; they promised me their aid, on condition, however, I would choose what is called a Bread study.* But as this did not belong to the tendency of my nature, and as I lived in the firm conviction that man must only cultivate that to which he is directed by a constant internal impulse, I adhered to my own plans, and my friends refused their assistance, granting nothing beyond a free board.

I had now only to carry out my scheme with my own resources, and to set about a literary production of some importance.

Müllner's "Schuld" (Crime) and Grillparzer's "Ahnfrau" (the Ancestress)† were then the order of the day, and attracted much attention. To my natural feeling these artificial works were repugnant, and still less could I reconcile myself to the ideas of destiny which they contained, and which I thought would have a demoralizing effect on the public; I therefore resolved to appear against them, and to show that destiny depends on character. However, I intended to fight not by words,

---

* That is a course of study for the express purpose of gaining a subsistence, as distinguished from that study which seeks learning for its own sake. —*Trans.*

† Two plays.—*Trans.*

but in act. A piece was to be produced which should utter the truth, that man in the present sows seeds for the future, which brings forth good or evil fruit according to his sowing. Being unacquainted with the history of the world, I had to invent the character and the course of the action. I carried it in my head for a full year, and imagined the single scenes and acts down to the minutest details, till at last I wrote it, in the winter of 1820, in the morning hours of a few weeks. I was supremely happy in doing this, for the whole flowed forth easily and naturally. But, in opposition to the above-named poets, I had my eye too steadily fixed on real life, and never thought of the theatre. Thus it was more a quiet delineation of situations than a rapidly progressive action, and only poetical and rhythmical, where characters and situations required it. Subordinate persons had too much room, and the whole piece too much breadth.

I showed it to my most intimate friends and acquaintance, but it was not received as I wished; they objected that some scenes belonged to comedy, and, further, that I had read too little. As I had expected a better reception, I was at first quietly offended, but I gradually came to the conviction that my friends were not so very wrong, and that my piece, even if the characters were correctly drawn, and the whole was well designed, and produced with some degree of care and facility, was of far too small merit to be fit for public representation, with respect to the views of life which it developed.

When I consider my origin, and the little I had studied, this was not to be wondered at. I determined to remodel the piece, and arrange it for the theatre;

but first to progress in my studies, that I might be capable to give everything a higher character. My anxiety to go to the university, where I hoped to attain all I wanted, and through which I expected to improve my position in life, became a positive passion. I resolved to publish my poems, as a chance of obtaining my wishes. As I had not that established reputation which would lead me to expect a handsome sum from a publisher, I chose the way of subscription as more suitable to my position.

This was conducted by my friends, and had the happiest result. I again went before my superiors with my views as to Göttingen, and asked for my dismissal. As they were convinced that I was really in earnest, and would not give way, they favoured my designs. On the representations of my chief, Colonel von Berger, the war-office *(*Kriegs-Canzlei*)* granted me my dismissal, and also a hundred and fifty dollars yearly for two years, to aid me in the prosecution of my studies.

I was now happy in the realization of the schemes I had cherished for years. I had the poems printed and sent off as quickly as possible, and derived from them, after deducting all expenses, a clear profit of one hundred and fifty dollars. In May 1821, I went to Göttingen, leaving one behind me I dearly loved.

My first attempt to reach the university had failed, because I obstinately refused any " Bread study," as it is called. Now, however, grown wiser by experience, and only too well aware of the unspeakable struggles which then awaited me, both on the side of my nearest acquaintance and on that of higher persons of influence,

I was prudent enough to submit to the views of a too-potent world, and to declare that I would choose a "Bread study," and devote myself to jurisprudence.

My powerful patrons, and all who set their heart on my worldly advancement, while they had no notion of the urgency of my mental wants, found my plan very rational. All opposition was now at an end. I found everywhere kind advances, and a ready furtherance of my views. To confirm me in such good intentions, they did not fail to allege that the juridical studies were by no means of such a kind as to preclude higher mental advantages. They said that I should thus gain an insight into civil and social relations, such as I could attain in no other way; that this study was by no means so extensive as to hinder my pursuing many so-called higher studies; and they told me of various celebrated persons, who had studied all the departments of law, and also attained the highest proficiency in other ways.

However, both my friends and myself overlooked the fact that such men not only came to the University well stored with school-learning, but had, besides, a much longer time to expend on their studies than the imperious necessity of my circumstances would permit to me.

Suffice it to say, that, as I deceived others, I gradually deceived myself also, and really fancied that I might seriously study law, and, at the same time, attain my own peculiar ends.

Under this delusion, of seeking that which I had no wish to possess and apply, I began with jurisprudence as soon as I reached the University. I found the science by no means of a repulsive kind, but rather such that, if my head had not been already too full of other plans and wishes, I could willingly have given myself up to it. But I was like a maiden, who finds abundant reasons for objecting to a proposed marriage, merely because she unfortunately has a secret love in her heart.

At the lectures on the Institutes and Pandects, I was often absorbed in inventing dramatic scenes and acts. I zealously tried to fix my mind on the matter delivered by the lecturer, but it always wandered. I really thought of nothing but poetry and art, and the higher human culture to attain which I had for years passionately endeavoured to reach the University.

Heeren was the person who most assisted me in my immediate objects during this first year at the University. His ethnography and history laid the best foundation for farther studies of the same kind, while the clearness and closeness of his style was of important advantage to me in other respects. I attended every lecture with delight, and never left one without being penetrated with the highest veneration and affection for that eminent man.

I judiciously began my second academic year by setting aside entirely the study of jurisprudence, which was, indeed, much too important to be made subordinate to others, and which was too great a hindrance with regard to my principal object. I devoted myself to philology, and was now as much indebted to Dissen as I had been in the first year to Heeren. For not only because his lectures gave my studies the food most needed and desired, did I find myself daily enlightened and advanced, and receive safe directions for my future works, but I had also the happiness of becoming personally acquainted with this excellent man, and of receiving from him guidance and encouragement in my studies.

My daily intercourse with the best minds among the students, and the conversations on the noblest subjects during our walks and often till late at night, were to me invaluable, and exercised a most favourable influence on the development of my faculties.

In the mean while, the end of my pecuniary means drew near. On the other hand, during the past year and a half, I had accumulated daily new treasures of knowledge; and to heap more together, without any practical application, would not have suited my natural disposition and my course of life. Hence, my passionate desire now was, by some literary undertaking, to make myself once more free, and sharpen my appetite for further study.

I intended to complete my dramatic work, which still interested me, as far as the subject was concerned, but which was to be elevated both in form and import, and also to bring forward some ideas relating to the principles of poetry, which had developed themselves in opposition to the views then prevalent. These two labours were to be undertaken in succession.

I, therefore, left the University in the autumn of 1822, and took lodgings in the country near Hanover. I first wrote my theoretical essays, which I hoped might aid youthful talents, not only in production, but in criticising poetical works, and gave them the title of " Beyträge zur Poesie."*

In May 1823, I had completed this work. As I

---

* Contributions to Poetry.

needed not only a good publisher, but also a handsome remuneration, I took the resolution at once to send my work to Goethe, and ask him to say some words of recommendation to Herr von Cotta.

Goethe was still, as formerly, the poet to whom I daily looked up as my infallible polar star; whose utterance harmonized with my thought, and led me constantly to a higher and higher point of view; whose high art in treating the most varied subjects I was ever striving to fathom and imitate; and towards whom my love and veneration had almost the nature of a passion.

Soon after my arrival in Göttingen, I had sent him a copy of my poems, accompanied by a slight sketch of the progress of my life and culture, and had the great joy, not only to receive some lines written by his own hand, but to hear from travellers that he had a good opinion of me, and proposed to make mention of me in the numbers of "Kunst und Alterthum."*

In my situation, at that time, the knowledge of this fact was of great importance, and gave me courage to show him the manuscript I had just completed.

I had no other desire at present than to see him personally for some moments; to attain which object I set off, about the end of May, and went on foot over Göttingen and the Werrathal to Weimar.

During this journey, which the heat of the weather often made fatiguing, I frequently felt within me the consolatory belief that I was under the especial guidance of kindly powers, and that this journey would be of great importance to my success in life.

* Art and Antiquity.

CONVERSATIONS OF GOETHE.

1822.

1822.

(Sup.*)   Saturday, September 21, 1822.

THIS evening at Goethe's, with Counsellor (Hofrath) Meyer. The conversation turned principally upon mineralogy, chemistry, and natural science (physik). The phenomena of the polarization of light appeared to interest him particularly. He showed me various preparations, chiefly after his own designs, and expressed a wish to make some experiments with me.

In the course of our conversation, Goethe became more and more free and communicative. I remained more than an hour, and at my departure he said many kind things to me.

His figure is still to be called handsome; his forehead and eyes are extremely majestic. He is tall and well built, and so vigorous in appearance that one can scarcely comprehend how he has been able for some years to declare himself too old to enter into society, and to go to court.

(Sup.*)   Tuesday, September 24, 1822.

The evening spent at Goethe's, with Meyer, Goethe's son, Frau von Goethe, and his physician, Counsellor (Hofrath) Rehbein. To-day, Goethe was particularly lively. He showed me some splendid lithographs from Stuttgard, the most perfect things of the kind I had ever seen. After that we conversed on scientific subjects, especially on the advancement of chemistry. Iodine and chlorine occupied him particularly; he spoke about these substances as if the new discoveries in chemistry had quite taken him by surprise. He had some iodine brought in, and volatilized it, before our eyes, in the flame of a taper; by which means he did not fail to make us admire the violet-vapour as a pleasing confirmation of a law in his theory of colours.

(Sup.*) Thursday, October 1, 1822.

To an evening party at Goethe's. I found amongst the assembled guests, Chancellor von Müller, President Peucer, Dr. Stephan Schütze, and Counsellor (Regierungsrath) Schmidt, which last played some sonatas of Beethoven's with rare perfection. I also derived great enjoyment from the conversations of Goethe and his daughter-in-law, who had all the cheerfulness of youth, and in whom an amiable disposition was united with infinite intelligence.

(Sup.*) Thursday, October 10, 1822.

To an evening party at Goethe's, with the renowned Blumenbach from Göttingen. Blumenbach is old, but with an animated and cheerful expression. He has contrived to preserve the whole activity of youth. His deportment is such, that no one would know that a learned man stood before him. His cordiality is frank and jovial; he is quite unceremonious, and one is soon upon an easy footing with him. His acquaintance was to me as interesting as agreeable.

(Sup.*) Tuesday, November 5, 1822.

An evening party at Goethe's. Amongst the assembled guests was the artist Kolbe. We were shown a beautifully executed painting by him,—a copy of Titian's Venus, from the Dresden Gallery.

This evening, I also found with Goethe, Herr von Eschwege, and the celebrated Hummel. Hummel improvised for nearly an hour upon the piano, with a force and a talent of which it is impossible to form a conception unless one has heard him. I found his conversation simple and natural, and himself, for a virtuoso of such celebrity, surprisingly modest.

(Sup.*) Tuesday, December 3, 1822.

At an evening party at Goethe's. Herren Riemer, Coudray, and Meyer, Goethe's son, and Frau von Goethe, were amongst those assembled.

The students at Jena are in an uproar, and a company of artillery has been sent to quiet them. Riemer read a collection of songs, which were prohibited, and which had thus given occasion or pretext to the revolt. All these songs, being read aloud, received decisive applause, on account of the great talent they displayed. Goethe himself thought well of them, and promised me a private inspection of them.

After we had spent some time in examining copper-plates and valuable books, Goethe, to our great delight, read to us the poem of " Charon." I could not but admire the clear, distinct, and energetic manner in which Goethe read the poem. I have never heard so beautiful a declamation. What fire! what a glance! and what a voice! Alternately like thunder, and then soft and mild. Perhaps, in some parts, he displayed too much force for the small room in which we were assembled; but yet there was nothing in his delivery which we could wish otherwise. Goethe afterwards conversed upon literature, and upon his works, also upon Madame de Stael, and kindred subjects. He is at present occupied with the translation and arrangement of the fragments of the " Phaëton" of Euripides. He began this work about a year ago, and has lately resumed it.

(Sup.*) Thursday, December 5, 1822.

This evening, at Goethe's, I heard the rehearsal of the first act of an opera which will shortly be produced, "The Count of Gleichen," by Eberwein. Since Goethe resigned the direction of the theatre, this is the first time, I have been told, that he has had at his house so great an operatic company. Herr Eberwein directed the singing. Some ladies of Goethe's acquaintance joined in the choruses, whilst the solo parts were sung by members of the operatic company. Some pieces appeared to me very remarkable, especially a canon for four voices.

(Sup.*) Tuesday, December 17, 1822.

In the evening at Goethe's. He was very cheerful, and treated with much spirit the theme that the follies of fathers are lost for their children.

The investigations which are now being made touching the discovery of salt springs evidently interested him. He inveighed against the stupidity of certain projectors, who totally disregard the outward signs, and the position and order of the strata under which rock-salt lies, and through which the auger must pass, and who, without knowing or seeking to discover the right spot, obstinately continue to work at random at the same shaft and in the same place.

CONVERSATIONS OF GOETHE.

1823.

1823.

(Sup.*) Monday, February 9, 1823.

THIS evening at Goethe's, whom I found alone, in conversation with Meyer. I perused an album belonging to bygone times, containing the handwriting of several renowned men, such as Luther, Erasmus, Mosheim, and others. The last-mentioned has written, in Latin, the following remarkable words: " Renown is a source of toil and sorrow; obscurity is a source of happiness."

(Sup.*) Monday, February 23, 1823.

Goethe has been for some days dangerously ill; yesterday he lay in a hopeless condition. To-day, however, a crisis has arrived, by which he appears to be saved. Still, this morning he said that he considered himself lost; later, at noon, he seemed to hope that he might recover; and again, in the evening, he said that, if he escaped, it must be allowed that, for an old man, he had played too high a game.

(Sup.*) Tuesday, February 24, 1823.

This day has been an anxious one on account of Goethe, because there was not at noon the same improvement in him which was observable yesterday. In a paroxysm of weakness he said to his daughter-in-law, "I feel that the moment is come in which the struggle between life and death begins within me." Still, in the evening the invalid retained his full intellectual consciousness, and even displayed a playful levity. "You are too timid with your remedies," said he to Rehbein; "you spare me too much: when one has a patient like me to deal with, one must set to work a little in the Napoleon fashion." Thereupon he drank off a cup of a decoction of arnica, which, employed by Huschke at the most dangerous moment yesterday, had brought on the favourable crisis. Goethe gave a beautiful description of this plant, and extolled its powerful effect to the skies. He was told that the physicians would not allow the grand-duke to see him: "Were I the grand-duke," exclaimed Goethe, "I would have asked a great deal, and troubled myself a great deal about you." At a moment when he felt better, and when his chest appeared less oppressed, he spoke with facility and clear intelligence; whereupon Rehbein whispered in the ear of a bystander, "A better respiration generally brings with it a better inspiration." Goethe, who heard this, immediately exclaimed, very pleasantly, "I knew that long ago; but this truth does not apply to you, you rogue."

Goethe sat upright in his bed, facing the open door of his workroom, where his nearest friends were assembled without his knowledge. His features appeared to me little altered; his voice was clear and distinct, still there was a solemnity in its tone like that of a dying man. "You seem to believe," said he to his children, "that I am better, but you deceive yourselves." We endeavoured playfully to reason him out of his apprehensions, and he appeared to take it in good part. More persons were constantly entering the chamber, which appeared to me by no means desirable, for the presence of so many people would needlessly deteriorate the air, and hinder the attendants on the patient. I could not forbear to speak of it, and went down into the lower room, whence I issued my bulletins to her imperial highness.

(Sup.*) Wednesday, February 25, 1823.

Goethe has caused an account to be given of the treatment which has been employed towards him up to the present time; he has also read a list of the persons who have made inquiries concerning the state of his health, of whom the number daily was very great. He afterwards received the grand-duke, and did not appear fatigued by his visit. I found fewer persons in his workroom to-day; whereupon I observed, to my joy, that my remark yesterday had been productive of some good. Now that the disease is removed, people seem to dread the consequences. His left hand is swollen, and there appear threatening precursors of the dropsy. We shall not know for some days what will be the final result of the illness. To-day, for the first time, Goethe has inquired after one of his friends; namely, his oldest friend Meyer. He wished to show him a scarce medal which he has received from Bohemia, and with which he is enraptured.

I came at twelve o'clock; and when Goethe heard that I had arrived, he had me called to his side. He gave me his hand, saying—"You see in me one risen from the dead." He then commissioned me to thank her imperial highness for the sympathy which she had shown him during his illness. "My recovery will be very slow," he added; "but to the physicians, notwithstanding, belongs the honour of having worked a little miracle upon me."

After a few minutes I withdrew. His colour is good; only he has much fallen away, and still breathes with some pain. It appeared to me that he spoke with greater difficulty than yesterday. The swelling of the left arm is very conspicuous. He keeps his eyes closed, and only opens them when he speaks.

(Sup.*) Monday, March 2, 1823.

This evening at Goethe's, whom I had not seen for several days. He sat in his arm-chair, and had with him his daughter and Riemer. He was strikingly better. His voice had recovered its natural tone; his breathing was free; his hand was no longer swollen; his appearance again was what it had been in a state of health; and his conversation was easy. He rose and walked, without effort, into his sleeping-room and back. We took tea with him; and as this was the first time, I playfully reproached Frau von Goethe with having forgotten to place a nosegay on the tea-tray. Frau von Goethe directly took a coloured ribbon from her hat, and bound it on the tea-urn. This joke appeared to give Goethe much pleasure.

We afterwards examined a collection of imitated jewels, which the grand-duke had received from Paris.

(Sup.*) *Saturday, March 22, 1823.*

To-day, in celebration of Goethe's recovery, his Tasso was represented at the theatre, with a prologue by Riemer, spoken by Frau von Heigendorf. His bust was adorned with a crown of laurel, amidst the loud exclamations of the excited spectators. After the performance was over, Frau von Heigendorf went to Goethe's. She was still in the costume of Leonora, and presented to Goethe the crown of Tasso; which he took, to adorn with it the bust of the Grand-Duchess Alexandra.

(Sup.*) *Wednesday, April 1, 1823.*

I brought Goethe, from her imperial highness, a number of the French "Journal des Modes," in which a translation of his works was discussed. On this occasion we conversed on " Rameau's Neffe" (Rameau's Nephew), the original of which has long been lost. Many Germans believe that the original never existed, and that it is all Goethe's own invention. Goethe, however, affirms that it would have been impossible for him to imitate Diderot's spirited style and manner, and that the German Rameau is nothing but a very faithful translation.

(Sup.*) *Friday, April 3, 1823.*

A portion of this evening was passed at Goethe's, in company with Herr Coudray, the government architect. We talked about the theatre, and the improvements which have taken place in it lately. " I have remarked it without going there," said Goethe, laughing. " Two months ago my children always came home in an ill-humour; they were never satisfied with the entertainment which had been provided. But now they have turned over a new leaf; they come with joyful countenances, *because for once and away they can have a good cry.* Yesterday, they owed this " pleasure in weeping " * to a drama by Kotzebue.

(Sup.*) Monday, April 13, 1823.

This evening alone with Goethe. We talked about literature, Lord Byron, his Sardanapalus and Werner. We then came to Faust, a subject on which Goethe frequently and willingly speaks. He wished that it might be translated into French, in the style of Marot's period. He considers it as the source whence Byron derived the tone of his " Manfred." Goethe thinks that Byron has made decided progress in his two last tragedies; because in these he appears less gloomy and misanthropical. We afterwards spoke about the text of " Zauberflöte," to which Goethe has written a sequel; but he has not yet found a composer to treat the subject properly. He admits that the well-known first part is full of improbabilities and jests which every one cannot understand and appreciate; still we must at all events allow that the author understood, to a high degree, the art of producing great theatrical effects by means of *contrasts.*

(Sup.*) Wednesday, April 15, 1823.

This evening at Goethe's, with the Countess Caroline

* These words " Wonne der Thränen" are put in inverted commas, probably with reference to " Wonne der Wehmuth," the title of a little poem by Goethe.—*Trans.*

Egloffstein. Goethe joked about the German almanacs, and some other periodical publications; all pervaded by a ridiculous sentimentality, which appears to be the order of the day. The countess remarked that German novelists had made the beginning, by spoiling the taste of their numerous readers; and that now the readers spoil the novelists, because, in order to find a publisher for their manuscripts, they must suit the prevailing bad taste of the public.

(Sup.*) Sunday, April 26, 1823.

I found Coudray and Meyer at Goethe's. We conversed on various subjects. "The library of the grand-duke," said Goethe among other things, "contains a globe, which was made by a Spaniard in the reign of Charles V. There are some remarkable inscriptions upon it, as, for example, 'the Chinese are a people bearing a strong resemblance to the Germans.'

"In former times," continued Goethe, "the African deserts were depicted on the maps, with representations of the wild beasts. In the present day, this custom is abandoned; the geographers prefer to leave us *carte blanche.*"

(Sup.*) Wednesday, May 6, 1823.

This evening at Goethe's. He endeavoured to give me an idea of his theory of colours. "Light," said he, "is by no means a compound of different colours; neither can light alone produce any colour; for that requires a certain modification and blending of light and *shade.*"

(Sup.*) Tuesday, May 13, 1823.

I found Goethe occupied with collecting his little poems and short addresses (*Blättchen*) to persons. "In earlier times," said he, "when I was more careless with my things, and neglected to make copies, I lost hundreds of such verses."

(Sup.*) Monday, June 2, 1823.

The chancellor, Riemer, and Meyer were with Goethe. We discussed Béranger's poems; and Goethe commented upon, and paraphrased some of them, with great originality and good humour.

The conversation then turned on natural science *(physik)* and meteorology. Goethe is on the point of working out a theory of the weather, in which he will ascribe the rise and fall of the barometer entirely to the action of the earth, and to her attraction and repulsion of the atmosphere.

"The scientific men, and especially the mathematicians," continued Goethe, "will not fail to consider my ideas perfectly ridiculous; or else they will do still better: they will totally ignore them in a most stately manner. But do you know why? Because they say that I am not one of the craft."

"The caste spirit of the learned by profession," I replied, "is very pardonable. When errors have crept into their theories, and have been borne along with them, we must seek for the cause in this: that such errors were handed down to them as dogmas, at a time when they themselves were still seated on their school-benches."

"That is true," exclaimed Goethe; "your learned men act like the bookbinders of Weimar. The masterpiece that is required of them to be admitted into the corporation is not a pretty binding, in the newest style. No; far from that. There must always be supplied a thick folio bible, just in the fashion of two or three hundred years ago, with clumsy covers, and in strong leather. The task is an absurdity. But it would go hard with the poor workman if he were to affirm that his examiners were blockheads."

Weimar, June 10, 1823.*

I arrived here a few days ago, but did not see Goethe till to-day. He received me with great cordiality; and the impression he made on me was such, that I consider this day as one of the happiest in my life.

Yesterday, when I called to inquire, he fixed to-day at twelve o'clock as the time when he would be glad to see me. I went at the appointed time, and found a servant waiting for me, preparing to conduct me to him.

The interior of the house made a very pleasant impression upon me; without being showy, everything was extremely simple and noble; even the casts from antique statues, placed upon the stairs, indicated Goethe's especial partiality for plastic art, and for Grecian antiquity. I saw several ladies moving busily about in the lower part of the house, and one of Ottilia's beautiful boys, who came familiarly up to me, and looked fixedly in my face.

After I had cast a glance around, I ascended the

---

* This is the first day in Eckermann's first book, and the first time in which he speaks in this book, as distinguished from Soret.—*Trans.*

stairs, with the very talkative servant, to the first floor. He opened a room, on the threshold of which the motto *Salve* was stepped over as a good omen of a friendly welcome. He led me through this apartment and opened another, somewhat more spacious, where he requested me to wait, while he went to announce me to his master. The air here was most cool and refreshing; on the floor was spread a carpet: the room was furnished with a crimson sofa and chairs, which gave a cheerful aspect; on one side stood a piano; and the walls were adorned with many pictures and drawings, of various sorts and sizes.

Through an open door opposite, one looked into a farther room, also hung with pictures, through which the servant had gone to announce me.

It was not long before Goethe came in, dressed in a blue frock-coat, and with shoes. What a sublime form! The impression upon me was surprising. But he soon dispelled all uneasiness by the kindest words. We sat down on the sofa. I felt in a happy perplexity, through his look and his presence, and could say little or nothing.

He began by speaking of my manuscript. " I have just come from *you*," said he; " I have been reading your writing all the morning; it needs no recommendation—it recommends itself." He praised the clearness of the style, the flow of the thought, and the peculiarity, that all rested on a solid basis, and had been thoroughly considered. " I will soon forward it," said he; " to-day I shall write to Cotta by post, and send him the parcel to-morrow." I thanked him with words and looks.

We then talked of my proposed excursion. I told him that my design was to go into the Rhineland, where I intended to stay at a suitable place, and write something new. First, however, I would go to Jena, and there await Herr von Cotta's answer.

Goethe asked whether I had acquaintance in Jena. I replied that I hoped to come in contact with Herr von Knebel; on which he promised me a letter which would insure me a more favourable reception. "And, indeed," said he, "while you are in Jena, we shall be near neighbours, and can see or write to one another as often as we please."

We sat a long while together, in a tranquil affectionate mood. I was close to him; I forgot to speak for looking at him—I could not look enough. His face is so powerful and brown! full of wrinkles, and each wrinkle full of expression! And everywhere there is such nobleness and firmness, such repose and greatness! He spoke in a slow, composed manner, such as you would expect from an aged monarch. You perceive by his air that he reposes upon himself, and is elevated far above both praise and blame. I was extremely happy near him; I felt becalmed like one who, after many toils and tedious expectations, finally sees his dearest wishes gratified.

He then spoke of my letter, and remarked that I was perfectly right, and that, if one can treat *one* matter with clearness, one is fitted for many things besides.

"No one can tell what turn this may take," said he; "I have many good friends in Berlin, and have lately thought of you in that quarter." Here he smiled pleasantly to himself. He then pointed out to me what I ought now to see in Weimar, and said he would desire secretary Kräuter to be my cicerone. Above all, I must not fail to visit the theatre. He asked me where I lodged, saying that he should like to see me once more, and would send for me at a suitable time.

We bade each other an affectionate farewell; I was supremely happy; for every word of his spoke kindness, and I felt that he was thoroughly well-intentioned towards me.

Wednesday, June 11, 1823.

This morning I received a card from Goethe, written by his own hand, desiring me to come to him. I went and staid an hour. He seemed quite a different man from that of yesterday, and had the impetuous and decided manner of a youth.

He entered, bringing two thick books. "It is not well," said he, "that you should go from us so soon; let us become better acquainted. I wish more ample opportunity to see and talk with you. But, as the field of generalities is so wide, I have thought of something in particular, which may serve as a ground-work for intercourse. These two volumes contain the 'Frankfurter Gelehrte Anzeigen' (Frankfort Literary Notices) of the years 1772 and 1773, among which are almost all my little critiques written at that time. These are not marked; but, as you are familiar with my style and tone of thought, you will easily distinguish them from the others. I would have you examine somewhat more closely these youthful productions, and tell me what you think of them. I wish to know whether they deserve a place in a future edition of my works. From my present self these things stand so far, that I have no judgment about them. But you younger people can tell whether they are to you of any value, and how far they suit our present literary point of view. I have already had copies taken of them, which you can have by-and-by to compare with the originals. Afterwards, by a careful survey, we might ascertain whether here and there some trifle might not be left out, or touched up with advantage, and without injuring the general character of the whole."

I replied that I would gladly make the attempt, and that nothing could gratify me more than to proceed according to his intention.

" You will find yourself perfectly competent," said he, " when you have once entered on the employment; it will come quite naturally to you."

He then told me that he intended to set off for Marienbad in a week, and that he should be glad if I could remain at Weimar till then; that we might see one another in the mean time, and become better acquainted.

" I wish, too," said he, " that you would not merely pass a few days or weeks in Jena, but would live there all the summer, till I return from Marienbad towards the autumn. Already I have written about a lodging for you, and other things of the kind necessary to make your stay convenient and pleasant.

" You will find there the most various resources and means for further studies, and a very cultivated social circle; besides, the country presents so many aspects, that you may take fifty walks, each different from the others, each pleasant, and almost all suited for undisturbed meditation. You will find there plenty of leisure and opportunity to write many new things for yourself, and also to accomplish my designs."

I could make no objection to such good proposals, and consented joyfully to them all. When I departed he was especially amiable, and he fixed another hour the day after to-morrow for further converse.

Monday, June 16, 1823.

I have lately been frequently with Goethe. To-day, we talked principally of business. I declared my opinion also of his Frankfort criticisms, calling them echoes of his academic years, an expression which seemed to please him, as marking the point of view from which these youthful productions should be regarded.

He then gave me the first eleven numbers of " Kunst und Alterthum,"* that I might take them with me to Jena, together with the Frankfort critiques as a second task.

"It is my wish," said he, "that you should study carefully these numbers, and not only make a general index of contents, but also set down what subjects are not to be looked upon as concluded, that I may thus see at once what threads I have to take up again and spin longer. This will be a great assistance to me, and so far an advantage to you, that, in this practical way, you will more keenly observe and apprehend the import of each particular treatise, than by common perusal, regulated solely by inclination."

* Art and Antiquity.

I found these remarks judicious, and said that I would willingly undertake this labour also.

Thursday, June 19, 1823.

I was to have gone to Jena to-day; but Goethe yesterday requested earnestly that I would stay till Sunday, and then go by the post. He gave me yesterday the letters of recommendation, and also one for the family of Frommann. " You will enjoy their circle," said he; " I have passed many delightful evenings there. Jean Paul, Tieck, the Schlegels, and all the other distinguished men of Germany, have visited there, and always with delight; and even now it is the union-point of many learned men, artists, and other persons of note. In a few weeks, write to me at Marienbad, that I may know how you are going on, and how you are pleased with Jena. I have requested my son to visit you there during my absence."

I felt very grateful to Goethe for so much care, and was very happy to see that he regarded me as one of his own, and wished me to be so considered.

Saturday, the 21st June, I bade farewell to Goethe, and on the following day went to Jena, where I established myself in a rural dwelling, with very good, respectable people. In the families of von Knebel and Frommann, I found, on Goethe's recommendation, a cordial reception and very instructive society. I made the best possible progress with the work I had taken with me, and had, besides, the pleasure of receiving a letter from Herr von Cotta, in which he not only declared himself ready to publish my manuscript which had been sent him, but promised me a handsome remuneration, adding that I myself should superintend the printing at Jena.

Thus my subsistence was secured for at least a year, and I felt the liveliest desire to produce something new at this time, and so to found my future prosperity as an author. I hoped that I had already, in my "Beyträge zur Poesie," come to an end with theory and criticism; I had in them endeavoured to get clear views as to the principal laws of art, and my whole inner nature now urged me to a practical application. I had plans for innumerable poems, both long and short, also for dramas of various sorts; and I had now, as I thought, only to think which way I should turn, to produce one after the other, with some degree of convenience to myself.

I was not long content in Jena; my life there was too quiet and uniform. I longed for a great city, where there was not only a good theatre, but where a popular life was developed on a great scale, that I might seize upon important elements of life, and advance my own mental culture as rapidly as possible. In such a town, too, I hoped to live quite unobserved, and to be free always to isolate myself for completely undisturbed production.

Meanwhile, I had sketched the index which Goethe wished for the first four volumes of "Kunst und Alterthum," and sent it to Marienbad with a letter, in which I openly expressed my plans and wishes. I received in answer the following lines:—

"The index arrived just at the right time, and

corresponds precisely with my wishes and intentions. Let me, when I return, find the Frankfort criticisms arranged in a like manner, and receive my best thanks, which I already silently pay beforehand, by carrying about with me your views, situation, wishes, aims, and plans, so that, on my return, I may be able to discuss more solidly your future welfare. To-day I will say no more. My departure from Marienbad gives me much to think of and to do, while my stay, all too brief, with persons of interest, occasions painful feelings.

"May I find you in that state of tranquil activity, from which, after all, views of the world and experiences are evolved in the surest and purest manner. Farewell. Rejoice with me in the anticipation of a prolonged and more intimate acquaintance.

"GOETHE.

"Marienbad, August 14, 1823."

By these lines of Goethe's, the reception of which made me extremely happy, I felt tranquillized as to the future. They determined me to take no step for myself, but to be wholly resigned to his will and counsel. Meanwhile, I wrote some little poems, finished arranging the Frankfort criticisms, and expressed my opinion of them in a short treatise, intended for Goethe. I looked forward with eagerness to his return from Marienbad; for my "Beyträge zur Poesie" was almost through the press, and I wished, at all events, to refresh myself this autumn, by going for a few weeks to the Rhine.

Jena, September 15, 1823.

Goethe is returned safe from Marienbad, but, as his country-house in this place is not so convenient as he requires, he will only stay here a few days. He is well and active, so that he can take walks several miles long, and it is truly delightful to see him.

After an interchange of joyful greetings, Goethe commenced speaking on the subject of my affairs:—

"To speak out plainly," he began, "it is my wish that you should pass this winter with me in Weimar." These were his first words. Approaching closer to me, he continued thus:—"With respect to poetry and criticism, you are in the best possible condition. You have a natural foundation for them. They are your profession, to which you must adhere, and which will soon bring you a good livelihood. But yet there is much, not strictly appertaining to this department, which you ought to know. It is, however, a great point that you should not expend much time upon this, but get over it quickly. This you shall do with us this winter in Weimar, and you will wonder to find what progress you have made by Easter. You shall have the best of everything; because the best means are in my hands. Thus you will have laid a firm foundation for life. You will have attained a feeling of comfort, and will be able to appear anywhere with confidence."

I was much pleased by this proposal, and replied, that I would regulate myself entirely by his views and wishes.

"With a home in my neighbourhood," continued Goethe, "I will provide you; you shall pass no unprofitable moment during the whole winter. Much that is good is brought together in Weimar, and you will gradually find, in the higher circles, a society equal to the best in any of the great cities. Besides, many eminent men are personally connected with me. With them you will gradually make acquaintance, and you will find their conversation in the highest degree useful and instructive."

Goethe then mentioned many distinguished men, indicating, in a few words, the peculiar merits of each.

"Where else," he continued, "would you find so much good in such a narrow space. We also possess an excellent library, and a theatre which, in the chief requisites, does not yield to the best in other German towns. Therefore,—I repeat it,—stay with us, and not only this winter, but make Weimar your home. From thence proceed highways to all quarters of the globe. In summer you can travel, and see, by degrees, what you wish. I have lived there fifty years; and where have I not been? But I was always glad to return to Weimar."

I was very happy in being again with Goethe, and hearing him talk, and I felt that my whole soul was devoted to him. If I could only have *thee*, thought I, all else will go well with me. So I repeated to him the assurance that I was ready to do whatever he, after weighing the circumstances of my peculiar situation, should think right.

Jena, Thursday, September 18, 1823.

Yesterday morning, before Goethe's return to Weimar, I had the happiness of another interview with him.

What he said at that time was highly important; to me it was quite invaluable, and will have a beneficial influence on all my life. All the young poets of Germany should know it, as it may be of great profit to them.

He introduced the conversation by asking me whether I had written any poems this summer. I replied that I had indeed written some, but that on the whole I lacked the feeling of ease requisite for production. "Beware," said he, " of attempting a large work. It is exactly that which injures our best minds, even those distinguished by the finest talents and the most earnest efforts. I have suffered from this cause, and know how much it injured me. What have I not let fall into the well! If I had written all that I well might, a hundred volumes would not contain it.

" The Present will have its rights; the thoughts and feelings which daily press upon the poet will and should be expressed. But, if you have a great work in your head, nothing else thrives near it, all other thoughts are repelled, and the pleasantness of life itself is for the time lost. What exertion and expenditure of mental force are required to arrange and round off a great whole, and then what powers, and what a tranquil, undisturbed situation in life, to express it with the proper fluency. If you have erred as to the whole, all your toil is lost; and further, if, in treating so extensive a subject, you are not perfectly master of your material in the details, the whole will be defective, and censure will be incurred. Thus, for all his toil and sacrifice, the poet gets, instead of reward and pleasure, nothing but discomfort and a paralysis of his powers. But if he daily seizes the present, and always treats with a freshness of feeling what is offered him, he always makes sure of something good, and if he sometimes does not succeed, has, at least, lost nothing.

"There is August Hagen, in Königsberg, a splendid talent: have you ever read his 'Olfried und Lisena?' There you may find passages which could not be better; the situations on the Baltic, and the other particulars of that locality, are all masterly. But these are only fine passages; as a whole, it pleases nobody. And what labour and power he has lavished upon it; indeed, he has almost exhausted himself. Now, he has been writing a tragedy." Here Goethe smiled, and paused for a moment. I took up the discourse, and said that, if I was not mistaken, he had advised Hagen (in 'Kunst und Alterthum') to treat only small subjects. "I did so, indeed," he replied; "but do people conform to the instructions of us old ones? Each thinks he must know best about himself, and thus many are lost entirely, and many for a long time go astray. Now it is no more the time to blunder about—*that* belonged to us old ones; and what was the use of all our seeking and blundering, if you young people choose to go the very same way over again. In this way we can never get on at all. Our errors were endured because we found no beaten path; but from him who comes later into the world more is required; he must not be seeking and blundering, but should use the instructions of the old ones to proceed at once on the right path. It is not enough to take steps which may some day lead to a goal; each step must be itself a goal, and a step likewise.

"Carry these words about with you, and see how you can apply them to yourself. Not that I really feel uneasy about you, but perhaps by my advice I help you quickly over a period which is not suitable to your present situation. If you treat, at present, only small subjects, freshly dashing off what every day offers you, you will generally produce something good, and each day will bring you pleasure. Give what you do to the pocket-books and periodicals, but never submit yourself to the requisition of others; always follow your own sense.

"The world is so great and rich, and life so full of variety, that you can never want occasions for poems. But they must all be occasional* poems; that is to say, reality must give both impulse and material for their production. A particular case becomes universal and poetic by the very circumstance that it is treated by a poet. All my poems are occasional poems, suggested by real life, and having therein a firm foundation. I attach no value to poems snatched out of the air.

"Let no one say that reality wants poetical interest; for in this the poet proves his vocation, that he has the art to win from a common subject an interesting side. Reality must give the motive, the points to be expressed,—the kernel, as I may say; but to work

---

* The word "Gelegenheitsgedicht" (occasional poem) properly applies to poems written for special occasions, such as birthdays, weddings, &c., but Goethe here extends the meaning, as he himself explains. As the English word "occasional" often implies no more than "occurrence now and then," the phrase "occasional poem" is not very happy, and is only used for want of a better. The reader must conceive the word in the limited sense, "produced on some special event."—*Trans.*

out of it a beautiful, animated whole, belongs to the poet. You know Fürnstein, called the Poet of Nature; he has written the prettiest poem possible, on the cultivation of hops. I have now proposed to him to make songs for the different crafts of working-men, particularly a weaver's song, and I am sure he will do it well, for he has lived among such people from his youth; he understands the subject thoroughly, and is therefore master of his material. That is exactly the advantage of small works; you need only choose those subjects of which you are master. With a great poem, this cannot be: no part can be evaded; all which belongs to the animation of the whole, and is interwoven into the plan, must be represented with precision. In youth, however, the knowledge of things is only one-sided. A great work requires many-sidedness, and on that rock the young author splits."

I told Goethe that I had contemplated writing a great poem upon the seasons, in which I might interweave the employments and amusements of all classes. "Here is the very case in point," replied Goethe; "you may succeed in many parts, but fail in others which refer to what you have not duly investigated. Perhaps you would do the fisherman well, and the huntsman ill; and if you fail anywhere, the whole is a failure, however good single parts may be, and you have not produced a perfect work. Give separately the single parts to which you are equal, and you make sure of something good.

"I especially warn you against great inventions of your own; for then you would try to give a view of things, and for that purpose youth is seldom ripe. Further, character and views detach themselves as sides from the poet's mind, and deprive him of the fulness requisite for future productions. And, finally, how much time is lost in invention, internal arrangement, and combination, for which nobody thanks us, even supposing our work is happily accomplished.

"With a *given* material, on the other hand, all goes easier and better. Facts and characters being provided, the poet has only the task of animating the whole. He preserves his own fulness, for he needs to part with but little of himself, and there is much less loss of time and power, since he has only the trouble of execution. Indeed, I would advise the choice of subjects which have been worked before. How many Iphigenias have been written! yet they are all different, for each writer considers and arranges the subject differently; namely, after his own fashion.

"But, for the present, you had better lay aside all great undertakings. You have striven long enough; it is time that you should enter into the cheerful period of life, and for the attainment of this, the working out of small subjects is the best expedient."

During this conversation, we had been walking up and down the room. I could do nothing but assent, for I felt the truth of each word through my whole being. At each step I felt lighter and happier, for I must confess that various grand schemes, of which I had not as yet been able to take a clear view, had been no little burden to me. I have now thrown them aside, and shall let them rest till I can take up and sketch off one subject and one part after another in cheerfulness, as by study of the world I gradually become master of the several parts of the material.

I feel, through these words of Goethe's, several years wiser, and perceive, in the very depths of my soul, the good fortune of meeting with a true master. The advantage is incalculable.

What shall I not learn from him this winter! what shall I not gain merely from intercourse with him, even in times when he does not speak what is so very important! His personality, his mere presence, seems to educate me, even when he does not speak a word.

Weimar, Thursday, October 2, 1823.

I came here yesterday from Jena, favoured by very agreeable weather. Immediately after my arrival, Goethe, by way of welcoming me to Weimar, sent me a season-ticket for the theatre. I passed yesterday in making my domestic arrangements; and the rather, as they were very busy at Goethe's; for the French Ambassador from Frankfort, Count Reinhard, and the Prussian State Counsellor (*Staatsrath*), Schultz, from Berlin, had come to visit him.

This forenoon I was again at Goethe's. He was rejoiced to see me, and was in every way kind and amiable. As I was about to take my leave, he said he would first make me acquainted with the State Counsellor, Schultz. He took me into the next room, where I found that gentleman busy in looking at the works of art, introduced me, and then left us together for further discourse.

"I am very glad," said Schultz, "that you are to stay in Weimar, and assist Goethe in arranging his unpublished works. He has been telling me how much advantage he promises himself from your assistance, and that he now hopes to complete many new plans."

I replied that I had no other aim in life than to aid German literature; and that, in the hope of being useful here, I had willingly laid aside, for the present, my own literary designs. I added, that a practical intercourse with Goethe, would have a most favourable effect on my own culture. I hoped, by this means, to gain a certain maturity in some years, and thus, in the end, better to perform those tasks for which I was at present less perfectly prepared.

"Certainly," replied Schultz, "the personal influence of so extraordinary a man and master as Goethe is quite invaluable. I, too, have come hither to refresh myself once more from his great mind."

He then inquired about the printing of my book, concerning which Goethe had written to him last summer. I said that I hoped, in a few days, to receive the first copies from Jena, and would not fail to present him with one, and to send it to Berlin, if he should not be here.

We separated with a cordial shake of the hand.

Tuesday, October 14, 1823.

This evening, I went for the first time to a large tea-party at Goethe's. I arrived first, and enjoyed the view of the brilliantly lighted apartments, which, through open doors, led one into the other. In one of the farthest, I found Goethe, who came to meet me, with a cheerful air. He was dressed in black, and wore his star, which became him so well. We were for a while alone, and went into the so-called "covered room" (*Deckenzimmer*), where the picture of the Aldobrandine Marriage, which was hung above a red couch, especially attracted my attention. On the green curtains being drawn aside, the picture was before my eyes in a broad light, and I was delighted to contemplate it quietly.

"Yes," said Goethe, "the ancients had not only great intentions, but they carried them into effect. On the contrary, we moderns have also great intentions, but are seldom able to bring them out with such power and freshness as we have thought them."

Now came Riemer, Meyer, Chancellor von Müller, and many other distinguished gentlemen and ladies of the court. Goethe's son and Frau von Goethe, with whom I was now for the first time made acquainted, also entered. The rooms filled gradually, and there was life and cheerfulness in them all. Some pretty youthful foreigners were present, with whom Goethe spoke French.

The society pleased me, all were so free and unconstrained; each stood or sat, laughed and talked with this person and that, just as he pleased. I had a lively conversation with young Goethe about Houwald's "Bild" (picture),* which was given a few days since. We had the same opinion about the piece, and I was greatly pleased to see this young man expound the different points with so much animation and intelligence.

Goethe himself appeared very amiable in society. He went about from one to another, and seemed to prefer listening, and hearing his guests talk, to talking

* A drama of some celebrity.—*Trans.*

much himself. Frau von Goethe would often come and lean upon him, and kiss him. I had lately said to him that I enjoyed the theatre highly, and that I felt great pleasure in giving myself up to the impression of the piece, without reflecting much upon it. This to him seemed right, and suited to my present state.

He came to me with Frau von Goethe. "This is my daughter-in-law," said he; "do you know each other?"

We told him that we had just become acquainted.

"He is as much a child about the theatre as you, Ottilia!" said he; and we exchanged congratulations upon this taste which we had in common. "My daughter," continued he, "never misses an evening."

"That is all very well," said I, "as long as they give good lively pieces; but when the pieces are bad, they try the patience."

"But," said Goethe, "it is a good thing that you cannot leave, but are forced to hear and see even what is bad. By this means, you are penetrated with the hatred for the bad, and come to a clearer insight into the good. In reading, it is not so,—you throw aside the book, if it displeases you; but at the theatre you must endure." I gave my assent, and thought how the old gentleman always said something opportune.

We now separated, and joined the rest, who were loudly and merrily amusing themselves about us,— now in this room, now in that. Goethe went to the ladies, and I joined Riemer and Meyer, who told us much about Italy.

Afterwards, Counsellor Schmidt seated himself at the piano, and played some of Beethoven's pieces, which seemed to be received with deep sympathy by the company. An intelligent lady then related many interesting particulars respecting Beethoven. Ten o'clock came at last, and thus had passed an extremely pleasant evening.

Sunday, October 19, 1823.

To-day, I dined for the first time with Goethe. No one was present except Frau von Goethe, Fräulein Ulrica, and little Walter, and thus we were all very comfortable. Goethe appeared now solely as father of a family, helping to all the dishes, carving the roast fowls with great dexterity, and not forgetting between whiles to fill the glasses. We had much lively chat about the theatre, young English people, and other topics of the day; Fräulein Ulrica was especially lively and entertaining. Goethe was generally silent, coming out only now and then with some pertinent remark. From time to time he glanced at the newspaper, now and then reading us some passages, especially about the progress of the Greeks.

They then talked about the necessity of my learning English, and Goethe earnestly advised me to do so, particularly on account of Lord Byron; saying, that a character of such eminence had never existed before, and probably would never come again. They discussed the merits of the different teachers here, but found none with a thoroughly good pronunciation; on which account they deemed it better to go to some young Englishman.

After dinner, Goethe showed me some experiments relating to his theory of colours. The subject was, however, new to me; I neither understood the phenomena, nor what he said about them. Nevertheless, I hoped that the future would afford me leisure and opportunity to initiate myself a little into this science.

Tuesday, October 21, 1823.

I went to see Goethe this evening. We talked of his "Pandora." I asked him whether this poem was to be regarded as a whole, or whether there was anything further. He said there was nothing further in existence, and that he had written no more for the very reason that the first part was planned on so large a scale, that he could not afterwards get through with a second. Besides, what was done might be regarded as a whole, so he felt quite easy about the matter.

I said that I had only penetrated the meaning of this difficult poem by degrees, namely, after I had read it so many times as almost to know it by heart. Goethe smiled, and said, "I can well believe that; for all its parts are, as one may say, wedged one within another."

I added, that I could not be perfectly satisfied with Schubarth's remarks upon this poem, who found there united all which had been said separately in "Werther," "Wilhelm Meister," "Faust," and the "Elective Affinities," thus making the matter very incomprehensible and difficult. "Schubarth," said Goethe, "often goes a little deep, but he is very clever, and all his words are fraught with deep meaning."

We spoke of Uhland, and Goethe said, "When I see great effects, I am apt to suppose great causes; and, with a popularity so extensive as that of Uhland, there must be something superior about him. However, I can scarcely form a judgment as to his poems ("Gedichte.") I took up his book with the best intentions, but fell immediately on so many weak and gloomy poems that I could not proceed. I then tried his ballads, where I really did find distinguished talent, and could plainly see that there was some foundation for his celebrity."

I then asked Goethe his opinion as to the kind of verse proper for German tragedy. "People in Germany," he replied, "will scarcely come to an agreement on that point. Every one does just as he likes, and as he finds somewhat suitable to his subject. The Iambic trimeter would be the most dignified measure, but it is too long for us Germans, who, for want of epithets, generally find five feet quite enough. The English, on account of their many monosyllables, cannot even get on so far as we do."

Goethe then showed me some copperplates, and afterwards talked about old German architecture, adding that, by degrees, he would show me a great deal in this way.

"We see in the works of the old German architecture," he said, "the flower of an extraordinary state of things. Whoever comes immediately close to such a flower, will only stare at it with astonishment ; but he who sees into the secret inner life of the plant, into the stirring of its powers, and observes how the flower gradually unfolds itself, sees the matter with quite different eyes,—he knows what he sees.

"I will take care that in the course of this winter you attain more insight into this important subject, that when you visit the Rhine next summer, the sight of the Minster of Strasburg and the Cathedral of Cologne may do you some good."

(Sup. *) Friday, October 24, 1823.

This evening at Goethe's. Madame Szymanowska, whose acquaintance he made this summer, at Marienbad, played a fantasia on the piano. Goethe, absorbed in listening, seemed at times much affected.

Saturday, October 25, 1823.

At twilight, I passed half an hour at Goethe's. He sat in a wooden arm-chair before his table. I found him in a singularly gentle mood, as one who is quite filled with celestial peace, or who is recalling a delicious happiness which he has enjoyed, and which again floats before his soul in all its fulness. Stadelman gave me a seat near him.

We talked of the theatre, which was one of the topics which chiefly interested me this winter. The "Erdennacht" (Night on Earth) of Raupach was the last piece I had seen. I gave it as my opinion that the piece was not brought before us as it existed in the mind of the poet; that the Idea was more predominant than Life; that it was rather lyric than dramatic; and that what was spun out through five acts would have been far better in two or three. Goethe added that the idea of the whole which turned upon aristocracy and democracy, was by no means of universal interest to humanity.

I then praised those pieces of Kotzebue's which I had seen — namely, his "Verwandschaften" (Affinities), and his "Versöhnung" (Reconciliation). I praised in them the quick eye for real life, the dexterity at seizing its interesting side, and the genuine and forcible representation of it. Goethe agreed with me. "What has kept its place for twenty years, and enjoys the favour of the people," said he, "must have something in it. When Kotzebue contented himself with his own sphere, and did not go beyond his powers, he usually did well. It was the same with him as with Chodowiecky, who always succeeded perfectly with the scenes of common citizens' life, while if he attempted to paint Greek or Roman heroes it proved a failure."

He named several other good pieces of Kotzebue's, especially "die beiden Klinsberge" (the two Klingsbergs). "None can deny," said he, "that Kotzebue has looked about a great deal in life, and ever kept his eyes open.

"Intellect, and some poetry, cannot be denied to our modern tragic poets, but most of them are incapable of an easy, living representation; they strive after something beyond their powers; and for that reason I might call them *forced* talents."

"I doubt," said I, "whether such poets could write a piece in prose, and am of opinion that this would be the true touchstone of their talent." Goethe agreed with me, adding that versification enhanced, and even called forth poetic feeling.

We then talked about various works. The conversation turned upon his "Journey through Frankfort and Stuttgard to Switzerland," which he has lying by him in three parts, in sheets, and which he will send me, in order that I may read the details, and plan how they may be formed into a whole. "You will see," said he, "that it was all written off on the impulse of the moment; there was no thought of plan or artistical rounding: it was like pouring water from a bucket."

I was pleased with this simile, which seemed very appropriate, to illustrate a thing utterly without plan.

Monday, October 27, 1823.

This morning, I was invited to a tea-party and concert, which were to be given at Goethe's house this evening. The servant showed me the list of persons to be invited, from which I saw that the company would be very large and brilliant. He said a young Polish lady had arrived, who would play on the piano. I accepted the invitation gladly.

Afterwards the bill for the theatre was brought, and I saw that the "Schachmaschine" (Chess-machine) was to be played. I knew nothing of this piece; but my landlady was so lavish in its praise, that I was seized with a great desire to see it. Besides, I had not been in my best mood all day, and the feeling grew upon me that I was more fit for a merry comedy than for such good society.

In the evening, an hour before the theatre opened, I went to Goethe. All was already in movement throughout the house. As I passed I heard them tuning the piano, in the great room, as preparation for the musical entertainment.

I found Goethe alone in his chamber; he was already dressed, and I seemed to him to have arrived at the right moment. "You shall stay with me here," he said, "and we will entertain one another till the arrival of the others." I thought, "Now I shall not be able to get away: stop, I must; and, though it is very pleasant to be with Goethe alone, yet, when a quantity of strange gentlemen and ladies come, I shall feel quite out of my element."

I walked up and down the room with Goethe. Soon the theatre became the subject of our discourse, and I had an opportunity of repeating that it was to me a source of new delight, especially as I had seen scarce anything in early years, and now almost every piece made quite a fresh impression upon me. "Indeed," added I, "I feel so much about it, that I have had a severe contest with myself, notwithstanding the great attractions of your evening party."

"Well," said Goethe, stopping short, and looking at me with kindness and dignity, "go then; do not constrain yourself; if the lively play this evening suits you best, is more suitable to your mood, go there. You have music here, and that you will often have again." "Then," said I, "I will go; it will, perhaps, do me good to laugh." "Stay with me, however," said Goethe, "till six o'clock: we shall have time to say a word or two."

Stadelman brought in two wax lights, which he set on the table. Goethe desired me to sit down, and he would give me something to read. And what should this be but his newest, dearest poem, his "Elegy from Marienbad!"

I must here go back a little for a circumstance connected with this poem. Immediately after Goethe's return from Marienbad, the report had been spread that he had there made the acquaintance of a young lady equally charming in mind and person, and had been inspired with a passion for her. When her voice was heard in the Brunnen-Allee, he had always seized his hat, and hastened down to join her. He had missed no opportunity of being in her society, and had passed happy days: the parting had been very painful, and he had, in this excited state, written a most beautiful poem, which, however, he looked upon as a sort of consecrated thing, and kept hid from every eye.

I believed this story, because it not only perfectly accorded with his bodily vigour, but also with the productive force of his mind, and the healthy freshness of his heart. I had long had a great desire to see the poem itself, but naturally felt unwilling to ask Goethe. I had, therefore, to congratulate myself on the fortunate moment which brought it before me.

He had, with his own hand, written these verses, in Roman characters, on fine vellum paper, and fastened them with a silken cord into a red morocco case; so that, from the outside, it was obvious that he prized this manuscript above all the rest.

I read it with great delight, and found that every line confirmed the common report. The first verse, however, intimated that the acquaintance was not first made, but only renewed, at this time. The poem revolved constantly on its own axis, and seemed always to return to the point whence it began. The close, wonderfully broken off, made quite a deep and singular impression.

When I had finished, Goethe came to me again. "Well," said he, " there I have shown you something good. But you shall tell me what you think a few days hence." I was very glad that Goethe, by these words, excused me from passing a judgment at the moment; for the impression was too new, and too hastily received, to allow me to say anything that was appropriate.

Goethe promised to let me see it again in some tranquil hour. The time for the theatre had now arrived, and we separated with an affectionate pressure of the hand.

The "Chess-machine" was, perhaps, a good piece, well-acted, but I saw it not—my thoughts were with Goethe.

When the play was over, I passed by his house; it was all lighted up; I heard music from within, and regretted that I had not stayed there.

The next day, I was told that the young Polish lady, Madame Szymanowska, in whose honour the party had been given, had played on the piano in most excellent style to the enchantment of the whole company. I learned, also, that Goethe became acquainted with her last summer at Marienbad, and that she had now come to visit him.

At noon, Goethe sent me a little manuscript, "Studies by Zauper," in which I found some very apt remarks. I sent him some poems I had written this summer at Jena, and of which I had spoken to him.

Wednesday, October 29, 1823.

This evening I went to Goethe just as they were lighting the candles. I found him in a very animated state of mind: his eyes sparkled with the reflection of the candle light; his whole expression was one of cheerfulness, youth, and power.

As he walked up and down with me he began immediately to speak of the poems which I sent him yesterday.

"I understand now," said he, "why you talked to me at Jena, of writing a poem on the seasons. I now advise you to do so; begin at once with Winter. You seem to have a special sense and feeling for natural objects.

"Only two words would I say about your poems. You stand now at that point where you must necessarily break through to the really high and difficult part of art—the apprehension of what is individual. You must do some degree of violence to yourself to get out of the *Idea*. You have talent, and have got so far; now you *must* do this. You have been lately at Tiefurt; that might now afford a subject for the attempt. You may perhaps go to Tiefurt and look at it three or four times before you win from it the characteristic side, and bring all your means (*motive**) together; but spare not your toil; study it throughout, and then represent it; the subject is well worth this trouble. I should have used it long ago, but I could not; for I have lived through those important circumstances, and my being is so interwoven with them, that details press upon me with too great fulness. But you come as a stranger; you let the Castellan tell you the past, and you will see only what is present, prominent, and significant."

---

* The word "motive," which is of frequent occurrence in critical disquisition, is exactly defined in Heyse's "Fremdwörterbuch," a means in art calculated to produce an effect.—*Trans.*

I promised to try, but could not deny that this subject seemed to me very far out of my way, and very difficult.

"I know well," said he, "that it is difficult; but the apprehension and representation of the individual is the very life of art. Besides, while you content yourself with generalities, every one can imitate you; but, in the particular, no one can—and why? because no others have experienced exactly the same thing.

"And you need not fear lest what is peculiar should not meet with sympathy. Each character, however peculiar it may be, and each object which you can represent, from the stone up to man, has generality; for there is repetition everywhere, and there is nothing to be found only once in the world.

"At this step of representing what is individual," continued Goethe, "begins, at the same time, what we call composition."

This was not at once clear to me, though I refrained from questions. "Perhaps," thought I, "he means the blending of the Ideal with the Real,—the union of that which is external with that which is innate. But perhaps he means something else." Goethe continued:

"And be sure you put to each poem the date at which you wrote it." I looked at him inquiringly, to know why this was so important. "Your poems will thus serve," he said, "as a diary of your progress. I have done it for many years, and can see its use."

It was now time for the theatre. "So you are going to Finland?" called he, jestingly, after me; for the piece was "Johann von Finland" (John of Finland), by Frau von Weissenthurn.

The piece did not lack effective situations, but it was so overloaded with pathos, and the design was so obvious in every part, that, on the whole, it did not impress me favourably. The last act, however, pleased me much, and reconciled me to the rest.

This piece suggested to me the following remark: Characters which have been but indifferently drawn by the poet gain on the stage, because the actors, as living men, make them living beings, and impart to them some sort of individuality. But the finely drawn characters of the great poet, which already stand out with a sharply marked individuality, must lose on the stage, because actors are not often perfectly fitted for such parts, and very few can completely lay aside their own individualities. If the actor be not the counterpart of the character, or if he do not possess the power of utterly laying aside his own personality, a mixture ensues, and the character loses its purity. Therefore, the play of a really great poet only appears in single figures, just as it was originally intended.

Monday, November 3, 1823.

I went to Goethe at five o'clock. I heard them, as I came up stairs, laughing very loud, and talking in the great room. The servant said that the Polish lady dined there to-day, and that the company had not yet left the table. I was going away, but he said he had orders to announce me, and that perhaps his master would be glad of my arrival, as it was now late. I let him have his way, and waited a while, after which Goethe came out in a very cheerful mood, and took me to the opposite room. My visit seemed to please him. He had a bottle of wine brought at once, and filled for me, and occasionally for himself.

"Before I forget it," said he, looking about the table for something, "let me give you a concert-ticket. Madame Szymanowska gives, to-morrow evening, a public concert at the Stadthaus, and you must not fail to be there." I replied that I certainly should not repeat my late folly. "They say she plays very well," I added. "Admirably," said Goethe. "As well as Hummel?" asked I. "You must remember," said Goethe, "that she is not only a great performer, but a beautiful woman; and this lends a charm to all she does. Her execution is masterly,—astonishing, indeed." "And has she also great power?" said I. "Yes," said he, "great power; and that is what is most remarkable in her, because we do not often find it in ladies." I said that I was delighted with the prospect of hearing her at last.

Secretary Kräuter came in to consult about the library. Goethe, when he left us, praised his talent and integrity in business.

I then turned the conversation to the "Journey through Frankfort and Stuttgard into Switzerland, in 1797," the manuscript of which he had lately given me, and which I had already diligently studied. I spoke of his and Meyer's reflections on the *subjects* of plastic art.

"Ay," said Goethe, "what can be more important than the subject, and what is all the science of art without it? All talent is wasted if the subject is unsuitable. It is because modern artists have no worthy subjects, that people are so hampered in all the art of modern times. From this cause we all suffer. I myself have not been able to renounce my modernness.

"Very few artists," he continued, "are clear on this point, or know what will really be satisfactory. For instance, they paint my 'Fisherman' as the subject of a picture, and do not think that it cannot be painted. In this ballad, nothing is expressed but the charm in water which tempts us to bathe in summer; there is nothing else in it: and how can that be painted?"

I mentioned how pleased I was to see how, in that journey, he had taken an interest in everything, and apprehended everything; shape and situation of mountains, with their species of stone; soil, rivers, clouds, air, wind, and weather; then cities, with their origin and growth, architecture, painting, theatres, municipal regulations and police, trade, economy, laying out of streets, varieties of human race, manner of living, peculiarities; then again, politics, martial affairs, and a hundred things beside.

He answered, "But you find no word upon music, because that was not within my sphere. Each traveller should know what he has to see, and what properly belongs to him, on a journey."

The Chancellor came in. He talked a little with Goethe, and then spoke to me very kindly, and with much acuteness, about a little paper which he had lately read. He soon returned to the ladies, among whom I heard the sound of a piano.

When he had left us, Goethe spoke highly of him,

and said, "All these excellent men, with whom you are now placed in so pleasant a relation, make what I call a home, to which one is always willing to return."

I said that I already began to perceive the beneficial effect of my present situation, and that I found myself gradually leaving my ideal and theoretic tendencies, and more and more able to appreciate the value of the present moment.

"It would be a pity," said Goethe, "if it were not so. Only persist in this, and hold fast by the present. Every situation—nay, every moment—is of infinite worth; for it is the representative of a whole eternity."

After a short pause, I turned the conversation to Tiefurt, and the mode of treating it. "The subject," said I, "is complex, and it will be difficult to give it proper form. It would be most convenient to me to treat it in prose."

"For that," said Goethe, "the subject is not sufficiently significant. The so-called didactic, descriptive form, would, on the whole, be eligible; but even that is not perfectly appropriate. The best method will be to treat the subject in ten or twelve separate little poems, in rhyme, but in various measures and forms, such as the various sides and views demand, by which means light will be given to the whole." This advice I at once adopted as judicious. "Why, indeed," continued he, "should you not for once use dramatic means, and write a conversation or so with the gardener? By this fragmentary method you make your task easy, and can better bring out the various characteristic sides of the subject. A great, comprehensive whole, on the other hand, is always difficult; and he who attempts it seldom produces anything complete."

Wednesday, November 10, 1823.

Goethe has not been very well for the last few days; it seems he cannot get rid of a very bad cold. He coughs a great deal, very loud, and with much force; but, nevertheless, the cough seems to be painful, for he generally has his hand on his left side.

I passed half an hour with him this evening before the theatre. He sat in an arm-chair, with his back sunk in a cushion, and seemed to speak with difficulty.

After we had talked a little, he wished me to read a poem with which he intended to open a new number of "Kunst und Alterthum." He remained sitting, and showed me where it was kept. I took the light, and sat down at his writing-table to read it, at a little distance from him.

This poem was singular in its character, and, though I did not fully understand it on the first reading, it affected me in a peculiar manner. The glorification of the Paria was its subject, and it was treated as a Trilogy. The prevailing tone seemed to me that of another world, and the mode of representation such, that I found it very difficult to form a lively notion of the subject. The personal presence of Goethe was also unfavourable to thorough abstraction: now I heard him cough; now I heard him sigh; and thus I was, as it were, divided in two—one half read, and the other felt his presence. I was forced to read the poem again and again, only to approximate to it.

However, the more I penetrated into it, the more significant in character, and the higher in art, did it seem to be.

At last I spoke to Goethe, both as to the subject and treatment, and he gave me much new light by some of his remarks.

"Indeed," said he, "the treatment is very terse, and one must go deep into it to seize upon its meaning. It seems, even to me, like a Damascene blade hammered out of steel wire. I have borne this subject about with me for forty years; so that it has had time to get clear of everything extraneous."

"It will produce an effect," said I, "when it comes before the public."

"Ah, the public!" sighed Goethe.

"Would it not be well," said I, "to aid the comprehension, and to add an explanation as we do to pictures, when we endeavour to give life to what is actually present, by describing the preceding circumstances?"

"I think not," said he; "with pictures it is another matter; but, as a poem is already expressed in words, one word only cancels another."

I thought Goethe was here very happy in pointing out the rock on which those who interpret poems are commonly wrecked. Still it may be questioned whether it be not possible to avoid this rock, and affix some explanatory words to a poem without at all injuring the delicacy of its inner life.

When I went away, he asked me to take the sheets of "Kunst und Alterthum" home with me, that I might read the poem again, and also the "Roses from the East" (Oestliche Rosen) of Rückert, a poet whom he seems highly to value, and to regard with great expectation.

(Sup.*) Tuesday, November 11, 1823.

No evening company at Goethe's, who has again been suffering for some time. His feet were wrapped in a woollen coverlet, which he had taken with him everywhere since the campaign in Champagne. Apropos of this coverlet, he related an anecdote of the year 1806, when the French had occupied Jena, and the chaplain of a French regiment required some hangings to adorn his altar. "He was supplied with a splendid piece of crimson stuff," said Goethe; "but this was not good enough for him. He complained of this to me. 'Send me the stuff,' said I; 'I will see if I can procure something better.' In the mean time, we were just bringing out a new piece at the theatre, and I made use of the magnificent red stuff to decorate my actors. As for my chaplain, he received nothing else; he was forgotten; and he must have seen what good he got."

Wednesday, November 12, 1823.

Towards evening, I went to see Goethe; but heard, before I went up stairs, that the Prussian minister, von Humboldt, was with him, at which I was pleased, being convinced that this visit of an old friend would cheer him up and do him good.

I then went to the theatre, where "Die Schwestern von Prag" (the Sisters of Prague), got up to perfection, was done admirably, so that it was impossible to leave off laughing throughout the whole piece.

Thursday, November 13, 1823.

Some days ago, as I was walking one fine afternoon towards Erfurt, I was joined by an elderly man, whom I supposed, from his appearance, to be an opulent citizen. We had not talked together long, before the conversation turned upon Goethe. I asked him whether he knew Goethe. "Know him?" said he, with some delight; "I was his valet almost twenty years!" He then launched into the praises of his former master. I begged to hear something of Goethe's youth, and he gladly consented to gratify me.

"When I first lived with him," said he, "he might have been about twenty-seven years old; he was thin, nimble, and elegant in his person. I could easily have carried him in my arms."

I asked whether Goethe, in that early part of his life here, had not been very gay. "Certainly," replied he; "he was always gay with the gay, but never when they passed a certain limit; in that case he usually became grave. Always working and seeking; his mind always bent on art and science; that was generally the way with my master. The duke often visited him in the evening, and then they often talked on learned topics till late at night, so that I got extremely tired, and wondered when the duke would go. Even then he was interested in natural science.

"One time he rang in the middle of the night, and when I entered his room I found he had rolled his iron bed to the window, and was lying there, looking out upon the heavens. 'Have you seen nothing in the sky?' asked he; and when I answered in the negative, he bade me run to the guard-house, and ask the man on duty if he had seen nothing. I went there; the guard said he had seen nothing, and I returned with this answer to my master, who was still in the same position, lying in his bed, and gazing upon the sky. 'Listen,' said he to me; 'this is an important moment; there is now an earthquake, or one is just going to take place;' then he made me sit down on the bed, and showed me by what signs he knew this."

I asked the good old man " what sort of weather it was."

" It was very cloudy," he replied; " no air stirring; very still and sultry."

I asked if he at once believed there was an earthquake on Goethe's word.

" Yes," said he, " I believed it, for things always happened as he said they would. Next day he related his observations at court, when a lady whispered to her neighbour, 'Only listen, Goethe is dreaming.' But the duke, and all the men present, believed Goethe, and the correctness of his observations was soon confirmed; for, in a few weeks, the news came that a part of Messina, on that night, had been destroyed by an earthquake."

Friday, November 14, 1823.

Towards evening Goethe sent me an invitation to call upon him. Humboldt, he said, was at court, and therefore I should be all the more welcome. I found him, as I did some days ago, sitting in his arm-chair; he gave me a friendly shake of the hand, and spoke to me with heavenly mildness. The chancellor soon joined us. We sat near Goethe, and carried on a light conversation, that he might only have to listen. The physician, Counsellor (Hofrath) Rehbein, soon came also. To use his own expression, he found Goethe's pulse quite lively and easy. At this we were highly pleased, and joked with Goethe on the subject. "If I could only get rid of the pain in my left side!" he said. Rehbein prescribed a plaster there; we talked on the good effect of such a remedy, and Goethe consented to it. Rehbein turned the conversation to Marienbad, and this appeared to awaken pleasant reminiscences in Goethe. Arrangements were made to go there again, it was said that the great duke would join the party, and these prospects put Goethe in the most cheerful mood. They also talked about Madame Szymanowska, and mentioned the time when she was here, and all the men were solicitors for her favour.

When Rehbein was gone, the chancellor read the Indian poems, and Goethe, in the mean while, talked to me about the Marienbad Elegy.

At eight o'clock, the chancellor went, and I was going too, but Goethe bade me stop a little, and I sat down. The conversation turned on the stage, and the fact that "Wallenstein" was to be done to-morrow. This gave occasion to talk about Schiller.

"I have," said I, "a peculiar feeling towards Schiller. Some scenes of his great dramas I read with genuine love and admiration; but presently I meet with something which violates the truth of nature, and I can go no further. I feel this even in reading 'Wallenstein.' I cannot but think that Schiller's turn for philosophy injured his poetry, because this led him to consider the idea far higher than all nature; indeed, thus to annihilate nature. What he could conceive must happen, whether it were in conformity with nature or not."

"It was sad," said Goethe, "to see how so highly gifted a man tormented himself with philosophical disquisitions which could in no way profit him. Humboldt has shown me letters which Schiller wrote to him in those unblest days of speculation. There we see how he plagued himself with the design of perfectly separating sentimental from *naïve* poetry. For the former he could find no proper soil, and this brought him into unspeakable perplexity. As if," continued he, smiling, "sentimental poetry could exist at all without the *naïve* ground in which, as it were, it has its root.

"It was not Schiller's plan," continued Goethe, "to go to work with a certain unconsciousness, and as it were instinctively; he was forced, on the contrary, to reflect on all he did. Hence it was that he never could leave off talking about his poetical projects, and thus he discussed with me all his late pieces, scene after scene.

"On the other hand, it was contrary to my nature to talk over my poetic plans with anybody—even with Schiller. I carried everything about with me in silence, and usually nothing was known to any one till the whole was completed. When I showed Schiller my 'Hermann and Dorothea' finished, he was astonished, for I had said not a syllable to him of any such plan.

"But I am curious to hear what you will say of 'Wallenstein' to-morrow. You will see noble forms, and the piece will make an impression on you such as you probably do not dream of."

Saturday, November 15, 1823.

In the evening I was in the theatre, where I for the first time saw "Wallenstein." Goethe had not said too much; the impression was great, and stirred my inmost soul. The actors, who had almost all belonged to the time when they were under the personal influence of Schiller and Goethe, gave an *ensemble* of significant personages, such as on a mere reading were not presented to my imagination with all their individuality. On this account the piece had an extraordinary effect upon me, and I could not get it out of my head the whole night.

Sunday, November 16, 1823.

In the evening at Goethe's; he was still sitting in his elbow-chair, and seemed rather weak. His first question was about "Wallenstein." I gave him an account of the impression the piece had made upon me as represented on the stage, and he heard me with visible satisfaction.

M. Soret came in, led in by Frau von Goethe, and remained about an hour. He brought from the duke some gold medals, and by showing and talking about these seemed to entertain Goethe very pleasantly.

Frau von Goethe and M. Soret went to court, and I was left alone with Goethe.

Remembering his promise to show me again his Marienbad Elegy at a fitting opportunity, Goethe arose, put a light on the table, and gave me the poem. I was delighted to have it once more before me. He quietly seated himself again, and left me to an undisturbed perusal of the piece.

After I had been reading a while, I turned to say something to him, but he seemed to be asleep. I therefore used the favourable moment, and read the poem again and again with a rare delight. The most youthful glow of love, tempered by the moral elevation of the mind, seemed to me its pervading characteristic. Then I thought that the feelings were more strongly expressed than we are accustomed to find in Goethe's other poems, and imputed this to the influence of Byron—which Goethe did not deny.

"You see the product of a highly impassioned mood," said he. "While I was in it I would not for the world have been without it, and now I would not for any consideration fall into it again.

"I wrote that poem immediately after leaving Marienbad, while the feeling of all I had experienced there was fresh. At eight in the morning, when we stopped at the first stage, I wrote down the first strophe; and thus I went on composing in the carriage, and writing down at every stage what I had just composed in my head, so that by the evening the whole was on paper. Thence it has a certain directness, and is, as I may say, poured out at once, which may be an advantage to it as a whole."

"It is," said I, "quite peculiar in its kind, and recalls no other poem of yours."

"That," said he, "may be, because I staked upon the present moment as a man stakes a considerable sum upon a card, and sought to enhance its value as much as I could without exaggeration."

These words struck me as very important, inasmuch as they threw a light on Goethe's method so as to explain that many-sidedness which has excited so much admiration.

It was now near nine o'clock; Goethe bade me call Stadelmann, which I did.

He then let Stadelmann put the prescribed plaster on his left side. I turned to the window, but heard him lamenting to Stadelmann that his illness was not lessening, but assumed a character of permanence. When the process was over, I sat down by him again for a little while. He now complained to me also that he had not slept for some nights, and had no appetite. "The winter," said he, "thus passes away; I can put nothing together; my mind has no force." I tried to soothe him, requesting him not to think so much of his labours at present, and representing that there was reason to hope he would soon be better. "Ah," said he, "I am not impatient; I have lived through too many such situations not to have learned to suffer and to endure." He was in his white flannel gown, and a woollen coverlet was laid on his knees and feet. "I shall not go to bed," he said, "but will pass the night thus in my chair, for I cannot properly sleep."

In the mean while the time for my departure was come, he extended his dear hand to me, and I left.

When I went down into the servants' room, to fetch my cloak, I found Stadelmann much agitated. He said he was alarmed about his master, for if *he* complained, it was a bad sign indeed! His feet, too, which had lately been a little swollen had suddenly become thin. He was going to the physician early in the morning, to tell him these bad signs." I endeavoured to pacify him, but he would not be talked out of his fears.

(Sup.*) Sunday, November 16, 1823.

Goethe is not any better. The grand-duchess sent him, this evening, by me, some very beautiful medals, the examination of which might perhaps divert and cheer him. Goethe was manifestly pleased at this delicate attention on the part of the duchess. He complained to me that he felt the same pain in the left side, which had preceded his severe illness last winter. "I cannot work," said he, " I cannot read, and even thinking only succeeds with me in my happy moments of alleviation."

(Sup.*) Monday, November 17, 1823.

Humboldt is here. I have spent a few moments with Goethe to-day; when it appeared to me that Humboldt's presence and conversation had a favourable effect upon him. His disease does not appear to be merely of a physical kind. It seems more likely that the violent affection which he formed for a young lady, at Marienbad, in the summer, and which he is now trying to overcome, may be considered as the principal cause of his present illness.

Monday, November 17, 1823.

When I entered the theatre this evening, many persons pressed towards me, asking very anxiously how Goethe was. His illness must have spread rapidly over the town, and perhaps has been exaggerated.

Some said he had water on the chest. I felt depressed all the evening.

Wednesday, November 19, 1823.

Yesterday, I walked about in a state of great anxiety. No one besides his family was admitted to see him.

In the evening I went to his house, and he received me. I found him still in his arm-chair; his outward appearance was quite the same as when I left him on Sunday, but he was in good spirits.

We talked of Zauper, and the widely differing results which proceed from the study of ancient literature.

Friday, November 21, 1823.

Goethe sent for me. To my great joy I found him walking up and down in his chamber. He gave me a little book, the "Ghazels" of Count Platen. "I had intended," said he, "to say something of this in ' Kunst und Alterthum,' for the poems deserve it; but my present condition will not allow me to do anything. Just see if you can fathom the poems and get anything out of them."

I promised to make the attempt.

"'Ghazels,'" continued he, "have this peculiarity, that they demand great fulness of meaning. The constantly recurring similar rhymes must find ready for them a store of similar thoughts. Therefore it is not every one that succeeds in them; but these will please you." The physician came in, and I departed.

Monday, November 24, 1823.

Saturday and Sunday I studied the poems: this morning I wrote down my view of them, and sent it to Goethe; for I had heard that no one had been admitted to him for some days, the physician having forbidden him to talk.

However, he sent for me this evening. When I entered, I found a chair already placed for me near him; he gave me his hand, and was extremely affectionate and kind. He began immediately to speak of my little critique. "I was much pleased with it," said he; "you have a fine talent. I wish now to tell you something," he continued; "if literary proposals should be made to you from other quarters, refuse them, or at least consult me before deciding upon them; for, since you are now linked with me, I should not like to see you connected with others also."

I replied that I wished to belong to him alone, and had at present no reason to think of new connections.

This pleased him, and he said that we should this winter get through much pleasant work together.

We then talked of the "Ghazels." Goethe expressed his delight at the completeness of these poems, and that our present literature produced so much that was good.

"I wish," said he, "to recommend the newest talent to your especial study and observation. I wish you to become acquainted with whatever our literature brings forth worthy of note, and to place before me whatever is meritorious, that we may discuss it in the numbers of 'Kunst und Alterthum,' and mention what is good, sound, and elevated, with due acknowledgment. For, with the best intentions, I cannot, at my advanced age, and with my manifold duties, do this without aid from others."

I said I would do this, and was very glad to find that our latest writers and poets were more interesting to Goethe than I had supposed.

He sent me the latest literary periodicals to assist in the proposed task. I did not go to him for several days, nor was I invited. I heard his friend Zelter had come to visit him.

(Sup.*) Friday, November 28, 1823.

The first part of Meyer's " History of Art," which has just appeared, seems to occupy Goethe very agreeably. He spoke of it to-day in terms of the highest praise.

Monday, December 1, 1823.

To-day, I was invited to dine with Goethe. I found Zelter sitting with him when I arrived. Both advanced to meet me, and gave me their hands. "Here," said Goethe, "we have my friend Zelter. In him you make a valuable acquaintance. I shall send you soon to Berlin; he will take excellent care of you." "Is Berlin a good place?" said I. "Yes," replied Zelter, laughing; "a great deal may be learned and unlearned there."

We sat down and talked on various subjects. I asked after Schubarth. "He visits me at least every week," said Zelter. "He is married now, but has no appointment, because he has offended the philologists in Berlin."

Zelter asked me then if I knew Immermann. I said I had often heard his name, but as yet knew nothing of his writings. "I made his acquaintance at Münster," said Zelter; "he is a very hopeful young man, and it is a pity that his appointment leaves him no more time for his art." Goethe also praised his talent. "But we must see," said he, "how he comes out; whether he will submit to purify his taste, and, with respect to form, adopt the acknowledged best models as his standard. His original striving has its merit, but leads astray too easily."

Little Walter now came jumping in, asking many questions, both of Zelter and his grandfather. "When thou comest, uneasy spirit," said Goethe, "all conversation is spoiled." However, he loves the boy, and was unwearied in satisfying his wishes.

Frau von Goethe and Fräulein Ulrica now came in, and with them, young Goethe, in his uniform and sword, ready for court. We sat down to table. Fräulein Ulrica and Zelter were very gay, and rallied each other in the pleasantest way during the whole of dinner. The person and presence of Zelter had an agreeable effect on me. As a healthy, happy man, he could give himself up wholly to the influence of the moment, and always had the word fit for the occasion. Then he was very lively and kindly, and so perfectly unconstrained, that he could speak out whatever was in his mind, sometimes giving a hard hit. He imparted to others his own freedom of spirit, so that all narrowing views were soon dispelled by his presence. I silently thought how much I should like to live with him a while, and I am sure it would do me good.

Zelter went away soon after dinner. He was invited to visit the grand-duchess that evening.

Thursday, December 4, 1823.

This morning, Secretary Kräuter brought me an invitation to dine with Goethe; at the same time, by Goethe's desire, giving me a hint to present Zelter with a copy of my " Beyträge zur Poesie." I took the copy to him at his hotel. Zelter, in return, put Immermann's poems into my hands. " I would willingly make you a present of this copy," said he, " but, you see, the author has dedicated it to me, and I must therefore keep it as a valuable memorial."

Before dinner, I walked with Zelter through the park towards Upper Weimar. Many spots recalled to him former days, and he told me much of Schiller, Wieland, and Herder, with whom he had been on terms of great intimacy, which he considered had been one of the great benefits of his life.

He then talked much of musical composition, and recited many of Goethe's songs. " If I am to compose music for a poem," said he, " I first try to penetrate into the meaning of the words, and to bring before me a living picture of the situation. I then read it aloud till I know it by heart, and thus, when I again recite it, the melody comes of its own accord."

Wind and rain obliged us to return sooner than we wished. I accompanied him to Goethe's house, where he went up to Frau von Goethe to sing with her before dinner.

About two, I returned there to dinner, and found Goethe and Zelter already engaged in looking at engravings of Italian scenery. Frau von Goethe came in, and we sat down to dinner. Fräulein Ulrica was absent to-day; and so was young Goethe, who just came in to say Good-day, and then returned to court.

The conversation at table was especially varied. Many very original anecdotes were told both by Zelter and Goethe, all illustrating the peculiarities of their common friend, Friedrich August Wolf, of Berlin. There was a great deal of talk about the "Nibelungen," and then about Lord Byron and his hoped-for visit to Weimar, in which Frau von Goethe took especial interest. The Rochus festival at Bingen was also a very cheerful subject; and Zelter particularly remembered two beautiful girls, whose amiability had made a deep impression upon him, and the memory of whom seemed still to exhilarate him. Goethe's social song, "Kriegsglück" (Fortune of War), was then gaily talked over. Zelter was inexhaustible in his anecdotes of wounded soldiers and beautiful women, and they all tended to show the truthfulness of the poem. Goethe himself said that he had had no need to go far for such realities; he had seen them all at Weimar. Frau von Goethe maintained a lively opposition, saying that she would not admit women were so bad as that "nasty" poem represented them.

Thus the time at table passed pleasantly enough.

When, afterwards, I was alone with Goethe, he asked me about Zelter. "Well," said he, "how do you like him?" I described the good effect produced on me by his presence. "On a first acquaintance," said Goethe, "he may appear somewhat blunt, even rough; but that is only external. I scarcely know any man who is really so tender as Zelter. Besides, we must not forget that he has passed more than half a century in Berlin, where, as I remark generally, there is such an audacious set of men, that one cannot get on well with delicacy, but must have one's eyes wide open, and be a little rough now and then, only to keep one's head above water.

(Sup.*) Friday, December 5, 1823.

I brought Goethe some minerals; amongst them was a piece of clayey ochre, found by Deschamps in Cormayan, which Herr Massot praises very highly. How astonished was Goethe, when he recognised, in this colour, the very same which Angelica Kauffmann used to employ for the fleshy parts of her pictures. "She valued the little that she possessed," said he, "at its weight in gold. However, the place whence it came, and where it is to be found, was unknown to her." Goethe said to his daughter-in-law that I treated him like a sultan, to whom new presents are brought every day. "He treats you much more like a child," said Frau von Goethe; at which he could not help smiling.

(Sup.*) Sunday, December 7, 1823.

I asked Goethe how he felt to-day. "Not quite so bad as Napoleon on his island," was the answer he returned, with a sigh.

The long protraction of his indisposition seems gradually to produce an effect upon him.

(Sup.*) Sunday, December 21, 1823.

Goethe's good humour was again brilliant to-day. We have reached the shortest day; and the hope that, with each succeeding week, we shall see a considerable increase in the days, appears to have exerted a favourable effect on his spirits. "To-day we celebrate the regeneration of the sun!" exclaimed he, joyfully, as I entered his room this morning. I hear that it is his custom, every year, to pass the weeks before the shortest day in a most melancholy frame of mind,—to sigh them away, in fact.

Frau von Goethe entered, to inform her papa-in-law that she was on the point of travelling to Berlin, in order to meet her mother, who was just returning.

When Frau von Goethe was gone, Goethe joked with me on the lively imagination which characterizes youth. "I am too old," said he, "to contradict her, and to make her comprehend that the joy of seeing her mother again, for the first time, would be the same whether here or there. This winter journey is much trouble about nothing, but such a nothing is often of infinite importance in the minds of youth: and in the long run what difference does it make! One must often undertake some folly only to be able to live on again a little. In my youth I did no better, and still I have escaped with a tolerably whole skin."

(Sup.*) Tuesday, December 30, 1823.

This evening was spent alone with Goethe in diversified conversation. He told me that he had some intention of including in his works his journey into Switzerland in the year 1797. The conversation then turned upon "Werther," which he had only read once, about ten years after its publication. The same had been the case with his other works. We then talked upon translation, when he told me that he found it very difficult to render English poetry in German verse. "When we try to express a strong English monosyllable by German polysyllables or compounds, all force and effect are lost at once." He said that he had made the translation of his "Rameau" in four weeks, dictating every word.

We then talked about the natural sciences, especially about the narrow-mindedness with which learned men contend amongst themselves for priority. "There is nothing," said Goethe, "through which I have learned to know mankind better, than through my philosophical exertions. It has cost me a great deal, and has been attended with great annoyance, but I nevertheless rejoice that I have gained the experience."

I remarked, that in the sciences, the egotism of men appears to be excited in a peculiar manner; and when this is once called into action, all infirmities of character very soon appear.

"Scientific questions," answered Goethe, "are very often questions of existence. A single discovery may make a man renowned, and lay the foundation of his worldly prosperity. It is for this reason that, in the sciences, there prevails this great severity, this pertinacity, and this jealousy concerning the discovery of another. In the sphere of æsthetics, everything is deemed more venial; the thoughts are, more or less, an innate property of all mankind, with respect to which the only point is the treatment and execution—and, naturally enough, little envy is excited. A single idea may give foundation for a hundred epigrams; and the question is, merely, which poet has been able to embody this idea in the most effective and most beautiful manner."

"But in science the treatment is nothing, and all the effect lies in the discovery. There is here little that is universal and subjective, for the isolated manifestations of the laws of nature lie without us—all sphynx-like, motionless, firm, and dumb. Every new phenomenon that is observed is a discovery—every discovery a property. Now, only let a single person meddle with property, and man will soon be at hand with all his passions."

"However," continued Goethe, "in the sciences, that also is looked upon as property which has been handed down or taught at the universities. And if any one advances anything new which contradicts, perhaps threatens to overturn, the creed which we have for years repeated, and have handed down to others, all passions are raised against him, and every effort is made to crush him. People resist with all their might; they act as if they neither heard nor could comprehend; they speak of the new view with contempt, as if it were not worth the trouble of even so much as an investigation or a regard, and thus a new truth may wait a long time before it can make its way. A Frenchman said to a friend of mine, concerning my theory of colours,—' We have worked for fifty years to establish and strengthen the kingdom of Newton, and it will require fifty years more to overthrow it.' The body of mathematicians has endeavoured to make my name so suspected in science that people are afraid of even mentioning it. Some time ago, a pamphlet fell into my hands, in which subjects connected with the theory of colours were treated: the author appeared quite imbued with my theory, and had deduced everything from the same fundamental principles. I read the publication with great delight, but, to my no small surprise, found that the author did not once mention my name. The enigma was afterwards solved. A mutual friend called on me, and confessed to me that the clever young author had wished to establish his reputation by the pamphlet, and had justly feared to compromise himself with the learned world, if he ventured to support by my name the views he was expounding. The little pamphlet was successful, and the ingenious young author has since introduced himself to me personally, and made his excuses."

"This circumstance appears to me the more remarkable," said I, "because in everything else people have reason to be proud of you as an authority, and every one esteems himself fortunate who has the powerful protection of your public countenance. With respect to your theory of colours, the misfortune appears to be, that you have to deal not only with the renowned and universally acknowledged Newton, but also with his disciples, who are spread all over the world, who adhere to their master, and whose name is legion. Even supposing that you carry your point at last, you will certainly for a long space of time stand alone with your new theory."

"I am accustomed to it, and prepared for it," returned Goethe. "But say yourself," continued he, "have I not had sufficient reason to feel proud, when for twenty years I have been forced to own to myself that the great Newton, and all mathematicians and august calculators with him, have fallen into a decided error respecting the theory of colours; and that I, amongst millions, am the only one who knows the truth on this important subject? With this feeling of superiority, it was possible for me to bear with the stupid pretensions of my opponents. People endeavoured to attack me and my theory in every way, and to render my ideas ridiculous; but, nevertheless, I rejoiced exceedingly over my completed work. All the attacks of my adversaries only serve to expose to me the weakness of mankind."

While Goethe spoke thus, with such a force and a fluency of expression as I have not the power to reproduce with perfect truth, his eyes sparkled with unusual fire; an expression of triumph was observable in them; whilst an ironical smile played upon his lips. The features of his fine countenance were more imposing than ever.

(Sup.) Wednesday, December 31, 1823.

Dined at Goethe's; conversing on various subjects. He showed me a portfolio containing sketches; amongst which the first attempts of Henry Füssli* were especially remarkable.

We then spoke upon religious subjects, and the abuse of the divine name. "People treat it," said Goethe, "as if that incomprehensible and most high Being, who is even beyond the reach of thought, were only their equal. Otherwise, they would not say the *Lord God*, the *dear God*,† the *good God*. This expression becomes to them, especially to the clergy, who have it daily in their mouths, a mere phrase, a barren name, to which no thought is attached whatever. If they were impressed by His greatness they would be dumb, and through veneration unwilling to name Him."

---

* That is, Fuseli, as we call him —*Trans.*

† "The *dear* God" (der liebe Gott) is one of the commonest German expressions —*Trans.*

CONVERSATIONS OF GOETHE.

1824.

1824.

(Sup.) Friday, January 2, 1824.

DINED at Goethe's, and enjoyed some cheerful conversation. Mention was made of a young beauty belonging to the Weimar society, when one of the guests remarked, that he was on the point of falling in love with her, although her understanding could not exactly be called brilliant.

"Pshaw," said Goethe, laughing, "as if love had anything to do with the understanding. The things that we love in a young lady are something very different from the understanding. We love in her beauty, youthfulness, playfulness, trustingness, her character, her faults, her caprices, and God knows what '*je ne sais quoi*' besides; but we do not *love* her understanding. We respect her understanding when it is brilliant, and by it the worth of a girl can be infinitely enhanced in our eyes. Understanding may also serve to fix our affections when we already love; but the understanding is not that which is capable of firing our hearts, and awakening a passion."

We found much that was true and convincing in Goethe's words, and were very willing to consider the subject in that light. After dinner, and when the rest of the party had departed, I remained sitting with Goethe, and conversed with him on various interesting topics.

We discoursed upon English literature, on the greatness of Shakspeare; and on the unfavourable position held by all English dramatic authors who had appeared after that poetical giant.

"A dramatic talent of any importance," said Goethe, "could not forbear to notice Shakspeare's works, nay, could not forbear to study them. Having studied them, he must be aware that Shakspeare has already exhausted the whole of human nature in all its tendencies, in all its heights and depths, and that, in fact, there remains for him, the aftercomer, nothing more to do. And how could one get courage only to put pen to paper, if one were conscious in an earnest appreciating spirit, that such unfathomable and unattainable excellences were already in existence!

"It fared better with me fifty years ago in my own dear Germany. I could soon come to an end with all that then existed; it could not long awe me, or occupy my attention. I soon left behind me German literature, and the study of it, and turned my thoughts to life and to production. So on and on I went in my own natural development, and on and on I fashioned the productions of epoch after epoch. And at every step of life and development, my standard of excellence was not much higher than what at such step I was able to attain. But had I been born an Englishman, and had all those numerous masterpieces been brought before me in all their power, at my first dawn of youthful consciousness, they would have overpowered me, and I should not have known what to do. I could not have gone on with such fresh light-heartedness, but should have had to bethink myself, and look about for a long time, to find some new outlet."

I turned the conversation back to Shakspeare. "When one, to some degree, disengages him from English literature," said I, "and considers him transformed into a German, one cannot fail to look upon his gigantic greatness as a miracle. But if one seeks him in his home, transplants oneself to the soil of his country, and to the atmosphere of the century in which he lived; further, if one studies his contemporaries, and his immediate successors, and inhales the force wafted to us from Ben Jonson, Massinger, Marlow, and Beaumont and Fletcher, Shakspeare still, indeed, appears a being of the most exalted magnitude; but still, one arrives at the conviction, that many of the wonders of his genius are, in some measure, accessible, and that much is due to the powerfully productive atmosphere of his age and time."

"You are perfectly right," returned Goethe. "It is with Shakspeare as with the mountains of Switzerland. Transplant Mont Blanc at once into the large plain of Luneburg Heath, and we should find no words to express our wonder at its magnitude. Seek it, however, in its gigantic home, go to it over its immense neighbours, the Jungfrau, the Finsteraarhorn, the Eiger, the Wetterhorn, St. Gothard, and Monte Rosa; Mont Blanc will, indeed, still remain a giant, but it will no longer produce in us such amazement."

"Besides, let him who will not believe," continued Goethe, "that much of Shakspeare's greatness appertains to his great vigorous time, only ask himself the question, whether a phenomenon so astounding would be possible in the present England of 1824, in these evil days of criticising and hair-splitting journals?

"That undisturbed, innocent, somnambulatory production, by which alone anything great can thrive, is no longer possible. Our talents at present lie before the public. The daily criticisms which appear in fifty different places, and the gossip that is caused by them amongst the public, prevent the appearance of any sound production. In the present day, he who does not keep aloof from all this, and isolate himself by main force, is lost. Through the bad, chiefly negative, æsthetical and critical tone of the journals, a sort of half culture finds its way into the masses; but to productive talent it is a noxious mist, a dropping poison, which destroys the tree of creative power from the ornamental green leaves, to the deepest pith and the most hidden fibres.

"And then how tame and weak has life itself become during the last two shabby centuries. Where do we now meet an original nature? and where is the man who has the strength to be true, and to show himself as he is? This, however, affects the poet, who must find all within himself, while he is left in the lurch by all without."

The conversation now turned on "Werther." "That," said Goethe, "is a creation which I, like the pelican, fed with the blood of my own heart. It contains so much from the innermost recesses of my breast—so much feeling and thought, that it might easily be spread into a novel of ten such volumes. Besides, as I have often said, I have only read the book once since its appearance, and have taken good care not to read it again. It is a mass of congreve-rockets. I am uncomfortable when I look at it; and I dread lest I should once more experience the peculiar mental state from which it was produced."

I reminded him of his conversation with Napoleon, of which I knew by the sketch amongst his unpublished papers, which I had repeatedly urged him to give more in detail. "Napoleon," said I, "pointed out to you a passage in 'Werther,' which, it appeared to him, would not stand a strict examination; and this you allowed. I should much like to know what passage he meant."

"Guess!" said Goethe, with a mysterious smile.

"Now," said I, "I almost think it is where Charlotte sends the pistols to Werther, without saying a word to Albert, and without imparting to him her misgivings and apprehensions. You have given yourself great trouble to find a motive for this silence, but it does not appear to hold good against the urgent necessity where the life of the friend was at stake."

"Your remark," returned Goethe, "is really not bad; but I do not think it right to reveal whether Napoleon meant this passage or another. However, be that as it may, your observation is quite as correct as his."

I asked the question, whether the great effect produced by the appearance of "Werther" was really to be attributed to the period. "I cannot," said I, "reconcile to myself this view, though it is so extensively spread. 'Werther' made an epoch because it appeared—not because it appeared at a certain time. There is in every period so much unexpressed sorrow—so much secret discontent and disgust for life, and, in single individuals, there are so many disagreements with the world—so many conflicts between their natures and civil regulations, that 'Werther' would make an epoch even if it appeared to-day for the first time."

"You are quite right," said Goethe; "it is on that account that the book to this day influences youth of a certain age, as it did formerly. It was scarcely necessary for me to deduce my own youthful dejection from the general influence of my time, and from the reading of a few English authors. Rather was it owing to individual and immediate circumstances which touched me to the quick, and gave me a great deal of trouble, and indeed brought me into that frame of mind which produced 'Werther.' I had lived, loved, and suffered much—that was it."

"On considering more closely the much-talked-of 'Werther' period, we discover that it does not belong to the course of universal culture, but to the career of life in every individual who, with an innate free natural instinct, must accommodate himself to the narrow limits of an antiquated world. Obstructed fortune, restrained activity, unfulfilled wishes, are not the calamities of any particular time, but those of every individual man; and it would be bad, indeed, if every one had not, once in his life, known a time when 'Werther' seemed as if it had been written for him alone."

(Sup.) *Sunday, January 4, 1824.*

To-day, after dinner, Goethe went through a portfolio, containing some works of Raphael, with me. He often busies himself with Raphael, in order to keep up a constant intercourse with that which is best, and to accustom himself to muse upon the thoughts of a great man. At the same time, it gives him pleasure to introduce me to such things.

We afterwards spoke about the " Divan "*—especially about the " book of ill-humour," in which much is poured forth that he carried in his heart against his enemies.

" I have, however," continued he, " been very moderate: if I had uttered all that vexed me or gave me trouble, the few pages would soon have swelled to a volume.

" People were never thoroughly contented with me, but always wished me otherwise than it has pleased God to make me. They were also seldom contented with my productions. When I had long exerted my whole soul to favour the world with a new work, it still desired that I should thank it into the bargain for considering the work endurable. If any one praised me, I was not allowed, in self-congratulation, to receive it as a well-merited tribute; but people expected from me some modest expression, humbly setting forth the total unworthiness of my person and my work. However, my nature opposed this; and I should have been a miserable hypocrite, if I had so tried to lie and dis-

---

* Goethe's "West-östliche (west-eastern) Divan," one of the twelve divisions of which is entitled " Das Buch des Unmuths" (The Book of Ill-Humour).—*Trans.*

semble. Since I was strong enough to show myself in my whole truth, just as I felt, I was deemed proud, and am considered so to the present day.

"In religious, scientific, and political matters, I generally brought trouble upon myself, because I was no hypocrite, and had the courage to express what I felt.

"I believed in God and in Nature, and in the triumph of good over evil; but this was not enough for pious souls: I was also required to believe other points, which were opposed to the feeling of my soul for truth; besides, I did not see that these would be of the slightest service to me.

"It was also prejudicial to me that I discovered Newton's theory of light and colour to be an error, and that I had the courage to contradict the universal creed. I discovered light in its purity and truth, and I considered it my duty to fight for it. The opposite party, however, did their utmost to darken the light; for they maintained that *shade is a part of light*. It sounds absurd when I express it; but so it is: for they said that *colours*, which are shadow and the result of shade, *are light itself*, or, which amounts to the same thing, *are the beams of light, broken now in one way, now in another.*"

Goethe was silent, whilst an ironical smile spread over his expressive countenance. He continued:—

"And now for political matters. What trouble I have taken, and what I have suffered, on that account, I cannot tell you. Do you know my 'Aufgeregten?'*

"Yesterday, for the first time," returned I, "I read

---

* "Die Aufgeregten" (the Agitated, in a political sense) is an unfinished drama by Goethe.—*Trans.*

the piece, in consequence of the new edition of your works; and I regret from my heart that it remains unfinished. But, even as it is, every right-thinking person must coincide with your sentiments."

"I wrote it at the time of the French Revolution," continued Goethe, "and it may be regarded, in some measure, as my political confession of faith at that time. I have taken the countess as a type of the nobility; and, with the words which I put into her mouth, I have expressed how the nobility really ought to think. The countess has just returned from Paris; she has there been an eye-witness of the revolutionary events, and has drawn, therefore, for herself, no bad doctrine. She has convinced herself that the people may be ruled, but not oppressed, and that the revolutionary outbreaks of the lower classes are the consequence of the injustice of the higher classes. 'I will for the future,' says she, 'strenuously avoid every action that appears to me unjust, and will, both in society and at court, loudly express my opinion concerning such actions in others. In no case of injustice will I be silent, even though I should be cried down as a democrat.'

"I should have thought this sentiment perfectly respectable," continued Goethe; "it was mine at that time, and it is so still; but as a reward for it, I was endowed with all sorts of titles, which I do not care to repeat."

"One need only read 'Egmont,'" answered I, "to discover what you think. I know no German piece in which the freedom of the people is more advocated than in this."

"Sometimes," said Goethe, "people do not like to look on me as I am, but turn their glances from everything which could show me in my true light. Schiller, on the contrary—who, between ourselves, was much more of an aristocrat than I am, but who considered what he said more than I—had the wonderful fortune to be looked upon as a particular friend of the people. I give it up to him with all my heart, and console myself with the thought that others before me have fared no better.

"It is true that I could be no friend to the French Revolution; for its horrors were too near me, and shocked me daily and hourly, whilst its beneficial results were not then to be discovered. Neither could I be indifferent to the fact, that the Germans were endeavouring, artificially, to bring about such scenes here, as were, in France, the consequence of a great necessity.

"But I was as little a friend to arbitrary rule. Indeed, I was perfectly convinced that a great revolution is never a fault of the people, but of the government. Revolutions are utterly impossible as long as governments are constantly just and constantly vigilant, so that they may anticipate them by improvements at the right time, and not hold out until they are forced to yield by the pressure from beneath.

"Because I hated the Revolution, the name of *Friend of the powers that be* was bestowed upon me. That is, however, a very ambiguous title, which I would beg to decline. If the 'powers that be' were all that is excellent, good, and just, I should have no objection to the title; but, since with much that is good there is also much that is bad, unjust, and imperfect, a friend of the 'powers that be' means often little less than the friend of the obsolete and bad.*

"But time is constantly progressing, and human affairs wear every fifty years a different aspect; so that an arrangement which, in the year 1800, was perfection, may, perhaps, in the year 1850 be a defect.

"And, furthermore, nothing is good for a nation but that which arises from its own core and its own general wants, without apish imitation of another; since what to one race of people, of a certain age, is a wholesome nutriment, may perhaps prove a poison for another. All endeavours to introduce any foreign innovation, the necessity for which is not rooted in the core of the nation itself, are therefore foolish; and all premeditated revolutions of the kind are unsuccessful, *for they are without God, who keeps aloof from such bungling.* If, however, there exists an actual necessity for a great reform amongst a people, God is with it, and it prospers. He was visibly with Christ and his first adherents; for the appearance of the new doctrine of love was a necessity to the people. He was also visibly with Luther; for the purification of the doctrine corrupted by the priests was no less a necessity. Neither of the great powers whom I have named was, however, a friend of the permanent; much more were both of them convinced that the old leaven must be got rid of, and that it would be impossible to go on and remain in the untrue, unjust, and defective way."

* The German phrase "Freund des Bestehenden," which, for want of a better expression, has been rendered above "friend of the powers that be," literally means "friend of the permanent," and was used by the detractors of Goethe to denote the " enemy of the progressive."—*Trans.*

Tuesday, 27th January, 1824.

Goethe talked with me about the continuation of his memoirs, with which he is now busy. He observed, that this later period of his life would not be narrated with such minuteness as the youthful epoch of "Dichtung und Wahrheit."* "I must," said he, "treat this later period more in the fashion of annals: my outward actions must appear rather than my inward life. Altogether, the most important part of an individual's life is that of development, and mine is concluded in the detailed volumes of "Dichtung und Wahrheit." Afterwards begins the conflict with the world, and that is interesting only in its results.

"And then the life of a learned German—what is it? What may have been really good in my case cannot be communicated, and what can be communicated is not worth the trouble. Besides, where are the hearers whom one could entertain with any satisfaction?

"When I look back to the earlier and middle periods of my life, and now in my old age think how few are left of those who were young with me, I always think of a summer residence at a bathing-place. When you arrive, you make acquaintance and friends of those who have already been there some time, and who leave in a few weeks. The loss is painful. Then you turn to the second generation, with which you live a good while, and become most intimate. But this goes also, and leaves us alone with the third, which comes just as we are going away, and with which we have, properly, nothing to do.

"I have ever been esteemed one of Fortune's

---

* "Poetry and Truth," the title of Goethe's autobiography.—*Trans.*

chiefest favourites; nor will I complain or find fault with the course my life has taken. Yet, truly, there has been nothing but toil and care; and I may say that, in all my seventy-five years, I have never had a month of genuine comfort. It has been the perpetual rolling of a stone, which I have always had to raise anew. My annals will render clear what I now say. The claims upon my activity, both from within and without, were too numerous.

"My real happiness was my poetic meditation and production. But how was this disturbed, limited, and hindered by my external position! Had I been able to abstain more from public business, and to live more in solitude, I should have been happier, and should have accomplished much more as a poet. But, soon after my 'Goetz' and 'Werther,' that saying of a sage was verified for me—'If you do anything for the sake of the world, it will take good care that you shall not do it a second time.'

"A wide-spread celebrity, an elevated position in life, are good things. But, for all my rank and celebrity, I am still obliged to be silent as to the opinion of others, that I may not give offence. This would be but poor sport, if by this means I had not the advantage of learning the thoughts of others without their being able to learn mine."

Sunday, February 15, 1824.

Goethe invited me to take a walk before dinner to-day. I found him at breakfast when I entered the room: he seemed in excellent spirits.

"I have had a pleasant visit," said he cheerfully. "A promising young Westphalian, named Meyer, has just been with me. He has written poems which warrant high expectations. He is only eighteen, and has made incredible progress.

"I am glad," continued he, smiling, "that I am not eighteen now. When I was eighteen, Germany was in its teens also, and something could be done; but now an incredible deal is demanded, and every avenue is barred.

"Germany itself stands so high in every department, that we can scarcely survey all it has done; and now we must be Greeks and Latins, and English and French into the bargain. Not content with this, some have the madness of pointing to the East also; and surely this is enough to confuse a young man's head!

"I have, by way of consolation, shown him my colossal Juno, as a token that he had best stick to the Greeks, and find consolation there. He is a fine young man, and, if he takes care not to dissipate his energies, something will be made of him. However, as I said before, I thank Heaven that I am not young in so thoroughly finished a time. I could not stay here. Nay, if I sought refuge in America, I should come too late, for there is now too much light even there."

Sunday, February 22, 1824.

Dined with Goethe and his son. The latter related some pleasant stories of the time when he was a student at Heidelberg. He had often been with his friends on an excursion along the Rhine, in his vacations, and especially cherished the remembrance of a landlord, at whose house he and ten other students had once passed the night, and who provided them with wine gratis, merely that he might share the pleasures of a " Commerz."*

After dinner, Goethe showed us some coloured drawings of Italian scenery, especially that of Northern Italy, with the adjoining Swiss mountains, and the Lago Maggiore. The Borromean Isles were reflected in the water; near the shore were skiffs and fishing-tackle, which led Goethe to remark that this was the lake in the "Wanderjahre." On the northwest, towards Monte Rosa, stood the hills bordering the lake in black-blue heavy masses, as we are wont to see them soon after sunset.

I remarked that, to me, who had been born in the plains, the gloomy sublimity of these masses produced an uncomfortable feeling, and that I, by no means desired to explore such wild recesses.

"That feeling is natural," said Goethe. "Really that state is alone suitable to man, in which, and for which, he was born. He who is not led abroad by great objects is far happier at home. Switzerland, at first, made so great an impression upon me, that it disturbed and confused me. Only after repeated visits— only in after years, when I visited those mountains merely as a mineralogist—could I feel at my ease among them."

We looked, afterwards, at a long series of copperplates, from pictures by modern artists, in one of the French galleries. The invention displayed in these pictures was almost uniformly weak, and among forty, we barely found four or five good ones. These were

* The academical word for a student's drinking party.—*Trans.*

a girl dictating a love-letter; a woman in a house to let, which nobody will take; "catching fish;" and musicians before an image of the Madonna. A landscape, in Poussin's manner was not bad; on looking at this, Goethe said, "Such artists get a general idea of Poussin's landscapes, and work upon that. We cannot style their pictures good or bad: they are not bad, because, through every part, you catch glimpses of an excellent model. But you cannot call them good, because the artists usually want the great personal peculiarity of Poussin. It is just so among poets, and there are some who, for instance, would make a very poor figure in Shakspeare's grand style."

We ended, by examining and talking over for a long while, Rauch's model of Goethe's statue, which is designed for Frankfort.

Tuesday, February 24, 1824.

I went to Goethe's at one o'clock to-day. He showed me some manuscripts, which he had dictated for the first number of the fifth volume of "Kunst und Alterthum." I found that he had written an appendix to my critique of the German "Paria," in reference both to the French tragedy and to his own lyrical trilogy, by which this subject, was, to a certain extent, completed.

"You were quite right," said he, "to avail yourself of the occasion of your critique, to become acquainted with Indian matters, since, in the end, we retain from our studies only that which we practically apply."

I agreed with him, and said that I had made this experience at the university, since, of all that was said in the lectures, I had only retained that, of which I could, through the tendency of my nature, make a practical application; on the contrary, I had completely forgotten all that I had been unable to reduce to practice. "I have," said I "heard Heeren's lectures on ancient and modern history, and know now nothing about the matter. But if I studied a period of history for the sake of treating it dramatically, what I learned would be safely secured to me for ever."

"Altogether," said Goethe, "they teach in academies far too many things, and far too much that is useless. Then the individual professors extend their department too much—far beyond the wants of their hearers. In former days lectures were read in chemistry and botany as belonging to medicine, and the physician could manage them. Now, both these have become so extensive, that each of them requires a life; yet acquaintance with both is expected from the physician. Nothing can come of this; one thing must be neglected and forgotten for the sake of the other. He who is wise puts aside all claims which may dissipate his attention, confines himself to one branch, and excels in that."

Goethe then showed me a short critique, which he had written on Byron's "Cain," and which I read with great interest.

"We see," he said, "how the inadequate dogmas of the church work upon a free mind like Byron's, and how by such a piece he struggles to get rid of a doctrine which has been forced upon him. The English clergy will not thank him; but I shall be surprised if he does not go on treating biblical subjects of similar import, and if he lets slip a subject like the destruction of Sodom and Gomorrah."

After these literary observations, Goethe directed my attention to plastic art, by showing me an antique gem, of which he had already expressed his admiration the day before. I was enchanted to observe the *naïveté* of the design. I saw a man who had taken a heavy vessel from his shoulder to give a boy drink. But the boy finds it is not bent down conveniently for him; the drink will not flow; and while he has laid both his little hands on the vessel, he looks up to the man, and seems to ask him to incline it a little more towards him.

"Now, how do you like that?" said Goethe. "We moderns," continued he, "feel well enough the beauty of such a perfectly natural, perfectly *naïve motive;* we have the knowledge and the idea how such a thing is to be brought about, but we cannot do it; the understanding is always uppermost, and this enchanting grace is always wanting."

We looked then at a medal by Brandt of Berlin, representing young Theseus taking the arms of his father from under the stone. The attitude had much that was commendable, but we found the limbs not sufficiently strained to lift such a burden. It seemed, too, a mistake for the youth to have the arms in one hand while he lifted the stone with the other; for, according to the nature of things, he would first roll aside the heavy stone, and then take up the arms. "By way of contrast," said Goethe, "I will show you an antique gem, where the same subject is treated by an ancient."

He bade Stadelmann bring a box containing several

hundred copies of antique gems, which he had brought with him from Rome, on the occasion of his travels in Italy. I then saw the same subject, treated by an old Greek—and how different it was! The youth was exerting his whole strength upon the stone, and was equal to the task, for the weight was already visibly overcome, and the stone was raised to that point, where it would very soon be cast on one side. All his bodily powers were directed by the young hero against the heavy mass; only his looks were fixed on the arms which lay beneath.

We were pleased with the great natural truth of this treatment.

"Meyer," said Goethe, laughing, "always says, 'If thinking were not so hard.' And the worst is, that all the thinking in the world does not bring us to thought; we must be right by nature, so that good thoughts may come before us like free children of God, and cry, 'Here we are.'"

Wednesday, February 25, 1824.

To-day, Goethe showed me two very remarkable poems, both highly moral in their tendency, but in their several *motives* so unreservedly natural and true, that they are of the kind which the world styles immoral. On this account, he keeps them to himself, and does not intend to publish them.

"Could intellect and high cultivation," said he, "become the property of all, the poet would have fair play; he could be always thoroughly true, and would not be compelled to fear uttering his best thoughts. But, as it is, he must always keep on a certain level; must remember that his works will fall into the hands of a mixed society; and must, therefore, take care lest by over-great openness he may give offence to the majority of good men. Then, Time is a strange thing. It is a whimsical tyrant, which in every century has a different face for all that one says and does. We cannot, with propriety, say things which were permitted to the ancient Greeks; and the Englishmen of 1820 cannot endure what suited the vigorous contemporaries of Shakspeare; so that at the present day, it is found necessary to have a Family Shakspeare."

"Then," said I, "there is much in the form also. The one of these two poems, which is composed in the style and metre of the ancients, would be far less offensive than the other. Isolated parts would displease, but the treatment throws so much grandeur and dignity over the whole, that we seem to hear a strong ancient, and to be carried back to the age of the Greek heroes. But the other, being in the style and metre of Messer Ariosto, is far more hazardous. It relates an event of our day, in the language of our day, and as it thus comes quite unveiled into our presence, the particular features of boldness seem far more audacious."

"You are right," said he; "mysterious and great effects are produced by different poetical forms. If the import of my Romish elegies were put into the measure and style of Byron's 'Don Juan,' the whole would be found infamous."

The French newspapers were brought. The campaign of the French in Spain under the Duke D'Angouleme, which was just ended, had great interest for Goethe. "I must praise the Bourbons for this measure," said he; "they had not really gained the throne till they had gained the army, and that is now accomplished. The soldier returns with loyalty to his king; for he has, from his own victories, and the discomfitures of the many-headed Spanish host, learned the difference between obeying one and many. The army has sustained its ancient fame, and shown that it is brave in itself, and can conquer without Napoleon."

Goethe then turned his thoughts backward into history, and talked much of the Prussian army in the Seven Years' war, which, accustomed by Frederic the Great to constant victory, grew careless, so that, in after days, it lost many battles from over-confidence. All the minutest details were present to his mind, and I had reason to admire his excellent memory.

"I had the great advantage," said he, "of being born at a time when the greatest events which agitated the world occurred, and such have continued to occur during my long life; so that I am a living witness of the Seven Years' war, of the separation of America from England, of the French Revolution, and of the whole Napoleon era, with the downfall of that hero, and the events which followed. Thus I have attained results and insight impossible to those who are born now and must learn all these things from books which they will not understand.

"What the next years will bring I cannot predict; but I fear we shall not soon have repose. It is not given to the world to be contented; the great are not such that there will be no abuse of power; the masses not such that, in hope of gradual improvement, they will be contented with a moderate condition. Could we perfect human nature, we might also expect a perfect state of things; but, as it is, there will always be a wavering hither and thither; one part must suffer while the other is at ease, envy and egotism will be always at work like bad demons, and party strife will be without end.

" The most reasonable way is for every one to follow his own vocation to which he has been born, and which he has learned, and to avoid hindering others from following theirs. Let the shoemaker abide by his last, the peasant by his plough, and let the king know how to govern; for this is also a business which must be learned, and with which no one should meddle who does not understand it."

Returning to the French papers, Goethe said,— " The liberals may speak, for when they are reasonable we like to hear them; but with the royalists, who have the executive power in their hands, talking comes amiss—they should act. They may march troops, and behead and hang—that is all right; but attacking opinions, and justifying their measures in public prints, does not become them. If there were a public of kings, they might talk.

" For myself," he continued, " I have always been a royalist. I have let others babble, and have done as I saw fit. I understood my course, and knew my own object. If I committed a fault as a single individual, I could make it good again; but if I committed it jointly with three or four others, it would be impossible to make it good, for among many there are many opinions."

Goethe was in excellent spirits to-day. He showed

me Frau von Spiegel's album, in which he had written some very beautiful verses. A place had been left open for him for two years, and he rejoiced at having been able to perform at last an old promise. After I had read the " Poem to Frau von Spiegel," I turned over the leaves of the book, in which I found many distinguished names. On the very next page was a poem by Tiedge, written in the very spirit and style of his "Urania." "In a saucy mood," said Goethe, "I was on the point of writing some verses beneath those; but I am glad I did not. It would not have been the first time that, by rash expressions, I had repelled good people, and spoiled the effect of my best works.

"However," continued Goethe, "I have had to endure not a little from Tiedge's 'Urania;' for, at one time, nothing was sung and nothing was declaimed but this same 'Urania.' Wherever you went, you found 'Urania' on the table. 'Urania' and immortality were the topics of every conversation. I would by no means dispense with the happiness of believing in a future existence, and, indeed, would say, with Lorenzo de Medici, that those are dead even for this life who hope for no other. But such incomprehensible matters lie too far off to be a theme of daily meditation and thought-distracting speculation. Let him who believes in immortality enjoy his happiness in silence, he has no reason to give himself airs about it. The occasion of Tiedge's 'Urania' led me to observe that piety, like nobility, has its aristocracy. I met stupid women, who plumed themselves on believing, with Tiedge, in immortality, and I was forced to bear much dark examination on this point. They were vexed by my saying I should be well pleased *if*, after the close of this life, we were blessed with another, only I hoped I should hereafter meet none of those who had believed in it here. For how should I be tormented! The pious would throng around me, and say, 'Were we not right? Did we not predict it? Has not it happened just as we said?' And so there would be ennui without end even in the other world.

"This occupation with the ideas of immortality," he continued, "is for people of rank, and especially ladies, who have nothing to do. But an able man, who has something regular to do here, and must toil and struggle and produce day by day, leaves the future world to itself, and is active and useful in this. Thoughts about immortality are also good for those who have not been very successful here; and I would wager that, if the good Tiedge had enjoyed a better lot, he would also have had better thoughts."

Thursday, February 26, 1824.

I dined with Goethe. After the cloth had been removed, he bade Stadelmann bring in some large portfolios of copper-plates. Some dust had collected on the covers, and, as no suitable cloths were at hand to wipe it away, Goethe was much displeased, and scolded Stadelmann. "I tell you for the last time," said he, "if you do not go this very day to buy the cloths for which I have asked so often, I will go myself to-morrow; and you shall see that I will keep my word." Stadelmann went.

"A similar case occurred to me with Becker, the actor," added Goethe to me, in a lively tone, "when he refused to take the part of a trooper in 'Wallenstein.' I gave him warning that, if he would not play the part, I would play it myself. That did the business; for they knew me at the theatre well enough, and were aware that I did not understand jesting in such matters, and also that I was mad enough to keep my word in any case."

"And would you really have played the part?" asked I.

"Yes," said Goethe, "I would have played it, and would have eclipsed Herr Becker, too, for I knew the part better than he did."

We then opened the portfolios, and proceeded to the examination of the drawings and engravings. Goethe, in such matters, takes great pains on my account, and I see that it is his intention to give me a higher degree of penetration in the observation of works of art. He shows me only what is perfect in its kind, and endeavours to make me apprehend the intention and merit of the artist, that I may learn to pursue the thoughts of the best, and feel like the best. "This," said he, "is the way to cultivate what we call taste. Taste is only to be educated by contemplation, not of the tolerably good, but of the truly excellent. I, therefore, show you only the best works; and when you are grounded in these, you will have a standard for the rest, which you will know how to value, without overrating them. And I show you the best in each class, that you may perceive that no class is to be despised, but that each gives delight when a man of genius attains its highest point. For instance, this piece, by a French artist, is *galant*, to a degree which you see nowhere else, and is therefore a model in its way."

Goethe handed me the engraving, and I looked at it with delight. There was a beautiful room in a summer residence, with open doors and windows looking into a garden, where one might see the most graceful figures. A handsome lady, aged about thirty, was sitting with a music book, from which she seemed to have just sung. Sitting by her, a little further back, was a young girl of about fifteen. At the open window behind stood another young lady, holding a lute, which she seemed still to be sounding. At this moment a young gentleman was entering, to whom the eyes of the ladies were directed. He seemed to have interrupted the music; and his slight bow gave the notion that he was making an apology, which the ladies were gratified to hear.

"That, I think," said Goethe, "is as *galant* as any piece of Calderon's; and you have now seen the very best thing of this kind. But what say you to this?"

With these words he handed me some etchings by Roos, the famous painter of animals; they were all of sheep, in every posture and situation. The simplicity of their countenances, the ugliness and shagginess of the fleece,—all was represented with the utmost fidelity, as if it were nature itself.

"I always feel uneasy," said Goethe, "when I look at these beasts. Their state, so limited, dull, gaping, and dreaming, excites in me such sympathy, that I fear I shall become a sheep, and almost think the artist must have been one. At all events, it is most wonderful how Roos has been able to think and feel himself into the very soul of these creatures, so as to make the internal character peer with such force through the outward covering. Here you see what a great talent can do when it keeps steady to subjects which are congenial with its nature."

"Has not, then," said I, "this artist also painted dogs, cats, and beasts of prey with similar truth; nay, with this great gift of assuming a mental state foreign to himself, has he not been able to delineate human character with equal fidelity?"

"No," said Goethe, "all that lay out of his sphere; but the gentle, grass-eating animals, sheep, goats, cows, and the like, he was never weary of repeating; this was the peculiar province of his talent, which he did not quit during the whole course of his life. And in this he did well. A sympathy with these animals was born with him, a knowledge of their psychological condition was given him, and thus he had so fine an eye for their bodily structure. Other creatures were perhaps not so transparent to him, and therefore he felt neither calling nor impulse to paint them."

By this remark of Goethe's, much that was analogous was revived within me, and was presented in all its liveliness to my mind. Thus he had said to me, not long before, that knowledge of the world is inborn with the genuine poet, and that he needs not much experience or varied observation to represent it adequately. "I wrote 'Goetz von Berlichingen,'" said he, "as a young man of two-and-twenty, and was astonished, ten years after, at the truth of my delineation. It is obvious that I had not experienced nor seen anything of the kind, and therefore I must have acquired the knowledge of various human conditions by way of anticipation.

"Generally, I only took pleasure in painting my inward world before I became acquainted with the outer one. But when I found, in actual life, that the world was really just what I had fancied, it vexed me, and I no more felt delight in representing it. Indeed, I may say that if I had waited till I knew the world before I represented it, my representation would have had the appearance of persiflage.

"There is in every character," said he, another time, "a certain necessity, a sequence, which, together with this or that leading feature, causes secondary features. Observation teaches this sufficiently; but with some persons this knowledge may be innate. Whether with me experience and innate faculty are united, I will not inquire; but this I know, if I have talked with any man a quarter of an hour, I will let him talk two hours."

Goethe had likewise said of Lord Byron, that the world to him was transparent, and that he could paint by way of anticipation. I expressed some doubts whether Byron would succeed in painting, for instance, a subordinate animal nature, for his individuality seemed to me to be too powerful for him to give himself up, with any degree of predilection, to such a subject. Goethe admitted this, and replied, that the anticipation only went so far as the objects were analogous to the talent; and we agreed, that in the same proportion as the anticipation is confined or extended, is the representing talent of greater or smaller compass.

"If your excellency," said I, "maintains that the

world is inborn with the poet, you of course mean only the interior world, not the empirical world of appearances and conventions; if the poet is to give a successful representation of this also, an investigation into the actual will surely be requisite."

"Certainly," replied Goethe, "so it is; the region of love, hate, hope, despair, or by whatever other names you may call the moods and passions of the soul, is innate with the poet, and he succeeds in representing it. But it is not born with him to know by instinct how courts are held, or how a parliament or a coronation is managed; and if he will not offend against truth, while treating such subjects, he must have recourse to experience or tradition. Thus, in 'Faust,' I could, by anticipation, know how to describe my hero's gloomy weariness of life, and the emotions which love excites in the heart of Gretchen; but the lines,

> *Wie traurig steigt die unvollkommne Scheibe*
> *Des späten Monds mit feuchter Glut heran!*
>
> 'How gloomily does the imperfect disc
> Of the late moon with humid glow arise!'

required some observation of nature."

"Yet," said I, "every line of 'Faust' bears marks, not to be mistaken, of a careful study of life and the world; nor does one for a moment suppose otherwise than that the whole is only the result of the amplest experience."

"Perhaps so," replied Goethe; "yet, had I not the world already in my soul through anticipation, I should have remained blind with seeing eyes, and all experience and observation would have been dead, unproductive labour. The light is there, and the colours surround us; but, if we had no light and no colours in our own eyes, we should not perceive the outward phenomena."

Saturday, February 28, 1824.

"There are," said Goethe, "excellent men, who are unable to do anything impromptu, or superficially, but whose nature demands that they should quietly and deeply penetrate into every subject they may take in hand. Such minds often make us impatient, for we seldom get from them what we want at the moment; but in this way alone the noblest tasks are accomplished."

I turned the conversation to Ramberg. "He," said Goethe, "is an artist of quite a different stamp, of a most genial talent, and indeed unequalled in his power of impromptu. At Dresden, he once asked me to give him a subject. I gave him Agamemnon, at the moment when, on his return home from Troy, he is descending from his chariot, and is seized with a gloomy feeling, on touching the threshold of his house. You will agree that this is a subject of a most difficult kind, and with another artist, would have demanded the most mature deliberation. But the words had scarcely passed my lips, before Ramberg began to draw, and, indeed, I was struck with admiration, to see how correctly he at once apprehended his subject. I cannot deny that I should like to possess some drawings by Ramberg."

We talked then of other artists, who set to work in a superficial way, and thus degenerated into mannerism.

"Mannerism," said Goethe, "is always longing to have done, and has no true enjoyment in work. A genuine, really great talent, on the other hand, finds its greatest happiness in execution. Roos is unwearied in drawing the hair and wool of his goats and sheep, and you see by his infinite details that he enjoyed the purest felicity in doing his work, and had no wish to bring it to an end.

"Inferior talents do not enjoy art for its own sake; while at work they have nothing before their eyes but the profit they hope to make when they have done. With such worldly views and tendencies, nothing great was ever yet produced."

Sunday, February 29, 1824.

At twelve o'clock, I went to Goethe, who had invited me to take a walk before dinner. I found him at breakfast when I entered, and taking my seat opposite to him, turned the conversation upon those productions which occupy us both on account of the new edition of his works. I counselled him to insert both his "Gods, Heroes, and Wieland," and his "Letters of a Pastor," in this new edition.

"I cannot," said Goethe, "from my present point of view, properly judge the merit of those youthful productions. You younger people may decide, if you will. Yet I will not find fault with those beginnings; I was, indeed, then in the dark, and struggled on, unconscious of what I was seeking so earnestly; but I had a feeling of the right, a divining rod, that showed me where gold was to be found."

I observed that this must be the case with all great talents, since otherwise, on awaking in a mixed world, they would not seize upon the right and shun the wrong.

The horses had, in the mean while, been put to, and we rode towards Jena. We conversed on different subjects, and Goethe mentioned the last French newspapers. " The constitution of France," said he, " belonging to a people who have within themselves so many elements of corruption, rests upon a very different basis from that of England. Everything may be done in France by bribery; indeed the whole French revolution was directed by such means."

He then spoke of the death of Eugene Napoleon (Duke of Leuchtenberg), the news of which had arrived that morning, and which seemed to grieve him much. " He was one of those great characters," said Goethe, " which are becoming more and more rare; and the world is once more one important man the poorer. I knew him personally; only last summer I was with him at Marienbad. He was a handsome man, about forty-two, though he looked older, which was not to be wondered at when we call to mind all he went through, and how, through all his life, one campaign and one great deed pressed constantly on another. He told me at Marienbad of a plan, on the execution of which he conversed with me much. This was the union of the Rhine with the Danube, by means of a canal—a gigantic enterprise, when you consider the obstacles offered by the locality. But to a man who has served under Napoleon, and with him shaken the world, nothing appears impossible. Charlemagne had the same plan, and even began the work, but it soon came to a standstill. The sand would not hold, the banks were always falling in on both sides."

Monday, March 22, 1824.

To-day, before dinner, I went with Goethe into his garden.

The situation of this garden, on the other side of the Ilm, near the park, and on the western declivity of a hill, gives it a very inviting aspect. It is protected from the north and east winds, but open to the cheering influences of the south and west, which makes it a most delightful abode, especially in spring and autumn.

To the town, which lies north-west, one is so near that one can be there in a few minutes, and yet if one looks round, one does not anywhere see the top of a building, or even a spire, to remind one of such a proximity; the tall and thickly-planted trees of the park shut out every other object on that side. Under the name of the "Star," they go to the left, towards the north, close to the carriage-way, which leads immediately from the garden.

Towards the west and south-west, there is a free view over a spacious meadow, through which, at about the distance of a bow-shot, the Ilm winds silently along. On the opposite side of the river, the bank rises like a hill; on the summit and sides of which spreads the broad park, with the mixed foliage of alders, ash-trees, poplars, and birches, bounding the horizon at an agreeable distance on the south and west.

This view of the park over the meadow gives a feeling, especially in summer, as if one were near a wood which extended leagues round about. One thinks that every moment there will be deer bounding out upon the meadows. One feels transplanted into the peace of the deepest natural solitude, for the silence is often uninterrupted, except by the solitary notes of the blackbird, or the frequently-suspended song of the wood-thrush.

Out of this dream of profound solitude, we are, however, awakened by the striking of the tower-clock, the screaming of the peacocks from the park, or the drums and horns of the military in the barracks. And this is not unpleasant; for such tones comfortably remind one of the neighbourhood of the friendly city, from which one has fancied oneself distant so many miles.

At certain seasons, these meadows are the reverse of lonely. One sees sometimes country people going to Weimar to market, or to work, and returning thence; sometimes loungers of all sorts walking along the windings of the Ilm, especially in the direction towards Upper Weimar, which is on certain days much visited. The hay-making season also animates the scene very agreeably. In the back-ground, one sees flocks of sheep grazing, and sometimes the stately Swiss cows of the neighbouring farm.

To-day, however, there was no trace of these summer phenomena, which are so refreshing to the senses. On the meadows, some streaks of green were scarcely visible; the trees of the park as yet could boast nothing but brown twigs and buds; yet the note of the finch, with the occasional song of the blackbird and thrush, announced the approach of spring.

The air was pleasant and summerlike; a very mild south-west wind was blowing. Small, isolated thunderclouds passed along the clear sky; high above might be observed the dispersing cirrus-streaks. We accurately observed the clouds, and saw that the massive clouds of the lower region were likewise dispersing; from which Goethe inferred that the barometer must be rising.

Goethe then spoke much about the rising and falling of the barometer, which he called the affirmative and negative of water. He spoke of the inhaling and exhaling processes of the earth, according to eternal laws; of a possible deluge, if the "water-affirmative" continued. He said, besides, that, though each place has its proper atmosphere, there is great uniformity in the state of the barometer throughout Europe; nature, he said, was incommensurable, and with her great irregularities, it was often difficult to find her laws.

While he thus instructed me on such high subjects, we were walking up and down the broad gravel-walk of the garden. We came near the house, which he bade the servant to open, that he might show me the interior. Without, the whitewashed walls were covered with rose-bushes, which, trained on espaliers, reached to the roof. I went round the house, and saw with pleasure, on the branches of these rose-bushes, against the wall, a great number of birds' nests of various kinds, which had been there since the preceding summer, and, now that the bushes were bare of leaves, were exposed to the eye. There were especially to be observed the nests of the linnet and of various kinds of hedge-sparrows, built high or low according to the habits of the birds.

Goethe then took me inside the house, which I had

not seen since last summer. In the lower story, I found only one inhabitable room, on the walls of which were hung some charts and engravings, besides a portrait of Goethe, as large as life, painted by Meyer shortly after the return of both friends from Italy. Goethe here appears in the prime of his powers and his manhood, very brown, and rather stout. The expression of the countenance is not very animated, and is very serious; one seems to behold a man on whose mind lies the weight of future deeds.

We ascended the stairs to the upper-rooms. I found three, and one little cabinet; but all very small, and not very convenient. Goethe said that, in former years, he had passed a great deal of his time here with pleasure, and had worked very quietly.

These rooms were rather cool, and we returned into the open air, which was mild. As we walked up and down the chief pathway, in the noon-day sun, our conversation turned on modern literature, Schelling, and some new plays by Count Platen.

We soon returned to the natural objects. The crown-imperials and lilies were already far advanced; the mallows on both sides of the park were already green.

The upper part of the garden, on the declivity of the hill, is covered with grass, and here and there a few fruit-trees. Paths extend along the summit, and then return to the foot; which awakened in me a wish to ascend and look about me. Goethe, as he ascended these paths, walked swiftly before me, and I was rejoiced to see how active he was.

On the hedge above we found a pea-hen, which

seemed to have come from the prince's park; and Goethe remarked that, in summer time, he was accustomed to allure the peacocks, by giving them such food as they loved.

Descending on the winding path on the other side of the hill, I found a stone, surrounded by shrubs, on which was carved this line from the well-known poem—

Hier im stillen gedachte der Liebende seiner Geliebten ;

" Here in silence reflected the lover upon his beloved ;"

and I felt as if I were on classic ground.

Near this was a thicket of half-grown oaks, firs, birches, and beech-trees. Beneath the firs, I found the sign* of a bird of prey. I showed it to Goethe, who said he had often seen such in this place. From this I concluded that these firs were a favourite abode of some owls, which had been frequently seen in this place.

Passing round this thicket, we found ourselves once more on the principal path near the house. The oaks, firs, birches, and beeches, which we had just gone round, being mingled together, here form a semicircle, overarching like a grotto the inner space, in which we sat down on little chairs, placed about a round table. The sun was so powerful, that the shade even of these leafless trees was agreeable. "I know," said Goethe, "no better refuge, in the

---

* The word here rendered by the general expression " sign " is " Gewölle,"† a sporting term, which signifies the hair, feathers, or other indigestible matter swallowed by a bird of prey and afterwards vomited.— *Trans.*

heats of summer, than this spot. I planted all the trees, forty years ago, with my own hand; I have had the pleasure of watching their growth, and have now for a long time enjoyed their refreshing shade. The foliage of these oaks and beeches is impervious to the most potent sun. In hot summer days, I like to sit here after dinner; and often over the meadows and the whole park such stillness reigns, that the ancients would say, ' Pan sleeps.' "

We now heard the town-clock striking two, and returned to the house.

Tuesday, March 30, 1824.

This evening, I was with Goethe. I was alone with him; we talked on various subjects, and drank a bottle of wine. We spoke of the French drama, as contrasted with the German.

"It will be very difficult," said Goethe, "for the German public to come to a kind of right judgment, as they do in Italy and France. We have a special obstacle in the circumstance, that on our stage a medley of all sorts of things is represented. On the same boards where we saw Hamlet yesterday, we see Staberl* to-day; and if to-morrow we are delighted with 'Zauberflöte,' the day after we shall be charmed with the oddities of the next lucky wight. Hence the public becomes confused in its judgment, mingling together various species, which it never learns rightly to appreciate and to understand. Furthermore, every one has his own individual demands and personal wishes, and returns to the spot where he finds them

* A Viennese buffoon.—*Trans.*

realized. On the tree where he has plucked figs to-day, he would pluck them again to-morrow, and would make a long face if sloes had grown in their stead during the night. If any one is a friend to sloes, he goes to the thorns.

"Schiller had the happy thought of building a house for tragedy alone, and of giving a piece every week for the male sex exclusively. But this notion presupposed a very large city, and could not be realized with our humble means."

We talked about the plays of Iffland and Kotzebue, which, in their way, Goethe highly commended. "From this very fault," said he, "that people do not perfectly distinguish between *kinds* in art, the pieces of these men are often unjustly censured. We may wait a long time before a couple of such popular talents come again."

I praised Iffland's "Hagestolz" (Old Bachelor), with which I had been highly pleased on the stage. "It is unquestionably Iffland's best piece," said Goethe; "it is the only one in which he goes from prose into the ideal."

He then told me of a piece, which he and Schiller had made as a continuation to the "Hagestolz;" that is to say, in conversation, without writing it down. Goethe told me the progress of the action scene by scene; it was very pleasant and cheerful, and gave me great delight.

Goethe then spoke of some new plays by Platen. "In these pieces," said he, "we may see the influence of Calderon. They are very clever, and, in a certain sense, complete; but they want specific gravity, a certain weight of import. They are not of a kind to excite in the mind of the reader a deep and abiding interest; on the contrary, the strings of the soul are touched but lightly and transiently. They are like cork, which, when it swims on the water, makes no impression, but is easily sustained by the surface.

"The German requires a certain earnestness, a certain grandeur of thought, and a certain fulness of sentiment. It is on this account that Schiller is so highly esteemed by all. I do not in the least doubt the abilities of Platen; but those, probably from mistaken views of art, are not manifested here. He shows distinguished culture, intellect, pungent wit, and artistical completeness; but these, especially in Germany, are not enough.

"Generally, the personal character of the writer influences the public rather than his talents as an artist. Napoleon said of Corneille, ' *S'il vivait, je le ferais prince;*' yet he never read him. Racine he read, but did not say this of him. Lafontaine, too, is looked upon with a high degree of esteem by the French, not on account of his poetic merits, but of the greatness of character which he manifests in his writings."

We then talked of the "Elective Affinities" (Wahlverwandtschaften); and Goethe told me of a travelling Englishman, who meant to be separated from his wife when he returned to England. He laughed at such folly, and gave me several examples of persons who had been separated, and afterwards could not let each other alone.

"The late Reinhard of Dresden," said he, "often

wondered that I had such severe principles with respect to marriage, while I was so tolerant in everything else."

This expression of Goethe's was remarkable to me, because it clearly showed what he really intended by that often misunderstood work ("Die Wahlverwandtschaften").

We then talked about Tieck, and his personal relation to Goethe.

"I entertain the greatest kindness for Tieck," said Goethe; "and I think that, on the whole, he is well disposed towards me. Still, there is something not as it ought to be in his relation to me. This is neither my fault nor his, but proceeds from causes altogether foreign.

"When the Schlegels began to make themselves important, I was too strong for them; and to balance me, they were forced to look about for some man of talent, whom they might set up in opposition. Such a talent they found in Tieck; and that, when placed in contrast to me, he might appear sufficiently important in the eyes of the public, they were forced to make more of him than he really was. This injured our mutual relation; for Tieck, without being properly conscious of it himself, was thus placed in a false position with respect to me.

"Tieck is a talent of great importance, and no one can be more sensible than myself to his extraordinary merits; only when they raise him above himself, and place him on a level with me, they are in error. I can speak this out plainly; it matters nothing to me, for I did not make myself. I might just as well compare myself to Shakspeare, who likewise did not make himself, and who is nevertheless a being of a higher order, to whom I must look up with reverence."

Goethe was this evening full of energy and gaiety. He brought some manuscript poems, which he read aloud. It was quite a peculiar pleasure to hear him, for not only did the original force and freshness of the poems excite me to a high degree, but Goethe, by his manner of reading them, shewed himself to me on a side hitherto unknown, but highly important. What variety and force in his voice! What life and expression in the noble countenance, so full of wrinkles! And what eyes!

Wednesday, April 14, 1824.

I went out walking with Goethe about one. We discussed the styles of various writers.

"On the whole," said Goethe, "philosophical speculation is an injury to the Germans, as it tends to make their style vague, difficult, and obscure. The stronger their attachment to certain philosophical schools, the worse they write. Those Germans who, as men of business and actual life, confine themselves to the practical, write the best. Schiller's style is most noble and impressive whenever he leaves off philosophizing, as I observe every day in his highly interesting letters, with which I am now busy.

"There are likewise among the German women, genial beings who write a really excellent style, and, indeed, in that respect surpass many of our celebrated male writers.

"The English almost always write well; being

born orators and practical men, with a tendency to the real.

"The French, in their style, remain true to their general character. They are of a social nature, and therefore never forget the public whom they address; they strive to be clear, that they may convince their reader,—agreeable, that they may please him.

"Altogether, the style of a writer is a faithful representative of his mind; therefore, if any man wish to write a clear style, let him be first clear in his thoughts; and if any would write in a noble style, let him first possess a noble soul."

Goethe then spoke of his antagonists as a race which would never become extinct. "Their number," said he, "*is* legion; yet they may be in some degree classified. First, there are my antagonists from stupidity,—those who do not understand me, and find fault with me without knowing me. This large company has wearied me much in the course of my life; yet shall they be forgiven, for they knew not what they did.

"The second large class is composed of those who envy me. These grudge me the fortune and the dignified station I have attained through my talents. They pluck at my fame, and would like to destroy me. If I were poor and miserable, they would assail me no more.

"There are many who have been my adversaries, because they have failed themselves. In this class are men of fine talent, but they cannot forgive me for casting them into the shade.

"Fourthly, there are my antagonists from *reasons*.

For, as I am a human being, and as such have human faults and weaknesses, my writings cannot be free from them. Yet, as I was constantly bent on my own improvement, and always striving to ennoble myself, I was in a state of constant progress, and it often happened that they blamed me for faults which I had long since left behind. These good folks have injured me least of any, as they shot at me, when I was already miles distant. Generally when a work was finished, it became uninteresting to me; I thought of it no more, but busied myself with some new plan.

"Another large class comprises those who are adversaries, because they differ from me in their views and modes of thought. It is said of the leaves on a tree, that you will scarcely find two perfectly alike, and thus, among a thousand men, you will scarce find two, who harmonize entirely in their views and ways of thinking. This being allowed, I ought less to wonder at having so many opponents, than at having so many friends and adherents. My tendencies were opposed to those of my time, which were wholly subjective; while in my objective efforts, I stood quite alone to my own disadvantage.

"Schiller had, in this respect, great advantage over me. Hence, a certain well-meaning general once gave me plainly to understand, that I ought to write like Schiller. I replied by analyzing Schiller's merits, for I knew them better than he. I went quietly on in my own way, not troubling myself further about success, and taking as little notice as possible of my opponents."

We returned, and had a very pleasant time at dinner.

Frau von Goethe talked much of Berlin, where she had lately been. She spoke with especial warmth of the Duchess of Cumberland, who had shown her much kindness. Goethe remembered this princess, who, when very young, had passed some time with his mother, with particular interest.

In the evening, I had a musical treat of a high order at Goethe's house, where some fine singers, under the superintendence of Eberwein, performed part of Händel's Messiah. The Countess Caroline von Egloffstein, Fraulein von Froriep, with Frau von Pogwisch and Frau von Goethe, joined the female singers, and thus kindly gratified a wish which Goethe had entertained long since.

Goethe, sitting at some distance, wholly absorbed in hearing, passed a happy evening, full of admiration at this noble work.

Monday, April 19, 1824.

The greatest philologist of our time, Friedrich August Wolf, from Berlin, is here, on his way towards the south of France. Goethe gave, to-day, on his account, a dinner to his Weimar friends, at which General Superintendent Röhr, Chancellor von Müller, Oberbau-Director Coudray, Professor Riemer, and Hofrath Rehbein, and myself, were present. The conversation was very lively. Wolf was full of witty sallies, Goethe being constantly his opponent in the pleasantest way. "I cannot," said Goethe to me afterwards, " get on with Wolf at all, without assuming the character of Mephistophiles. Nothing else brings out his hidden treasures."

The *bon mots* at table were too evanescent, and too

much the result of the moment, to bear repetition. Wolf was very great in witty turns and repartees, but nevertheless it seemed to me that Goethe always maintained a certain superiority over him.

The hours at table flew by as if with wings, and six o'clock came before we were aware. I went with young Goethe to the theatre, where "Zauberflöte" was played. Afterwards I saw Wolf in the box, with the Grand Duke Carl August.

Wolf remained in Weimar till the 25th, when he set out for the south of France. The state of his health was such that Goethe did not conceal the greatest anxiety about him.

Sunday, May 2, 1824.

Goethe reproved me for not having visited a certain family of distinction. "You might," said he, "have passed there, during the winter, many delightful evenings, and have made the acquaintance of many interesting strangers; all which you have lost from God knows what caprice."

"With my excitable temperament," I replied, "and with my disposition to a broad sympathy with others, nothing can be more burdensome and hurtful to me than an overabundance of new impressions. I am neither by education nor habit fitted for general society. My situation in earlier days was such, that I feel as if I had never lived till I came near you. All is new to me. Every evening at the theatre, every conversation with you, makes an era in my existence. Things perfectly indifferent to persons of different education and habits, make the deepest impression on me, and as the desire of instructing myself is great, my mind seizes on every thing with a certain energy, and draws from it as much nourishment as possible. In this state of mind, I had quite enough in the course of this winter, from the theatre and my connection with you; and I should not have been able to give myself up to other connections and engagements, without disturbing my mind."

"You are an odd fellow," said Goethe, laughing. "Well, do as you please; I will let you have your way."

"And then," continued I, "I usually carry into society my likes and dislikes, and a certain need of loving and being beloved; I seek a nature which may harmonize with my own; I wish to give myself up to this, and to have nothing to do with the others."

"This natural tendency of yours," replied Goethe, "is indeed not of a social kind; but what would be the use of culture, if we did not try to control our natural tendencies. It is a great folly to hope that other men will harmonize with us; I have never hoped this. I have always regarded each man as an independent individual, whom I endeavoured to study, and to understand with all his peculiarities, but from whom I desired no further sympathy. In this way have I been enabled to converse with every man, and thus alone is produced the knowledge of various characters, and the dexterity necessary for the conduct of life. For it is in a conflict with natures opposed to his own that a man must collect his strength to fight his way through, and thus all our different sides are brought out and developed, so that we soon feel ourselves a match for every foe. You should do the same; you have more capacity for it than you imagine; indeed, you must at all events plunge into the great world, whether you like it or not."

I took due heed of these good, kind words, and determined to act in accordance with them as much as possible.

Towards evening, Goethe invited me to take a drive with him. Our road lay over the hills through Upper Weimar, by which we had a view of the park towards the west. The trees were in blossom, the birches already in full leaf, and the meadows were one green carpet, over which the setting sun cast a glow. We sought out picturesque groups, and could not look enough. We remarked that trees full of white blossoms should not be painted, because they make no picture, just as birches with their foliage are unfit for the foreground of a picture, because the delicate leaf does not sufficiently balance the white trunk; there are no large masses for strong effects of light and shade. "Ruysdael," said Goethe, "never introduced the birch with its foliage into his foregrounds, but only birch trunks broken off, without any leaves. Such a trunk is perfectly suited to a foreground, as its bright form comes out with most powerful effect."

After some slight discussion of other topics, we came upon the mistake of those artists who make religion art, while for them art should be religion. "Religion," said Goethe, " stands in the same relation to art as any other of the higher interests in life. It is merely to be looked upon as a material, with similar claims to any other vital material. Faith and want of faith are not the organs with which a work of art is to be apprehended. On the contrary, human powers and capacities of a totally different character are required. Art must address itself to those organs with which we apprehend it; otherwise it misses its effect. A religious material may be a good subject for art, but only in so far as it possesses general human interest. The Virgin with the Child is on this account an excellent subject, and one that may be treated a hundred times, and always seen again with pleasure."

In the mean while, we had gone round the thicket (the Webicht), and had turned by Tiefurt into the Weimar road, where we had a view of the setting sun. Goethe was for a while lost in thought; he then said to me, in the words of one of the ancients—

> *Untergehend sogar ist's immer dieselbige Sonne.*
> " Still it continues the self-same sun, e'en while it is sinking."

"At the age of seventy-five," continued he, with much cheerfulness, "one must, of course, think sometimes of death. But this thought never gives me the least uneasiness, for I am fully convinced that our spirit is a being of a nature quite indestructible, and that its activity continues from eternity to eternity. It is like the sun, which seems to set only to our earthly eyes, but which, ·in reality, never sets, but shines on unceasingly."

The sun had, in the mean while, sunk behind the Ettersberg; we felt in the wood the chill of the evening, and drove all the quicker to Weimar, and to Goethe's house. Goethe urged me to go in with him for a while, and I did so. He was in an extremely engaging, amiable mood. He talked a great deal about his theory of colours, and of his obstinate opponents; remarking that he was sure that he had done something in this science.

"To make an epoch in the world," said he, "two conditions are notoriously essential,—a good head, and a great inheritance. Napoleon inherited the French Revolution; Frederick the Great, the Silesian War; Luther, the darkness of the Popes; and I, the errors of the Newtonian theory. The present generation has no conception of what I have accomplished in this matter, but posterity will grant that I have by no means come into a bad inheritance!"

Goethe had sent me this morning a roll of papers relative to the theatre, among which I had found some detached remarks, containing the rules and studies which he had made with Wolff and Grüner to qualify them for good actors. I found these details important and highly instructive for young actors, and therefore proposed to put them together, and make from them a sort of theatrical catechism. Goethe consented, and we discussed the matter further. This gave us occasion to speak of some distinguished actors who had been formed in his school; and I took the opportunity to ask some questions about Frau von Heigendorf. "I may," said Goethe, "have influenced her, but, properly speaking, she is not my pupil. She was, as it were, born on the boards, and was as decided, ready, and adroit in anything as a duck in the water. She needed not my instruction, but did what was right instinctively, and perhaps without knowing it."

We then talked of the many years he had superintended the theatre, and the infinite time which had thus been lost to literary production. "Yes," said he, "I may have missed writing many a good thing, but when I reflect, I am not sorry. I have always regarded all I have done solely as symbolical; and, in fact, it has been tolerably indifferent to me whether I have made pots or dishes."

(Sup.) Wednesday, May 5, 1824.

The papers containing the studies which Goethe prosecuted with the actors Wolff and Grüner have occupied me very pleasantly during the last few days; and I have succeeded in bringing these dismembered notices into a sort of form, so that something has arisen from them which may be regarded as the beginning of a catechism for actors. I spoke with Goethe about this work to-day, and we went through the various topics in detail. The remarks concerning pronunciation, and the laying aside of provincialisms, appeared to us particularly important.

"I have, in my long practice," said Goethe, "become acquainted with beginners from all parts of Germany. The pronunciation of the North German leaves little to be desired: it is pure, and may in many respects be looked upon as a model. On the contrary, I have often had a great deal of trouble with native Suabians, Austrians, and Saxons. The natives of our beloved town, Weimar, have also given me a great deal to do. Among these have arisen the most ridiculous mistakes; because in schools here they are not forced to distinguish, by a marked pronunciation, *b* from *p*, and *d* from *t*. One would scarcely believe that *b*, *p*, *d*, and *t* are generally considered to be *four* different letters; for they only speak of a hard and a soft *b*, and of a hard and a soft *d*, and thus seem tacitly to intimate that *p* and *t* do not exist. With such people, *Pein* (pain) sounds like *Bein* (leg), *Pas* (pass) like *Bass* (bass), and *Teckel* * like *Deckel* (cover)."

"An actor of this town," added I, "who did not properly distinguish *t* from *d*, lately made a mistake of the kind, which appeared very striking. He was playing a lover, who had been guilty of a little infidelity; whereupon the angry young lady showered upon him various violent reproaches. Growing impatient, he had to exclaim, ' *O ende!* ' (O cease!); but being unable to distinguish the T from the D, he exclaimed, ' *O ente!* ' (O duck!) which excited general laughter."

"The circumstance is very quaint," returned Goethe, "and will do well to mention in our ' Theatrical Catechism.' "

"Lately, a young singer, likewise of this town," continued I, "who could not make the distinction between the *t* and the *d*, had to say, ' *Ich will dich den Eingeweihten übergeben* ' (I will give you up to the initiated); but as she pronounced the *t* as *d*, it sounded as if she said, ' *Ich will dich den Eingeweiden übergeben* ' (I will give you up to the bowels).

"Again, an actor of this town," continued I, "who played the part of a servant, had to say to a stranger, ' *Mein Herr ist nicht zu Haus, er sitzt im Rathe* ' (my master is not at home, he sits in council); but as he could not distinguish the *t* from the *d*, it sounded as if he said, ' *Mein Herr ist nicht zu Haus, er sitzt*

* A provincial word for a terrier.

im Rade' (my master is not at home, he sits in the wheel)."

"These incidents," said Goethe, "are not bad, and we will notice them. Thus, if any one who does not distinguish the *p* from the *b*, has to call out, '*Packe ihn an!*' (seize him), but, instead of this, exclaims, '*Backe ihn an!*' (stick him on), it is very laughable.

"In a similar manner," said Goethe, "the *ü* is frequently pronounced like *i*, which has been the cause of not a few scandalous mistakes. I have frequently heard said, instead of *Küstenbewohner* (inhabitant of the coast), *Kistenbewohner* (inhabitant of the box); instead of *Thürstück* (a painting over a door), *Thierstück* (animal-picture); instead of *Trübe* (gloomy), *Triebe* (impulses); and instead of *Ihr müsst* (you must), *Ihr misst* (you miss);—not, however, without a hearty laugh."

"I lately noticed at the theatre," said I, "a very ludicrous case of the kind, in which a lady, in a critical situation, has to follow a man, whom she had never seen before. She had to say, '*Ich kenne Dich zwar nicht, aber ich setze mein ganzes Vertrauen in den Edelmuth Deiner Züge*' (I do not know you, but I place entire confidence in the nobility of your countenance); but as she pronounced the *ü* like *i*, she said, '*Ich kenne Dich zwar nicht, aber ich setze mein ganzes Vertrauen in den Edelmuth Deiner Ziege*' (I do not know you, but I place entire confidence in the nobility of your goat). This caused great laughter."

"This anecdote is not bad," returned Goethe, "and we will notice it also. Thus, too," continued he, "*g* and *k* are here frequently confounded; *g* being used instead of *k*, and *k* instead of *g*, possibly from uncertainty whether the letter should be hard or soft, a result of the doctrine so much in vogue here. You have probably often heard, or will hear, at some future time, in our theatre, *Kartenhaus* (card-house) instead of *Gartenhaus* (garden-house), *Kasse* (chest) instead of *Gasse* (lane), *Klauben* (to pick out) instead of *Glauben* (to believe), *bekränzen* (to enwreath) instead of *begrenzen* (to bound), and *Kunst* (art) instead of *Gunst* (favour)."

"I have already heard something similar," returned I. "An actor of this town had to say '*Dein Gram geht mir zu Herzen*,' (thy grief touches my heart). But he pronounced the *g* like *k*, and said very distinctly, '*Dein Kram geht mir zu Herzen*' (thy goods* touch my heart)."

"Besides," answered Goethe, "we hear this substitution of *g* for *k*, not merely amongst actors, but even amongst very learned theologians. I once personally experienced an incident of this sort; and I will relate it to you.

"When I, some five years ago, stayed for some time at Jena, and lodged at the 'Fir Tree,' a theological student one morning presented himself to me. After he had conversed with me very agreeably for some time, he made, as he was just going, a request of a most peculiar kind. He begged me *to allow him to preach in my stead on the next Sunday.* I immediately discovered which way the wind blew, and that the hopeful youth was one of those who confound *g* for *k*. I, therefore, answered him in a friendly manner, that I

* Or lumber.—*Trans.*

could not personally assist him in this affair; but that he would be sure to attain his object, if he would be so good as to apply to Archdeacon Koethe."

Thursday, May 6, 1824.

When I came to Weimar, last summer, it was not, as I have said, my intention to remain here, I only intended to make Goethe's personal acquaintance, and then to visit the Rhine, where I intended to live some time in a suitable place.

However, I had been detained in Wiemar by Goethe's remarkable kindness, and my relation to him had become more and more practical, inasmuch as he drew me more and more into his own interest, and gave me much important work to do, preparatory to a complete edition of his works.

Thus in the course of last winter, I collected several divisions of "tame Xenia" (*zahme Xenien*) from the most confused bundles of paper, arranged a volume of new poems, and the "Theatrical Catechism," and also the outlines of a treatise on "Dillettantism," in the different arts.

I had, however, never forgotten my design of seeing the Rhine; and Goethe himself, that I might not carry within me the sting of an unsatisfied desire, advised me to devote some months of this summer to a visit to that region.

It was, however, decidedly his wish that I should return to Weimar. He observed that it was not good to break ties scarcely formed, and that everything in life to be of value must have a sequence. He, at the same time, plainly intimated to me that he had selected me and Riemer, not only to aid him in preparing a new and complete edition of his works, but to take the whole charge of it in case he should be suddenly called away, as might naturally happen at his advanced age.

He showed me this morning immense packages of letters, laid out in what is called the Chamber of Busts (*Büsten-Zimmer*). "These," said he, "are all letters which I have received since 1780, from the most distinguished men of our country. There lies hoarded in these a rich treasure of thoughts, which it shall some time be your office to impart to the public. I am now having a chest made, in which these letters will be put, together with the rest of my literary remains. I wish you, before you set out on your journey, to put them all in order, that I may feel easy about them, and have a care the less."

He then told me that he intended to visit Marienbad this summer, but did not intend to go till the end of July, the reasons for which he disclosed to me in confidence. He expressed a wish that I should be back before his departure, that he might speak to me.

A few weeks afterwards, I visited my friends in Hanover, then stopped during the months of June and July on the Rhine, where, especially at Frankfort, Heidelberg, and Bonn, I made many valuable acquaintances among Goethe's friends.*

(Sup.) Tuesday, May 18, 1824.

This evening at Goethe's, in company with Riemer.

* This short statement, though attached to the conversation of 6th May in the first volume, will be read more properly after 26th May (p. 173), which is taken from the supplemental volume.

Goethe talked to us about an English poem, of which geology was the subject. He made, as he went on, an impromptu translation of it, with so much spirit, imagination, and good humour, that every individual object stood before us, with as much life as if it were his own invention at the moment. The hero of the poem, King *Coal*, was seen, in his brilliant hall of audience, seated upon his throne, his consort *Pyrites*, by his side, waiting for the nobles of the kingdom. Entering according to their rank, they appeared one by one to the king, and were introduced as Duke *Granite*, Marquis *Slate*, Countess *Porphyry*, and so on with the rest, who were all characterized by some excellent epithet and joke. Then followed Sir Lorenzo *Chalk*, a man of great possessions, and well received at court. He excuses his mother, the Lady *Marble*, on the ground that her residence is rather distant. She is a very polished and accomplished lady, and a cause of her non-appearance at court, on this occasion, is, that she is involved in an intrigue with *Canova*, who likes to flirt with her. *Tufa*, whose hair is decked with lizards and fishes, appears rather intoxicated. Hans *Marl* and Jacob *Clay* do not appear till the end; the last is a particular favourite of the queen, because he has promised her a collection of shells. Thus the whole went on for a long time in the most cheerful tone; but the details were too minute for me to note the further progress of the story.

"Such a poem," said Goethe, "is quite calculated to amuse people of the world; while at the same time it diffuses a quantity of useful information, which no one ought properly to be without. A taste for science is thus excited amongst the higher circles; and no one knows how much good may ultimately result from such an entertaining half-joke. Many a clever person may be induced to make observations himself, within his own immediate sphere. And such individual observations, drawn from the natural objects with which we are in contact, are often the more valuable, the less the observer professionally belongs to the particular department of science."

"You appear, then, to intimate," returned I, "that the more one knows, the worse one observes."

"Certainly," said Goethe, "when the knowledge which is handed down is combined with errors. As soon as any one belongs to a certain narrow creed in science, every unprejudiced and true perception is gone. The decided Vulcanist always sees through the spectacles of a Vulcanist; and every Neptunist, and every professor of the newest elevation-theory, through his own. The contemplation of the world, with all these theorists, who are devoted to an exclusive tendency, has lost its innocence, and the objects no longer appear in their natural purity. If these learned men, then, give an account of their observations, we obtain, notwithstanding their love of truth as individuals, no actual truth with reference to the objects themselves; but we always receive these objects with the taste of a strong, subjective mixture.

"I am, however, far from maintaining that an unprejudiced, correct knowledge is a drawback to observation. I am much more inclined to support the old truth, that we, properly speaking, have only eyes and ears for what we know. The musician by profession hears, in an orchestral performance, every instrument and every single tone, whilst one unacquainted with the art is wrapped up in the massive effect of the whole. A man merely bent upon enjoyment sees in a green or flowery meadow only a pleasant plain, whilst the eye of a botanist discovers an endless detail of the most varied plants and grasses."

"Still everything has its measure and goal, and as it has been said in my 'Goetz von Berlichingen,' that the son, from pure learning, does not know his own father, so in science do we find people who can neither see nor hear through sheer learning and hypothesis. Such people look at once within; they are so occupied by what is revolving in themselves, that they are like a man in a passion, who passes his dearest friends in the street without seeing them. The observation of nature requires a certain purity of mind, which cannot be disturbed or pre-occupied by anything. The beetle on the flower does not escape the child; he has devoted all his senses to a single, simple interest; and it never strikes him that at the same moment, something remarkable may be going on in the formation of the clouds to distract his glances in that direction."

"Then," returned I, "children and the child-like would be good hod-men in science."

"Would to God!" exclaimed Goethe, "we were all nothing more than good hod-men. It is just because we will be more, and carry about with us a great apparatus of philosophy and hypothesis, that we spoil all."

Then followed a pause in the conversation, which Riemer broke by mentioning Lord Byron and his death. Goethe thereupon gave a brilliant elucidation of his writings, and was full of the highest praise and the purest acknowledgment.

"However," continued he, "although Byron has died so young, literature has not suffered an essential loss, through a hindrance to its further extension. Byron could, in a certain sense, go no further. He had reached the summit of his creative power, and whatever he might have done in the future, he would have been unable to extend the boundaries of his talent. In the incomprehensible poem, 'The Vision of Judgment,' he has done the utmost of which he was capable."

The discourse then turned upon the Italian poet, Torquato Tasso, and his resemblance to Lord Byron, when Goethe could not conceal the superiority of the Englishman, in spirit, grasp of the world, and productive power. "One cannot," continued he, "compare these poets with each other, without annihilating one by the other. Byron is the burning thorn-bush which reduces the holy cedar of Lebanon to ashes. The great epic poem of the Italian has maintained its fame for centuries; but yet, with a single line of 'Don Juan,' one could poison the whole of 'Jerusalem Delivered.'"

(Sup.) Wednesday, May 26, 1824.

To-day I took leave of Goethe, in order to visit my friends in Hanover, and thence to proceed to the Rhine, according to my long, meditated plan. Goethe was very affectionate, and pressed me in his arms. "If at Hanover, you should chance to meet at Rehberg's, Charlotte Kestner, the old friend of my youth, remember me to her kindly. In Frankfort, I commend you to my friends Willemers, the Count Reinhardt, and the Schlossers. Then both in Heidelberg and Bonn, you will find friends who are truly devoted to me, and from whom you will receive a most hearty welcome. I did intend again to spend some time at Marienbad this summer; but I shall not go until after your return."

The parting with Goethe was very trying to me; though I went away with the firm conviction of seeing him again, safe and sound, at the end of two months.

Nevertheless, I felt very happy next day when the carriage conveyed me towards my beloved home in Hanover, to which my heartiest wishes are constantly directed.

Tuesday, August 10, 1824.

About a week ago, I returned from my tour on the Rhine. Goethe expressed much joy at my arrival; and I, on my part, was not less pleased to be with him again. He had a great deal to say to me; so that for the first few days I stirred but little from his side. His design of going to Marienbad he has abandoned, and does not intend to travel this summer. "Now you are again here," he said, "I may have a very pleasant August."

A few days ago, he put into my hands the commencement of a continuation of "Wahrheit und Dichtung," written on quarto leaves, and scarcely a finger's breadth thick. Part is complete, but the greater part consists of mere indications. However, it is already divided into five books, and the leaves containing the sketch are so arranged that, with a little trouble, one can take a survey of the general import.

The portion that is already finished appears to me

so excellent, and the import of the sketched portion to be so valuable, that I regret exceedingly to see a work which promises so much instruction and enjoyment come to a stand-still, and I shall make every effort to urge Goethe to continue and complete it as soon as possible.

The plan of the whole has much of the character of a novel. A graceful, tender, passionate love-affair, cheerful in its origin, idyllic in its progress, tragic at the end, through a tacit but mutual renunciation, runs through four books, and combines them to an organized whole. The charm of Lili's character, described in detail, is of a sort to captivate every reader, just as it held the lover himself in such bonds that he could only save himself by repeated flight.

The epoch of life set forth is of a highly romantic nature, or, at least, becomes so as it is developed in the principal character. But it acquires special significance and importance from the circumstance that, as an epoch preceding the position at Weimar, it is decisive for the whole life. If, therefore, any section of Goethe's life has any interest, and raises a wish for a detailed description, it is precisely this.

To excite in Goethe a new ardour for this work, which has been interrupted and has lain untouched for years, I have not only talked with him on the subject, but have sent him the following notes, that he may see at once what is finished and what has still to be worked out and arranged.*

* The last five books of "Wahrheit und Dichtung" were afterwards published in Goethe's posthumous works, but Eckermann's arrangement was not adopted.—*Trans.*

FIRST BOOK.

This book, which, according to the original intention, may be regarded as complete, contains a sort of exposition, inasmuch as it expresses the wish for a participation in worldly affairs, the fulfilment of which takes place at the end of the whole epoch, through the invitation to Weimar. However, that it may be connected more closely with the whole, I suggest that the relation to Lili, which runs through the four following books, should begin in this first book, and continue as far as the excursion to Offenbach. Thus, too, this book would gain in compass and importance, and too great an increase of the second would be prevented.

SECOND BOOK.

The idyllic life at Offenbach would then open this second book, and would go through with the happy love affair, till it, at last, begins to assume a doubtful, earnest, and even tragical character. The contemplation of serious matters, promised by the sketch in reference to Stilling, is well placed here, and much that is instructive may be anticipated from the design, which is simply indicated by a few words.

THIRD BOOK.

The third book, which contains the plan of a continuation of "Faust," is to be regarded as an episode, but is connected with the other books, by the attempt at a separation from Lili, which remains to be carried out.

Whether the plan of "Faust" is to be communicated or kept back is a doubtful point, which cannot be resolved until we examine the fragments now ready, and make up our minds whether the hope of a continuation of "Faust" is to be given up or not.

FOURTH BOOK.

The third book would terminate with the attempt at a separation from Lili. This fourth book, therefore, very aptly begins with the arrival of the Stolbergs and of Haugwitz, by which the journey into Switzerland and the first flight from Lili are brought about. The complete sketch of this book promises the most interesting matter, and excites a wish for the most thorough details. The passion for Lili, which is constantly bursting forth, and which cannot be suppressed, glows through the whole book with the fire of youthful love, and gives a peculiar, pleasant, and magical light to the situation of the traveller.

FIFTH BOOK.

This beautiful book is likewise nearly finished; at least the latter part, up to the conclusion, which touches on the unfathomable nature of fate, may be regarded as quite finished; and only a little is wanting for the introduction, of which there is already a very clear sketch. The working-out is, however, the more necessary and desirable, as the first mention is made of the Weimar affairs, and thus our interest for them is first excited.

Monday, August 16, 1824.

My conversations with Goethe have lately been very abundant in matter, but I have been so much engaged with other things as to render it impossible to write down anything of importance, from the fulness of his discourse.

Only the following detached sentences are found noted down in my diary; the connection between them and the occasion that gave rise to them, I have forgotten.

Men are swimming pots, which knock against each other.

In the morning we are shrewdest, but also most anxious; for even anxiety is a species of shrewdness, though only a passive one. Stupidity is without anxiety.

We must not take the faults of our youth into our old age; for old age brings with it its own defects.

Court-life is like music, in which every one must keep time.

Courtiers would die of *ennui*, if they could not fill up their time with ceremonies.

It is not right to counsel a prince to give way, even in the most trivial matter.

He who would train actors must have infinite patience.

Tuesday, November 9, 1824.

I passed this evening with Goethe. We talked of

Klopstock and Herder; and I liked to listen to him, as he explained to me the merits of those men.

"Without those powerful precursors," said Goethe, "our literature could not have become what it now is. When they appeared, they were before their age, and were obliged, as it were, to drag it after them; but now the age has far outrun them, and they who were once so necessary and important have now ceased to be *means to an end*. A young man who would take Klopstock and Herder for his teachers nowadays would be far behindhand."

We talked over Klopstock's "Messiah" and his Odes, touching on their merits and their defects. We agreed that he had no faculty for observing and apprehending the visible world, or for drawing characters; and that he therefore wanted the qualities most essential to the epic and dramatic poet, or, perhaps it might be said, to the poet generally.

"An ode occurs to me," said Goethe, "where he makes the German Muse run a race with the British; and, indeed, when one thinks what a picture it is, where the two girls run one against the other, throwing about their legs, and kicking up the dust, one must assume that the good Klopstock did not really have before his eyes such pictures as he wrote, else he could not possibly have made such mistakes."

I asked how he had felt towards Klopstock in his youth.

"I venerated him," said Goethe, "with the devotion which was peculiar to me; I looked upon him as my uncle. I revered whatever he had done, and never thought of reflecting upon it, or finding fault with it

I let his fine qualities work upon me; for the rest, I went my own way."

We came back to Herder, and I asked Goethe which of his works he thought the best. "His 'Ideas for the History of Mankind'" (*Ideen zur Geschichte der Menschheit*), replied Goethe, "are undoubtedly the best. In after days, he took the negative side, and was not so agreeable."

"Considering the great weight of Herder," said I, "I cannot understand how he had so little judgment on some subjects. For instance, I cannot forgive him, especially at that period of German literature, for sending back the manuscript of 'Goetz von Berlichingen' without any praise of its merits, and with taunting remarks. He must have utterly wanted organs to perceive some objects."

"Yes, Herder was unfortunate in this respect," replied Goethe; "nay," added he, with vivacity, "if his spirit were present at this conversation, it would not understand us."

"On the other hand," said I, "I must praise Merck, who urged you to print 'Goetz.'"

"He was indeed an odd but important man," said Goethe. "'Print the thing,' quoth he, 'it is worth nothing, but print it.' He did not wish me to make any alteration in it, and he was right; for it would have been different, but not better."

Wednesday, November 24, 1824.

I went to see Goethe this evening, before going to the theatre, and found him very well and cheerful. He inquired about the young Englishmen who are here. I told him that I proposed reading with Mr. Doolan a German translation of Plutarch. This led the conversation to Roman and Grecian history; and Goethe expressed himself as follows:—

"The Roman history," said he, "is no longer suited to us. We have become too humane for the triumphs of Cæsar not to be repugnant to our feelings. Neither are we much charmed by the history of Greece. When this people turns against a foreign foe, it is, indeed, great and glorious; but the division of the states, and their eternal wars with one another, where Greek fights against Greek, are insufferable. Besides, the history of our own time is thoroughly great and important; the battles of Leipsic and Waterloo stand out with such prominence, that that of Marathon and others like it are gradually eclipsed. Neither are our individual heroes inferior to theirs; the French Marshals, Blücher, and Wellington, vie with any of the heroes of antiquity."

We then talked of the late French literature, and the daily increasing interest in German works manifested by the French.

"The French," said Goethe, "do well to study and translate our writers; for, limited as they are both in form and motives, they can only look without for means. We Germans may be reproached for a certain formlessness; but in matter we are their superiors. The theatrical productions of Kotzebue and Iffland are so rich in motives that they may pluck them a long time before all is used up. But, especially, our philosophical Ideality is welcome to them; for every Ideal is serviceable to revolutionary aims.

"The French have understanding and *esprit*, but neither a solid basis nor piety. What serves the moment, what helps his party, seems right to the Frenchman. Hence they praise us, never from an acknowledgment of our merits, but only when they can strengthen their party by our views."

We then talked about our own literature, and of the obstacles in the way of some of our latest young poets.

"The majority of our young poets," said Goethe, "have no fault but this, that their subjectivity is not important, and that they cannot find matter in the objective. At best, they only find a material, which is similar to themselves, which corresponds to their own subjectivity; but as for taking the material on its own account, when it is repugnant to the subjectivity, merely because it is poetical, such a thing is never thought of.

"Still, as I have said, if we only had important personages, formed by great studies and situations in life, it might still go well with us, at least as far as our young lyric poets are concerned."

Friday, December 3, 1824.

A proposal has lately reached me to write for an English periodical, on very favourable terms, monthly notices of the latest productions in German literature. I was much inclined to accept the proposal, but thought it would be good first to talk over the affair with Goethe.

I went to him this evening. The curtains were down, and he was seated before a table, on which dinner had been served, and on which burned two lights which illuminated at once his own face and a colossal bust which stood before him on the table, and at which he was looking. "Now," said Goethe, pointing at the bust, after greeting me in a friendly manner, "who is this?" "Apparently, a poet, and an Italian," I replied. "It is Dante," said he: "it is well done; a fine head, yet not very pleasing. He seems old, bowed down, and peevish; the features are lax, and drawn down, as if he had just come from hell. I have a medal, which was struck during his life, and there everything appears much better."

He rose and brought the medal. "Do you see what power there is in the nose and the swell of the upper lip, the energy of the chin, and its fine blending with the cheek bone? The part about the eyes and the forehead are the same in this bust; but all the rest is weaker and older. Yet I will not find fault with the new work, which, on the whole, has great merit, and deserves praise."

Goethe then inquired what I had been doing and thinking about of late. I told him that a proposal had reached me to write for an English periodical, on very advantageous terms, monthly notices of the newest productions of the German prose *belles lettres*, and that I was much inclined to accept the offer.

Goethe's face, which had hitherto worn so friendly an expression, clouded over at these words, and I could read in every movement his disapproval of my project.

"I wish," said he, "your friends would leave you in peace. Why should you trouble yourself with things which lie quite out of your way, and are contrary to the tendencies of your nature? We have gold, silver, and paper money, and each has its own value; but to do justice to each, you must understand the exchange. And so in literature. You understand the metallic, but not the paper currency: you are not equal to this; your criticisms will be unjust, and do hurt. If you wish to be just, and give everything its proper place, you must first become acquainted with our middle literature, and make up your mind to a study by no means trifling. You must look back and see what the Schlegels proposed and performed, and then read all our later authors, Franz Horn, Hoffmann, Clauren, &c. Even this is not enough. You must also take in all the journals of the day, from the 'Morgenblatt' to the 'Abend-Zeitung,' in order that nothing which comes out may escape you; and thus you will spoil your best days and hours. Then all new books, which you would criticise with any degree of profundity, you must not only skim over, but study. How would you relish that? And, finally, if you find that what is bad is bad, you must not say so, if you would not run the risk of being at war with all the world.

"No; as I have said, decline the proposal; it is not in your way. Generally, beware of dissipating your powers, and strive to concentrate them. Had I been so wise thirty years ago, I should have done very differently. How much time I lost with Schiller on his 'Horen' and 'Musen-Almanachs!' Now, when I have just been looking over our correspondence, I feel this most forcibly, and cannot think without chagrin on those undertakings which made the world abuse us, and which were entirely without result for ourselves.

Talent thinks it can do whatever it sees others doing; but this is not the case, and it will have to repent its *Faux-frais* (idle expenses). What good does it do to curl up your hair for a single night? You have paper in your hair, that is all; next night, it is straight again.

"The great point," he continued, "is to make a capital that will not be exhausted. This you will acquire by the study of the English language and literature, which you have already begun. Keep to that, and continually make use of the advantages you now possess in the acquaintance of the young Englishmen. You studied the ancient languages but little during your youth; therefore, seek now a stronghold in the literature of so able a nation as the English. And, besides, our own literature is chiefly the offspring of theirs! Whence have we our novels, our tragedies, but from Goldsmith, Fielding, and Shakspeare? And in our own day, where will you find in Germany three literary heroes, who can be placed on a level with Lord Byron, Moore, and Walter Scott? Once more, ground yourself in English, concentrate your powers for something good, and give up everything which can produce no result of consequence to you, and is not suited to you."

I rejoiced that I had thus made Goethe speak. I was perfectly satisfied in my mind, and determined to comply with his advice in every respect.

Chancellor von Müller was now announced, and sat down with us. The conversation turned once more on the bust of Dante, which stood before us, and on his life and works. The obscurity of this author was especially mentioned,—how his own countrymen had never understood him, so that it would be impossible for a foreigner to penetrate such darkness. "To you," said Goethe, turning towards me, with a friendly air, "the study of this poet is hereby absolutely forbidden by your father confessor."

Goethe also remarked that the difficult rhyme is, in a great measure, the cause of his obscurity. For the rest, he spoke of Dante with extreme reverence; and I observed that he was not satisfied with the word *talent*, but called him a *nature*, as if thus wishing to express something more comprehensive, more full of prescience, of deeper insight, and wider scope.

Thursday, December 9, 1824.

I went this evening to Goethe. He cordially held out his hand, and greeted me with praises of my poem on "Schellhorn's Jubilee." I told him that I had written to refuse the proposal from England.

"Thank Heaven!" said he; "then you are free and at peace once more. And now let me warn you against something else. The composers will come and want an opera; but you must be steadfast and refuse them, for that is a work which leads to nothing, and only loses time.

"Goethe then told me that he had sent the author of the 'Paria,' who is now at Bonn, the play bill, through Nees of Esenbeck, that the poet might see his piece had been played here. Life is short," he added; "we must try to do one another a good turn."

The Berlin Journals lay before him, and he told me of the great inundation at Petersburg. He gave me the paper to read, and talked about the bad situation of Petersburg, laughing approvingly at an expression of

Rousseau's, who said that we could not hinder an earthquake by building a city near a burning mountain. "Nature goes her own way," said he, "and all that to us seems an exception is really according to order."

We then talked of the great tempests which had raged on every coast, and of other violent outbreaks of nature, mentioned in the journals, and I asked Goethe, whether it was known how such things were connected. "That no one knows," replied Goethe; "we have scarcely a suspicion respecting such mysteries, much less can we speak about them."

Coudray and Professor Riemer were announced. Both joined us, and the inundation of Petersburg was again discussed. M. Coudray, by drawing the plan of that city, plainly showed us the position of the Neva, and the rest of the locality.

CONVERSATIONS OF GOETHE.

———

1825.

1825.

Monday, January 10, 1825.

GOETHE, consistently with his great interest for the English, has desired me to introduce to him the young Englishmen who are here at present. At five o'clock this afternoon, he expected me with Mr. H., the English engineer officer, of whom I had previously been able to say much good to him. We went at the expected hour, and were conducted by the servant to a pleasant, well-warmed apartment, where Goethe usually passes his afternoons and evenings. Three lights were burning on the table, but he was not there; we heard him talking in the adjoining saloon.

Mr. H. looked about him for a while, and observed, besides the pictures and a large chart of the mountains which adorned the walls, a book-case full of portfolios. These, I told him, contained many drawings from the hands of celebrated masters, and engravings after the best pictures of all schools, which Goethe had, during a long life, been gradually collecting, and the repeated contemplation of which afforded him entertainment.

After we had waited a few minutes, Goethe came

in, and greeted us cordially. He said to Mr. H., "I presume I may address you in German, as I hear you are already well versed in our language." Mr. H. answered with a few polite words, and Goethe requested us to be seated.

Mr. H.'s manners and appearance must have made a good impression on Goethe; for his sweetness and mild serenity were manifested towards the stranger in their real beauty. "You did well," said he, "to come hither to learn German; for here you will quickly and easily acquire, not only a knowledge of the language, but also of the elements on which it rests, our soil, climate, mode of life, manners, social habits, and constitution, and carry it away with you to England."

Mr. H. replied, "The interest taken in the German language is now great, so that there is now scarcely a young Englishman of good family who does not learn German."

"We Germans," said Goethe, good-humouredly, "have, however, been half a century before your nation in this respect. For fifty years I have been busy with the English language and literature; so that I am well acquainted with your writers, your ways of living, and the administration of your country. If I went over to England, I should be no stranger there.

"But, as I said before, your young men do well to come to us and learn our language; for, not only does our literature merit attention on its own account, but no one can deny that he who now knows German well, can dispense with many other languages. Of the French, I do not speak; it is the language of conversation, and is indispensable in travelling, because everybody understands it, and in all countries we can get on with it instead of a good interpreter. But as for Greek, Latin, Italian, and Spanish, we can read the best works of those nations in such excellent German translations, that, unless we have some particular object in view, we need not spend much time upon the toilsome study of those languages. It is in the German nature duly to honour after its kind, everything produced by other nations, and to accommodate itself to foreign peculiarities. This, with the great flexibility of our language, makes German translations thoroughly faithful and complete. And it is not to be denied that, in general, you get on very far with a good translation. Frederick the Great did not know Latin, but he read Cicero in the French translation with as much profit as we who read him in the original."

Then, turning the conversation on the theatre, he asked Mr. H. whether he went frequently thither. "Every evening," he replied, "and find that I thus gain much towards the understanding of the language."

"It is remarkable," said Goethe, "that the ear, and generally the understanding gets the start of speaking; so that a man may very soon comprehend all he hears, but by no means express it all."

"I experience daily," said Mr. H., "the truth of that remark. I understand very well whatever I hear or read; I even feel when an incorrect expression is made use of in German. But when I speak, nothing will flow, and I cannot express myself as I wish. In light conversation at court, jests with the ladies, a chat at balls, and the like, I succeed pretty well. But, if I try to express an opinion on any important topic, to say anything peculiar or luminous, I cannot get on."

"Be not discouraged by that," said Goethe, "since it is hard enough to express such uncommon matters in one's own mother tongue."

He then asked what Mr. H. read in German literature. "I have read 'Egmont,'" he replied, "and found so much pleasure in the perusal, that I returned to it three times. 'Torquato Tasso,' too, has afforded me much enjoyment. Now, I am reading 'Faust,' but find that it is somewhat difficult."

Goethe laughed at these last words. "Really," said he, "I would not have advised you to undertake 'Faust.' It is mad stuff, and goes quite beyond all ordinary feeling. But since you have done it of your own accord, without asking my advice, you will see how you will get through. Faust is so strange an individual, that only few can sympathize with his internal condition. Then the character of Mephistophiles is, on account of his irony, and also because he is a living result of an extensive acquaintance with the world, also very difficult. But you will see what lights open upon you. 'Tasso,' on the other hand, lies far nearer the common feelings of mankind, and the elaboration of its form is favourable to an easy comprehension of it."

"Yet," said Mr. H., "'Tasso' is thought difficult in Germany, and people have wondered to hear me say, that I was reading it."

"What is chiefly needed for 'Tasso,'" replied Goethe, "is, that one should be no longer a child, and should have been in good society. A young man of good family, with sufficient mind and delicacy, and also with enough outward culture, such as will be produced by intercourse with accomplished men of the higher class, wlll not find 'Tasso' difficult."

The conversation turning upon "Egmont," he said, "I wrote 'Egmont' in 1775,—fifty years ago. I adhered closely to history, and strove to be as accurate as possible. Ten years afterwards, when I was in Rome, I read in the newspapers that the revolutionary scenes in the Netherlands there described were exactly repeated. 1 saw from this that the world remains ever the same, and that my picture must have some life in it."

Amid this and similar conversation, the hour for the theatre had come. We rose, and Goethe dismissed us in a friendly manner.

As we went homeward, I asked Mr. H. how he was pleased with Goethe. "I have never," said he, "seen a man who, with all his attractive gentleness, had so much native dignity. However he may condescend, he is always the great man."

Tuesday, January 18, 1825.

I went to Goethe about five o'clock. I had not seen him for some days, and passed a delightful evening. I found him sitting in his working-room, and talking, during the twilight, with his son and Hofrath Rehbein, his physician. I seated myself at the table with them. We talked a while in the dusk; then lights were brought in, and I had the happiness to see Goethe looking perfectly fresh and cheerful.

As usual, he inquired with interest what had happened to me of late, and I replied that I had made the acquaintance of a poetess. I was able, at the same time, to praise her uncommon talent, and Goethe, who was likewise acquainted with some of her productions, agreed with my commendation.

"One of her poems," said he, "in which she describes the country near her home, is of a highly peculiar character. She has a good tendency towards outward objects, and is besides not destitute of valuable internal qualities. We might, indeed, find much fault with her; but we will let her alone, and not disturb her in the path which her talent will shew her."

The conversation now turned on poetesses in general; Hofrath Rehbein remarked that the poetical talent of ladies often seemed to him as a sexual instinct of the intellect. "Hear him," said Goethe, laughing, and looking at me; "sexual instinct, indeed! how the physician explains it!"

"I know not," said Rehbein, "whether I express myself right; but it is something of the sort. Usually, these beings have not been fortunate in love, and they now seek compensation in intellectual pursuits. Had they been married in time, and borne children, they would never have thought of poetical productions."

"I will not inquire," said Goethe, "how far you are right in this case; but, as to the talents of ladies in other departments, I have always found that they ceased on marriage. I have known girls who drew finely; but so soon as they became wives and mothers it was all over: they were busy with their children, and never touched a pencil.

"But our poetesses," continued he, with much

animation, " might write and poetize as they pleased if only our men would not write like women. This it is that does not please me. Look at our periodicals and annuals; see how all becomes weaker and weaker. Were a chapter of Cellini now printed in the 'Morgenblatt,' what a figure it would make!

"However," he continued, in a lively manner, "let us forget all that, and rejoice in our brave girl at Halle, who with masculine spirit introduces us into the Servian world. These poems are excellent. There are some among them worthy of a comparison with 'Solomon's Song,' and that is saying something. I have finished my essay on these poems, and it is already in type." With these words he showed me the first four proof-sheets of a new number of " Kunst und Alterthum," where I found the essay in question. " I have in a few words," said he, " characterized these poems according to their chief subjects, and I think you will be pleased with the valuable *motives*. Rehbein, too, is not ignorant of poetry—at least as to its import and material—and he may perhaps like to hear you read this aloud."

I read slowly the subjects of the single poems. The situations indicated were so marked and expressive, that at each word a whole poem was revealed to my eye. The following appeared to me especially charming:—

1. Modesty of a Servian girl, who never raises her beautiful eyelashes.
2. Conflict in the mind of a lover, who, as groomsman, is obliged to conduct his beloved to another.
3. Being distressed about her lover, the girl will not sing, lest she should seem gay.

4. Complaint of the corruption of manners; how youths marry widows, and old men virgins.

5. Complaint of a youth that a mother gives her daughter too much liberty.

6. Confidingly joyous talk of a girl with the steed, who betrays to her his master's inclinations and designs.

7. The maiden will not have him she cannot love.

8. The fair bar-maid: her lover is not among the guests.

9. Finding and tender awakening of the beloved.

10. What trade shall my husband be?

11. Joys of love lost by babbling.

12. The lover comes from abroad, watches her by day, surprises her at night.

I remarked that these mere *motives* excited in me such lively emotions, that I felt as if I were reading the poems themselves, and had no desire for the details.

"You are quite right," said Goethe, "so it is; and here you see the great importance of *motives*, which no one will understand. Our women have no notion of it. 'That poem is beautiful,' they say, and by this they mean nothing but the feelings, the words, the verses. No one dreams that the true power of a poem consists in the situation,—in the *motives*.* And

---

* This "motive" (German, *motiv*) is a very difficult and unmanageable word, and like many words of the sort does not seem always to preserve the same meaning. According to the definition of lexicographers, the German expression is almost the same as the English one, and a poem is said to be well "motived" (motivirt) when it is well organized as a whole, —that is to say, when there is a sufficient motive for the different effects produced. But in the passage above, "motive" seems rather to mean "theme" for a poem, and it will be remembered that "motive" has that

for this very reason, thousands of poems are written, where the *motive* is nothing at all, and which merely through feeling and sounding verse reflect a sort of existence. Dilettanti, and especially women, have very weak ideas of poetry. They usually think, if they could but get quit of the technical part, they would have the essential, and would be quite accomplished; but they are much mistaken."

Professor Riemer was announced, Rehbein took leave, and Riemer sat down with us. The conversation still turned on the *motives* of the Servian love-poems. Riemer was acquainted with the topic, and made the remark, that according to the table of contents given above, not only could poems be made, but that the same *motives* had been already used by the Germans, without any knowledge that they had been treated in Servia. He mentioned some poems of his own, and I mentioned some poems by Goethe, which had occurred to me during the reading.

" The world," said Goethe, " remains always the same ; situations are repeated; one people lives, loves, and feels like another; why should not one poet write like another ? The situations of life are alike ; why, then, should those of poems be unlike ?"

" This very similarity in life and sensation," said Riemer, " makes us all able to appreciate the poetry of other nations. If this were not the case, we should never know what foreign poems were about."

" I am, therefore," said I, " always surprised at

sense in music. Wherever *motiv* occurs it will be represented by *motive* in italics, and the reader will do his best to understand it from the context.— *Trans.*

the learned, who seem to suppose that poetizing proceeds not from life to the poem, but from the book to the poem. They are always saying, 'He got this here; he got that there.' If, for instance, they find passages in Shakspeare which are also to be found in the ancients, they say he must have taken them from the ancients. Thus there is a situation in Shakspeare, where, on the sight of a beautiful girl, the parents are congratulated who call her daughter, and the youth who will lead her home as his bride. And because the same thing occurs in Homer, Shakspeare, forsooth, has taken it from Homer. How odd! As if one had to go so far for such things, and did not have them before one's eyes, feel them, and utter them every day."

"Ah, yes," said Goethe, "it is very ridiculous."

"Lord Byron, too," said I, "is no wiser, when he takes 'Faust' to pieces, and thinks you found one thing here, the other there."

"The greater part of those fine things cited by Lord Byron," said Goethe, "I have never even read, much less did I think of them, when I was writing 'Faust.' But Lord Byron is only great as a poet; as soon as he reflects, he is a child. He knows not how to help himself against the stupid attacks of the same kind made upon him by his own countrymen. He ought to have expressed himself more strongly against them. 'What is there is mine,' he should have said, 'and whether I got it from a book or from life, is of no consequence; the only point is, whether I have made a right use of it.' Walter Scott used a scene from my 'Egmont,' and he had a right to do so; and because he did it well, he deserves praise. He has also copied the character of my Mignon in one of his romances; but whether with equal judgment, is another question. Lord Byron's transformed Devil* is a continuation of Mephistophiles, and quite right too. If, from the whim of originality, he had departed from the model, he would certainly have fared worse. Thus, my Mephistophiles sings a song from Shakspeare, and why should he not? Why should I give myself the trouble of inventing one of my own, when this said just what was wanted. If, too, the prologue to my 'Faust' is something like the beginning of Job, that is again quite right, and I am rather to be praised than censured."

Goethe was in the best humour. He sent for a bottle of wine, and filled for Riemer and me; he himself drank Marienbad water. He seemed to have appointed this evening for looking over, with Riemer, the manuscript of the continuation of his autobiography, perhaps in order to improve it here and there, in point of expression. "Let Eckermann stay and hear it too," said Goethe; which words I was very glad to hear, and he then laid the manuscript before Riemer, who began to read, commencing with the year 1795.

I had already, in the course of the summer, had the pleasure of repeatedly reading and reflecting on the still unpublished record of those years, down to the latest time. But now to hear them read aloud in Goethe's presence, afforded quite a new enjoyment.

* This, doubtless, means the "Deformed Transformed," and the fact that this poem was not published till January 1824, rendering it probable that Goethe had not actually seen it, accounts for the inaccuracy of the expression.—*Trans.*

Riemer paid especial attention to the mode of expression; and I had occasion to admire his great dexterity, and his affluence of words and phrases. But in Goethe's mind the epoch of life described was revived; he revelled in recollections, and, on the mention of single persons and events, filled out the written narrative by the details he orally gave us. That was a precious evening! The most distinguished of his contemporaries were talked over; but the conversation always came back to Schiller, who was so interwoven with this period, from 1795 to 1800. The theatre had been the object of their united efforts, and Goethe's best works belong to this time. " Wilhelm Meister" was completed; " Hermann und Dorothea" planned and written; " Cellini" translated for the " Horen;" the " Xenien" written by both for Schiller's " Musenalmanach;"—every day brought with it points of contact. Of all this we talked this evening, and Goethe had full opportunity for the most interesting communications.

" ' Hermann und Dorothea,' " said he, " is almost the only one of my larger poems which still satisfies me; I can never read it without strong interest. I love it best in the Latin translation; there it seems to me nobler, and as if it had returned to its original form."

" Wilhelm Meister" was often a subject of discourse. " Schiller blamed me for interweaving tragic elements which do not belong to the novel. Yet he was wrong, as we all know. In his letters to me, there are most important views and opinions with respect to ' Wilhelm Meister.' But this work is one of the most incalculable productions; I myself can scarcely be said to have the key to it. People seek a central point, and that is hard, and not even right. I should think a rich manifold life, brought close to our eyes, would be enough in itself, without any express tendency, which, after all, is only for the intellect. But if anything of the sort is insisted upon, it will perhaps be found in the words which Frederic, at the end, addresses to the hero, when he says,—' Thou seem'st to me like Saul, the son of Kish, who went out to seek his father's asses, and found a kingdom. Keep only to this; for, in fact, the whole work seems to say nothing more than that man, despite all his follies and errors, being led by a higher hand, reaches some happy goal at last?'"

We then talked of the high degree of culture which, during the last fifty years, had become general among the middle classes of Germany, and Goethe ascribed the merit of this not so much to Lessing as to Herder and Wieland. "Lessing," said he, "was of the very highest understanding, and only one equally great could truly learn of him. To a half faculty he was dangerous." He mentioned a journalist who had formed himself on Lessing, and, at the end of the last century, had played a part indeed, but far from a noble one, because he was so inferior to his great predecessor.

"All Upper Germany," said he, "is indebted to Wieland for its style. It has learned much from him; and the capability of expressing itself correctly is not the least."

On mentioning the "Xenien,"* he especially praised

* It need scarcely be mentioned that this is the name given to a collection of sarcastic epigrams by Goethe and Schiller.—*Trans.*

those of Schiller, which he called sharp and biting, while he called his own innocent and trivial.

"The 'Thierkreis' (Zodiac), which is by Schiller," said he, "I always read with admiration. The good effects which the 'Xenien' had upon the German literature of their time are beyond calculation." Many persons against whom the "Xenien" were directed, were mentioned on this occasion, but their names have escaped my memory.

After we had read and talked over the manuscript to the end of the year 1800, interrupted by these and innumerable other observations from Goethe, he put aside the papers, and had a little supper placed at one end of the table at which we were sitting. We partook of it, but Goethe did not touch a morsel; indeed, I have never seen him eat in the evening. He sat down with us, filled our glasses, snuffed the candles, and intellectually regaled us with the most agreeable conversation. His remembrance of Schiller was so lively, that the conversation during the latter part of the evening was devoted to him alone.

Riemer spoke of Schiller's personal appearance. "The build of his limbs, his gait in the street, all his motions," said he, "were proud; his eyes only were soft."

"Yes," said Goethe, "everything else about him was proud and majestic, only the eyes were soft. And his talent was like his outward form. He seized boldly on a great subject, and turned it this way and that, and handled it this way and that. But he saw his object, as it were, only in the outside; a quiet development from its interior was not within his province. His talent was more desultory. Thus he was never decided—could never have done. He often changed a part just before a rehearsal.

"And, as he went so boldly to work, he did not take sufficient pains about *motives*. I recollect what trouble I had with him, when he wanted to make Gessler, in 'Tell,' abruptly break an apple from the tree, and have it shot from the boy's head. This was quite against my nature, and I urged him to give at least some motive to this barbarity, by making the boy boast to Gessler of his father's dexterity, and say that he could shoot an apple from a tree at a hundred paces. Schiller, at first, would have nothing of the sort; but at last he yielded to my arguments and intentions, and did as I advised him. I, on the other hand, by too great attention to *motives*, kept my pieces from the theatre. My 'Eugenie,'* is nothing but a chain of *motives*, and this cannot succeed on the stage.

"Schiller's genius was really made for the theatre. With every piece he progressed, and became more finished; but, strange to say, a certain love for the horrible adhered to him from the time of the 'Robbers,' which never quite left him even in his prime. I still recollect perfectly well, that in the prison scene in my 'Egmont,' where the sentence is read to him, Schiller would have made Alva appear in the background, masked and muffled in a cloak, enjoying the effect which the sentence would produce on Egmont. Thus Alva was to shew himself insatiable in revenge and malice. I, however, protested, and prevented the apparition. He was a great, odd man.

* "Die Natürliche Tochter" (the Natural Daughter).—*Trans.*

"Every week he became different and more finished; each time that I saw him, he seemed to me to have advanced in learning and judgment. His letters are the fairest memorials of him which I possess, and they are also among the most excellent of his writings. His last letter I preserve as a sacred relic, among my treasures." He rose and fetched it. "See and read it," said he, giving it to me.

It was a very fine letter, written in a bold hand. It contained an opinion of Goethe's notes to "Rameau's Nephew," which exhibit French literature at that time, and which he had given Schiller to look over. I read the letter aloud to Riemer. "You see," said Goethe, "how apt and consistent is his judgment, and that the handwriting nowhere betrays any trace of weakness. He was a splendid man, and went from us in all the fulness of his strength. This letter is dated the 24th of April 1805. Schiller died on the 9th of May."

We looked at the letter by turns, and were pleased both with the clear style and the fine hand writing. Goethe bestowed several other words of affectionate reminiscence upon his friend, until it was nearly eleven o'clock, and we departed.

Thursday, Feb. 24, 1825.

"If I were still superintendent of the theatre," said Goethe, this evening, "I would bring out Byron's 'Doge of Venice.' The piece is indeed long, and would require shortening. Nothing, however, should be cut out, but the import of each scene should be taken, and expressed more concisely. The piece would thus be brought closer together, without being damaged by alterations, and it would gain a powerful effect, without any essential loss of beauty."

This opinion of Goethe's gave me a new view as to how we might proceed on the stage, in a hundred similar cases, and I was highly pleased with such a maxim, which, however, presupposes a fine intellect, —nay, a poet, who understands his vocation.

We talked more about Lord Byron, and I mentioned how, in his conversations with Medwin, he had said there was something extremely difficult and unthankful in writing for the theatre. "The great point is," said Goethe, "for the poet to strike into the path which the taste and interest of the public have taken. If the direction of his talent accords with that of the public, everything is gained. Houwald hit this path with his *Bild* (picture), and hence the universal applause he received. Lord Byron, perhaps, would not have been so fortunate, inasmuch as his tendency varied from that of the public. The greatness of the poet is by no means the important matter. On the contrary, one who is little elevated above the general public may often gain the most general favour precisely on that account."

We continued to converse about Byron, and Goethe admired his extraordinary talent. "That which I call invention," said he, "I never saw in any one in the world to a greater degree than in him. His manner of loosing a dramatic knot is always better than one would anticipate."

"That," said I, "is what I feel about Shakspeare, especially when Falstaff has entangled himself in such a net of falsehoods, and I ask myself what I should do to help him out; for I find that Shakspeare surpasses all my notions. That you say the same of Lord Byron, is the highest praise that can be bestowed on him. Nevertheless," I added, "the poet who takes a clear survey of beginning and end, has, by far, the advantage with the biassed reader."

Goethe agreed with me, and laughed to think that Lord Byron, who, in practical life, could never adapt himself, and never even asked about a law, finally subjected himself to the stupidest of laws,—that of the *three unities.*

"He understood the purpose of this law," said he, "no better than the rest of the world. *Comprehensibility** is the purpose, and the three unities are only so far good as they conduce to this end. If the observance of them hinders the comprehension of a work, it is foolish to treat them as laws, and to try to observe them. Even the Greeks, from whom the rule was taken, did not always follow it. In the 'Phaeton' of Euripides, and in other pieces, there is a change of place, and it is obvious that good representation of their subject was with them more important than blind obedience to law, which, in itself, is of no great consequence. The pieces of Shakspeare deviate, as far as possible, from the unities of time and place; but they are comprehensible—nothing more so—and on this account, the Greeks would have found no fault in them. The French poets have endeavoured to follow

---

* We unwillingly adopt this uncouth word as the equivalent for "das Fassliche." The American translator uses the word "illusion," but this would be rather a result of "das Fassliche" than the thing itself.—*Trans.*

most rigidly the laws of the three unities, but they sin against comprehensibility, inasmuch as they solve a dramatic law, not dramatically, but by narration."

"I call to mind the 'Feinde' (enemies) of Houwald. The author of this drama stood much in his own light, when, to preserve the unity of place, he sinned against comprehensibility in the first act, and altogether sacrificed what might have given greater effect to his piece to a whim, for which no one thanks him. I thought, too, on the other hand, of "Goetz von Berlichingen," which deviates as far as possible from the unity of time and place; but which, as everything is visibly developed to us, and brought before our eyes, is as truly dramatic and comprehensible as any piece in the world. I thought, too, that the unities of time and place were natural, and in accordance with the intention of the Greeks, only when a subject is so limited in its range that it can develop itself before our eyes with all its details in the given time; but that with a large action, which occurs in several places, there is no reason to be confined to one place, especially as our present stage arrangements offer no obstacle to a change of scene."

Goethe continued to talk of Lord Byron. "With that disposition," said he, "which always leads him into the illimitable, the restraint which he imposed upon himself by the observance of the three unities becomes him very well. If he had but known how to endure moral restraint also! That he could not was his ruin; and it may be aptly said, that he was destroyed by his own unbridled temperament.

"But he was too much in the dark about himself. He lived impetuously for the day, and neither knew nor thought what he was doing. Permitting everything to himself, and excusing nothing in others, he necessarily put himself in a bad position, and made the world his foe? At the very beginning, he offended the most distinguished literary men by his 'English Bards and Scotch Reviewers.' To be permitted only to live after this, he was obliged to go back a step. In his succeeding works, he continued in the path of opposition and fault-finding. Church and State were not left unassailed. This reckless conduct drove him from England, and would in time have driven him from Europe also. Everywhere it was too narrow for him, and with the most perfect personal freedom he felt himself confined; the world seemed to him a prison. His Grecian expedition was the result of no voluntary resolution; his misunderstanding with the world drove him to it.

"The renunciation of what was hereditary and patriotic not only caused the personal destruction of so distinguished a man, but his revolutionary turn, and the constant mental agitation with which it was combined, did not allow his talent a fair development. Moreover, his perpetual negation and fault-finding is injurious even to his excellent works. For not only does the discontent of the poet infect the reader, but the end of all opposition is negation; and negation is nothing. If I call *bad* bad, what do I gain? But if I call *good* bad, I do a great deal of mischief. He who will work aright must never rail, must not trouble himself at all about what is ill done, but only do well himself. For the great point is, not to pull down, but to build up, and in this humanity finds pure joy."

I was delighted with these noble words, and this valuable maxim.

"Lord Byron," continued Goethe, "is to be regarded as a man, as an Englishman, and as a great talent. His good qualities belong chiefly to the man, his bad to the Englishman and the peer, his talent is incommensurable.

"All Englishmen are, as such, without reflection, properly so called; distractions and party spirit will not permit them to perfect themselves in quiet. But they are great as practical men.

"Thus, Lord Byron could never attain reflection on himself, and on this account his maxims in general are not successful, as is shewn by his creed, 'much money, no authority,' for much money always paralyzes authority.

"But where he will create, he always succeeds; and we may truly say that with him inspiration supplies the place of reflection. He was always obliged to go on poetizing, and then everything that came from the man, especially from his heart, was excellent. He produced his best things, as women do pretty children, without thinking about it or knowing how it was done.

"He is a great talent, a born talent, and I never saw the true poetical power greater in any man than in him. In the apprehension of external objects, and a clear penetration into past situations, he is quite as great as Shakspeare. But as a pure individuality, Shakspeare is his superior. This was felt by Byron, and on this account, he does not say much of Shakspeare, although he knows whole passages by heart. He would willingly have denied him altogether; for Shakspeare's cheerfulness is in his way, and he feels that he is no match for it. Pope he does not deny, for he had no cause to fear him. On the contrary, he mentions him, and shews him respect when he can, for he knows well enough that Pope is a mere foil to himself."

Goethe seemed inexhaustible on the subject of Byron, and I felt that I could not listen enough. After a few digressions, he proceeded thus:—

"His high rank as an English peer was very injurious to Byron; for every talent is oppressed by the outer world,—how much more, then, when there is such high birth and so great a fortune. A certain middle rank is much more favourable to talent, on which account we find all great artists and poets in the middle classes. Byron's predilection for the unbounded could not have been nearly so dangerous with more humble birth and smaller means. But as it was, he was able to put every fancy into practice, and this involved him in innumerable scrapes. Besides, how could one of such high rank be inspired with awe and respect by any rank whatever? He spoke out whatever he felt, and this brought him into ceaseless conflict with the world.

"It is surprising to remark," continued Goethe, "how large a portion of the life of a rich Englishman of rank is passed in duels and elopements. Lord Byron himself says, that his father carried off three ladies. And let any man be a steady son after that.

"Properly speaking, he lived perpetually in a state of nature, and with his mode of existence the necessity for self-defence floated daily before his eyes. Hence his constant pistol-shooting. Every moment he expected to be called out.

"He could not live alone. Hence, with all his oddities, he was very indulgent to his associates. He one evening read his fine poem on the death of Sir John Moore, and his noble friends did not know what to make of it. This did not move him, but he put it away again. As a poet, he really shewed himself a lamb. Another would have commended them to the devil."

(Sup.) Tuesday, March 22, 1825.

Last night, soon after twelve o'clock, we were awoke by an alarm of fire; we heard cries, "the theatre is on fire!" I at once threw on my clothes, and hastened to the spot. The universal consternation was very great. Only a few hours before, we had been delighted by the excellent acting of La Roche in Cumberland's "Jew," and Seidel had excited universal laughter by his good humour and jokes. And now, in the place so lately the scene of intellectual pleasures, raged the most terrible element of destruction.

The fire, which was occasioned by the heating apparatus, appears to have broken out in the pit; it soon spread to the stage and the dry lath-work of the wings, and, as it fearfully increased by the great quantity of combustible material, it was not long before the flames burst through the roof, and the rafters gave way.

There was no deficiency of preparations for extinguishing the fire. The building was, by degrees, surrounded by engines, which poured an immense quantity of water upon the flames. All, however, was without avail. The flames raged upwards as before, and threw up to the dark sky an inexhaustible mass of glowing sparks and burning particles of light materials, which then, with a light breeze, passed sideways over the town. The noise of the cries and calls of the men working the fire-ladders and engines was very great. All seemed determined to subdue the flames. On one side, as near to the spot as the fire allowed, stood a man in a cloak and military cap, smoking a cigar with the greatest composure. At the first glance, he appeared to be an idle spectator, but such was not the case. There were several persons to whom, in a few words, he gave commands, which were immediately executed. It was the Grand Duke Charles Augustus. He had soon seen that the building itself could not be saved; he, therefore, ordered that it should be left to fall, and that all the superfluous engines should be turned upon the neighbouring houses, which were much exposed to the fire. He appeared to think with princely resignation—

> " Let *that* burn down,
> With greater beauty will it rise again."

He was not wrong. The theatre was old, by no means beautiful; and for a long time, it had ceased to be roomy enough to accommodate the annually increasing public. Nevertheless, it was lamentable to see this building thus irreparably destroyed, with which so many reminiscences of a past time, illustrious and endeared to Weimar, were connected.

I saw in beautiful eyes many tears, which flowed for

its downfal. I was no less touched by the grief of a member of the orchestra. He wept for his burnt violin. As the day dawned, I saw many pale countenances. I remarked several young girls and women of high rank, who had awaited the event of the fire during the whole night, and who now shivered in the cold morning air. I returned home to take a little rest, and in the course of the forenoon I called upon Goethe.

The servant told me that he was unwell and in bed. Still Goethe had me called to his side. He stretched out his hand to me. "We have all sustained a loss," said he; "what is to be done? My little Wolf came early this morning to my bed-side. He seized my hand, and looking full at me said, ' So is it with *human things*.' What more can be said, than these words of my beloved Wolf's, with which he sought to comfort me? The theatre, the scene of my love-labours for nearly thirty years, lies in ashes. But, as Wolf says, 'so is it with human things.' I have slept but little during the night; from my front windows, I saw the flames incessantly rising towards the sky.

"You can imagine that many thoughts of old times, of my many years' exertions with Schiller, and of the progress of many a favourite pupil, passed through my mind, and not without causing some emotion. Hence, I intend wisely to remain in bed to-day."

I praised him for his forethought. Still he did not appear to me in the least weak or exhausted, but in a very pleasant and serene mood. This lying in bed seemed to me to be an old stratagem of war, which he is accustomed to adopt on any extraordinary event, when he fears a crowd of visitors.

Goethe begged me to be seated on a chair before his bed, and to stay there a little time. "I have thought much of you, and pitied you," said he. "What will you do with your evenings now?"

"You know," returned I, "how passionately I love the theatre. When I came here, two years ago, I knew nothing at all, except three or four pieces which I had seen in Hanover.

"All was new to me, actors as well as pieces; and since, according to your advice, I have given myself up entirely to the impression of the subject, without much thinking or reflecting, I can say with truth, that I have, during these two winters, passed at the theatre the most harmless and most agreeable hours that I have ever known. I was, moreover, so infatuated with the theatre, that I not only missed no performance, but also obtained admission to the rehearsals; nay, not contented with this, if, as I passed in the day-time, I chanced to find the doors open, I would enter, and sit for half an hour upon the empty benches in the pit, and imagine scenes which might at some time be played there."

"You are a madman," returned Goethe, laughing; "but that is what I like. Would to God that the whole public consisted of such children! And in fact you are right. Any one who is sufficiently young, and who is not quite spoiled, could not easily find any place that would suit him so well as a theatre. No one asks you any questions; you need not open your mouth unless you choose; on the contrary, you sit quite at your ease like a king, and let everything pass before you, and recreate your mind and senses to your heart's content. There is poetry, there is painting, there are singing and music, there is acting, and what not besides. When all these arts, and the charm of youth and beauty heightened to an important degree, work in concert on the same evening, it is a bouquet to which no other can compare. But, even when part is bad and part is good, it is still better than looking out of window, or playing a game at whist in a close party amid the smoke of cigars. The theatre at Weimar is, as you feel, by no means to be despised; it is still an old trunk from our best time, to which new talents have attached themselves; and we can still produce something which charms and pleases, and at least gives the appearance of an organized whole."

"Would I had seen it twenty or thirty years ago," answered I. "That was certainly a time," replied Goethe, "when we were assisted by great advantages. Consider that the tedious period of the French taste had not long gone by; that the public was not yet spoiled by over-excitement; that the influence of Shakspeare was in all its first freshness; that the operas of Mozart were new; and lastly, that the pieces of Schiller were first produced here year after year, and were given at the theatre of Weimar in all their first glory, under his own superintendence. Consider all this, I say, and you will imagine that, with such dishes, a fine banquet was given to old and young, and that we always had a grateful public."

I remarked, "Older persons, who lived in those

times, cannot praise highly enough the elevated position which the Weimar theatre then held."

"I will not deny that it was something," returned Goethe. "The main point, however, was this, that the Grand Duke left my hands quite free, and I could do just as I liked. I did not look to magnificent scenery, and a brilliant wardrobe, but I looked to good pieces. From tragedy to farce, every species was welcome; but a piece was obliged to have something in it to find favour. It was necessary that it should be great and clever, cheerful and graceful, and, at all events, healthy and containing some pith. All that was morbid, weak, lachrymose, and sentimental, as well as all that was frightful, horrible, and offensive to decorum, was utterly excluded; I should have feared, by such expedients, to spoil both actors and audience.

"By means of good pieces, I raised the actors; for the study of excellence, and the perpetual practice of excellence, must necessarily make something of a man whom nature has not left ungifted. I was, also, constantly in personal contact with the actors. I attended the first rehearsals,* and explained to every one his part; I was present at the chief rehearsals, and talked with the actors as to any improvements that might be made; I was never absent from a performance, and pointed out the next day anything which did not appear to me to be right.

"By these means I advanced them in their art.

---

* The word "Leseprobe," which is here used, answers exactly to the English stage technicality — the "reading." The chief rehearsals, "Haupt proben," are by us simply called "rehearsals."—*Trans.*

"But I also sought to raise the whole class in the esteem of society, by introducing the best and most promising into my own circle, and thus showing to the world that I considered them worthy of social intercourse with myself. The result of this was, that the rest of the higher society in Weimar did not remain behind me, and that actors and actresses gained soon an honourable admission into the best circles. By all this, they acquired a great internal as well as external culture. My scholar Wolf, in Berlin, and our Dürand, are people of the finest tact in society. Oels and Graff have enough of the higher order of culture to do honour to the best circles.

"Schiller proceeded in the same spirit as myself. He had a great deal of intercourse with actors and actresses. He, like me, was present at every rehearsal; and after every successful performance of one of his pieces, it was his custom to invite the actors, and to spend a merry day with them. All rejoiced together at that which had succeeded, and discussed how anything might be done better next time. But even when Schiller joined us, he found both actors and the public already cultivated to a high degree; and it is not to be denied that this conduced to the rapid success of his pieces."

It gave me great pleasure to hear Goethe speak so circumstantially upon a subject which always possessed great interest for me, and which, in consequence of the misfortune of the previous night, was uppermost in my mind.

"This burning of the house," said I, "in which you and Schiller, during a long course of years, effected so much good, in some degree closes a great epoch, which will not soon return for Weimar. You must at that time have experienced great pleasure in your direction of the theatre, and its extraordinary success."

"And not a little trouble and difficulty," returned Goethe, with a sigh.

"It must be difficult," said I, "to keep such a many-headed being in proper order."

"A great deal," said Goethe, "may be done by severity, more by love, but most by clear discernment and impartial justice, which pays no respect to persons.

"I had to beware of two enemies, which might have been dangerous to me. The one was my passionate love of talent, which might easily have made me partial. The other I will not mention, but you can guess it. At our theatre there was no want of ladies, who were beautiful and young, and who were possessed of great mental charms. I felt a passionate inclination towards many of them, and sometimes it happened that I was met half way. But I restrained myself, and said, No further! I knew my position, and also what I owed to it. I stood here, not as a private man, but as chief of an establishment, the prosperity of which was of more consequence to me than a momentary gratification. If I had involved myself in any love affair, I should have been like a compass, which cannot point right when under the influence of a magnet at its side.

"By thus keeping myself quite clear, and always remaining master of myself, I also remained master of the theatre, and I always received that proper respect, without which all authority is very soon at an end."

This confession of Goethe's deeply impressed me. I had already heard something of this kind about him from others, and I rejoiced now to hear its confirmation from his own mouth. I loved him more than ever, and took leave of him with a hearty pressure of the hand.

I returned to the scene of the fire, where flames and columns of smoke were rising from the great heap of ruins. People were still occupied in extinguishing and pulling to pieces. I found near the spot a burnt fragment of a written part. It contained passages from Goethe's " Tasso."

(Sup.) Thursday, March 24, 1825.

I dined with Goethe. The loss of the theatre was almost the exclusive subject of conversation. Frau von Goethe and Fräulein Ulrica recalled to mind the happy hours they had enjoyed in the old house. They had been seeking some relics from amongst the rubbish, which they considered invaluable; but which were, after all, nothing but stones and burnt pieces of carpet. Still, these pieces were from the precise spot in the balcony, where they had been used to sit.

" The principal thing is," said Goethe, " to recover oneself, and get in order as soon as possible. I should like the performances to recommence next week, in the palace or in the great town-hall, no matter which. Too long a pause must not be allowed, lest the public should seek some other resource for its tedious evenings."

"But," it was observed, "there are scarcely any of the decorations saved."

"There is no need of much decoration," returned Goethe. "Neither is there a necessity for great pieces. It is not even necessary to perform whole pieces at all, much less a great whole.

"The main point is, to choose something in which no great change of scene takes place. Perhaps a one act comedy, or a one act farce, or operetta. Then, perhaps, some air, duet, or finale, from a favourite opera, and you will be very passably entertained. We have only to get tolerably through April, for in May you have the songsters of the woods.

"In the mean time," continued Goethe, "you will, during the summer months, witness the spectacle of the rearing of a new house. This fire appears to me very remarkable. I will now confess to you, that, during the long winter evenings, I have occupied myself with Coudray, in drawing the plan of a new handsome theatre suitable to Weimar.

"We had sent for the ground-plans and sections of some of the principal German theatres, and by taking what was best, and avoiding what appeared defective, we accomplished a sketch which will be worth looking at. As soon as the Grand Duke gives permission, the building may be commenced, and it is no trifle that this accident found us so wonderfully prepared."

We received this intelligence of Goethe's with great joy.

"In the old house," continued Goethe, "the nobility were accommodated by the balcony, and the servants and young artisans by the gallery. The great number of the wealthy and genteel middle class were not well provided for; for when, at the performance of certain pieces, the students occupied the pit, these respectable persons did not know where to go. The few small boxes behind the pit, and the few stalls, were not sufficient. Now we have managed much better. We have a whole tier of boxes running round the pit, and another tier, of the second rank, between the balcony and the gallery.

"By these means we gain a great many places, without enlarging the house too much."

We rejoiced at this communication, and praised Goethe for his kind consideration of the theatre and the public.

In order to lend my share of assistance to the future theatre, I went, after dinner, with my friend Robert Doolan, to Upper Weimar, and over a cup of coffee at the inn, began to make the libretto of an opera, after the "Issipile" of Metastasio. The first thing was to write a programme, so as to cast the piece with all the favourite singers, male and female, belonging to the Weimar theatre. This gave us great pleasure. It was almost as if we were again seated before the orchestra.

We then set to work in good earnest, and finished a great part of the first act.

(Sup.) Sunday, March 27, 1825.

I dined at Goethe's with a large party. He shewed us the design for the new theatre. It was as he had told us a few days ago; the plan promised a very beautiful building, both externally and internally.

It was remarked that so pretty a theatre required beautiful decorations, and better costumes than the former one. We were also of opinion that the company had gradually become incomplete, and that some distinguished young members should be engaged, both for the drama and the opera. At the same time, we did not shut our eyes to the fact, that all this would be attended with great expense, which the present state of the treasury would not allow.

"I know very well," said Goethe, "that under pretext of sparing the treasury, some insignificant persons will be engaged who will not cost much. But we cannot expect to benefit the treasury by such means.

"Nothing injures the treasury more than the endeavour to save in such essential matters. Our aim must be, to have a full house every evening. And a young singer, male or female, a clever hero, and a clever young heroine of distinguished talents and some beauty, will do much towards this end. Ay, if I still stood at the head of the direction, I would now go a step farther for the benefit of the treasury, and you would perceive that I should not be without the money required."

Goethe was asked what he meant by this.

"I would employ very simple means," returned he. "I would have performances on Sundays. I should thus have the receipts of at least forty more evenings, and it would be hard if the treasury did not thus gain ten or fifteen thousand dollars a year."

This expedient was thought very practical. It was mentioned, that to the great working-class, who are usually occupied until late at night on week days, Sunday is the only day of recreation, when they would prefer the more noble pleasures of a play to a dance, with beer, at a village inn. It was also the general opinion, that all the farmers and land-owners, as well as the officials and wealthy inhabitants of the small towns in the neighbourhood, would consider the Sunday as a desirable day to go to the theatre at Weimar. Besides, at the present time, a Sunday evening at Weimar was very dreary and tedious for every one who did not go to court, or was not a member of a happy family circle, or a select society; since isolated individuals did not know where to go. And still people said that there ought to be some place where they might, on a Sunday evening, be comfortable, and forget the annoyances of the week.

Goethe's idea of permitting Sunday performances, according to the custom in all other German towns, received perfect approbation, and was greeted as a very happy one. Only a slight doubt arose, as to whether the court would approve of it.

"The court of Weimar," returned Goethe, "is too good and too wise to oppose any regulation which would conduce to the benefit of the town and an important institution. The court will certainly make the small sacrifice of altering its Sunday *soirées* to another day. But if this were not agreeable, we could find for the Sundays enough pieces which the court does not like to see, but which would suit the common people, and would fill the treasury admirably."

The conversation then turned upon actors, and much was said about the use and abuse of their powers.

"I have, during my long practice," said Goethe, "found that the main point is never to allow any play, or scarcely an opera, to be studied, unless one can look forward with some certainty to a good success for years. No one sufficiently considers the expenditure of power, which is demanded for the study of a five act play, or even an opera of equal length. Yes, my good friends, much is required before a singer has thoroughly mastered a part through all the scenes and acts, much more before the choruses go as they ought.

"I am horrified, when I hear how lightly people often give orders for the study of an opera, of the success of which they truly know nothing, and of which they have only heard through some very uncertain newspaper notice. As we, in Germany, already possess very tolerable means of travelling, and are even beginning to have diligences, I would, on the intelligence of any new opera being produced and praised, send to the spot the *Regisseur*, or some other trustworthy member of the theatre, that by his presence, at an actual representation, he might be convinced how far the highly-praised new opera was good for anything, whether our forces were sufficient for it or not. The expense of such a journey would be inconsiderable in comparison with the enormous advantage to be derived from it, and the fatal mistakes, which, by these means, would be avoided.

"And then, when a good play or a good opera has once been studied, it should be represented at short intervals,—be allowed to 'run' as long as it draws, and continues at all to fill the house. The same plan would be applicable to a good old play, or a good old opera, which has, perhaps, been long laid aside, and which now requires not a little fresh study to be reproduced with success. Such a representation should be repeated at short intervals, as frequently as the public shews any interest in it. The desire always to have something new, and to see a good play or opera, which has been studied with excessive pains only once, or at the most twice, or even to allow the space of six or eight weeks to elapse between such repetitions, in which time a new study becomes necessary, is a real detriment to the theatre, and an unpardonable misuse of the talents of the performers engaged in it."

Goethe appeared to consider this matter very important, and it seemed to lie so near his heart that he became more warm than, with his calm disposition, is often the case.

"In Italy," continued Goethe, "they perform the same opera every evening for four or six weeks, and the great Italian children by no means desire any change. The polished Parisian sees the classical plays of his great poets so often that he knows them by heart, and has a practised ear for the accentuation of every syllable. Here, in Weimar, they have done me the honour to perform my 'Iphigenia' and my 'Tasso,' but how often ? Scarcely once in three or four years. The public finds them tedious. Very probably. The actors are not in practice to play the pieces, and the public is not in practice to hear them. If, through more frequent repetitions, the actors entered so much into the spirit of their parts that their representation gained life, as if it were not the result of study, and everything flowed from their own hearts, the public would, assuredly, no longer remain uninterested and unmoved.

"I really had the notion once that it was possible to form a German drama. Nay, I even fancied that I myself could contribute to it, and lay some foundation-stones for such an edifice. I wrote my 'Iphigenia' and my 'Tasso,' and thought, with a childish hope, that thus it might be brought about. But there was no emotion or excitement,—all remained as it was before. If I had produced an effect, and had met with applause, I would have written a round dozen of pieces such as 'Iphigenia' and 'Tasso.' There was no deficiency of material. But, as I said, actors were wanting to represent such pieces with life and spirit, and a public was wanting to hear and receive them with sympathy."

(Sup.) Wednesday, March 30, 1825.

This evening to a great tea party at Goethe's, where I found a young American, besides the young Englishmen. I also had the pleasure of seeing the Countess Julia von Egloffstein, and of conversing with her pleasantly on various subjects.

(Sup.) Wednesday, April 6, 1825.

Goethe's advice has been followed, and a performance has taken place this evening, for the first time, in the great hall of the town-house, consisting of small things and fragments, which were in accordance with the confined space and the want of decorations. The little opera, "Das Hausgesinde" (the domestic servants), went quite as well as at the theatre. Then a favourite quartet, from the opera "Graf von Gleichen" (Count von Gleichen), by Eberwein, was received with decided approbation. Our first tenor, Herr Moltke, then sang a well-known song from " Die Zauberflöte," after which, with a pause between, the grand finale to the first act of " Don Juan" came in with powerful effect, and nobly concluded this first substitute for an evening at the theatre.

(Sup.) Sunday, April 10, 1825.

Dined with Goethe. " I have the good news to tell you," said he, " that the Grand Duke has approved of our design for the new theatre, and that the foundation will be laid immediately."

I was very much pleased at this information.

" We had to contend with all sorts of obstacles," continued Goethe; " we are, at last, happily through them. We owe many thanks, on that account, to the Privy Counsellor, Schweitzer, who, as we might have expected of him, stood true to our cause with hearty good will. The sketch is signed in the Grand Duke's own handwriting, and is to undergo no further alteration. Rejoice, then, for you will obtain a very good theatre."

(Sup.) Thursday, April 14, 1825.

This evening at Goethe's. Since conversation upon the theatre and theatrical management were now the order of the day, I asked him upon what maxims he proceeded in the choice of a new member of the company.

" I can scarcely say," returned Goethe; " I had various modes of proceeding. If a striking reputation preceded the new actor, I let him act, and saw how he suited the others; whether his style and manner disturbed our *ensemble*, or whether he would supply a deficiency. If, however, he was a young man who had never trodden a stage before, I first considered his personal qualities; whether he had about him anything prepossessing or attractive, and, above all things, whether he had control over himself. For an actor who possesses no self-possession, and who cannot appear before a stranger in his most favourable light, has, generally speaking, little talent. His whole profession requires continual self-denial, and a continual existence in a foreign mask.

"If his appearance and his deportment pleased me, I made him read, in order to test the power and extent of his organ, as well as the capabilities of his mind. I gave him some sublime passage from a great poet, to see whether he was capable of feeling and expressing what was really great; then something passionate and wild, to prove his power. I then went to something marked by sense and smartness, something ironical and witty, to see how he treated such things, and whether he possessed sufficient freedom. Then I gave him something in which was represented the pain of a wounded heart, the suffering of a great soul, that I might learn whether he had it in his power to express pathos.

"If he satisfied me in all these numerous particulars, I had a well-grounded hope of making him a very important actor. If he appeared more capable in some particulars than in others, I remarked the line to which he was most adapted. I also now knew his weak points, and, above all, endeavoured to work upon him so that he might strengthen and cultivate himself here. If I remarked faults of dialect, and what are called provincialisms, I urged him to lay them aside, and recommended to him social intercourse and friendly practice with some member of the stage who was entirely free from them. I then asked him whether he could dance and fence; and if this were not the case, I would hand him over for some time to the dancing and fencing masters.

"If he were now sufficiently advanced to make his appearance, I gave him at first such parts as suited his individuality, and I desired nothing but that he should represent himself. If he now appeared to me of too fiery a nature, I gave him phlegmatic characters; if too calm and tedious, I gave him fiery and hasty characters, that he might thus learn to lay aside himself, and assume foreign individuality."

The conversation turned upon the casting of plays, upon which Goethe made, among others, the following remarkable observations:—

"It is a great error to think," said he, "that an indifferent piece may be played by indifferent actors. A second or third rate play can be incredibly improved by the employment of first-rate powers, and be made something really good. But if a second or third rate play be performed by second or third rate actors, no one can wonder if it is utterly ineffective.

"Second-rate actors are excellent in great plays. They have the same effect that the figures in half shade have in a picture; they serve admirably to show off more powerfully those which have the full light."

(Sup.) Saturday, April 16, 1825.

Dined at Goethe's with D'Alton, whose acquaintance I made last summer at Bonn, and whom it gave me great pleasure to meet again. D'Alton is a man quite after Goethe's own heart; there is also a very pleasant relation between them. In his own science he appears of great importance, so that Goethe esteems his observations, and honours every word he utters. Moreover, D'Alton is, as a man, amiable and witty, while in eloquence and abundance of flowing thoughts few can equal him, and one is never tired of hearing him.

Goethe, who in his endeavours to investigate nature would willingly encompass the Great Whole, stands in a disadvantageous position to every natural philosopher* of importance who has devoted a whole life to one special object. The latter has mastered a kingdom of endless details, whilst Goethe lives more in the contemplation of great universal laws. Thence it is that Goethe, who is always upon the track of some great synthesis, but who, from the want of knowledge of single facts, lacks a confirmation of his presentiments, seizes upon, and retains with such decided love, every connection with important natural philosophers. For in them he finds what he himself wants; in them he finds that which supplies his own deficiencies. He will in a few years be eighty years old; but he is not tired of inquiries and experiments. In none of his

---

* *Naturforscher*, literally "Investigator into Nature;" for the Germans do not, like us, honour experimentalists with the name of philosophers.—*Trans.*

tendencies has he come to a fixed point; he will always go on further and further. Still learning and learning. Thus he shews himself a man endowed with perpetual, imperishable youth.

These reflections were awakened to-day, by his animated conversation with D'Alton. D'Alton talked about Rodentia,* and the formation and modifications of their skeletons, and Goethe was unwearied in hearing new facts.

Wednesday, April 20, 1825.

Goethe shewed me this evening a letter from a young student, who begs of him the plan for the second part of "Faust," with the design of completing the work himself. In a straightforward, good-humoured, and candid tone, he freely sets forth his wishes and views, and at last, without reserve, utters his conviction that all other literary efforts of later years have been nought, but that in him a new literature is to bloom afresh.

If I met a young man who would set about continuing Napoleon's conquest of the world, or a young dilettante in architecture, who attempted to complete the Cathedral of Cologne, I should not be more surprised, nor find them more insane and ridiculous, than this young poetical amateur, who fancies he could write a second part of "Faust" merely because he has a fancy to do so.

Indeed, I think it more possible to complete the Cathedral of Cologne, than to continue "Faust" on Goethe's plan. For the former object might, at any

* This word of Cuvier's exactly corresponds to the German *Nagethier*.
—*Trans.*

rate, be attained mathematically; it stands visibly before our eyes, and may be touched with our hands; but what line or measure could avail for a mental invisible work, which wholly depends on the subjective peculiarity of the artist, in which the first discovery (aperçu) is everything, and which, for its material requires a great life actually experienced, and for its execution, a technical skill heightened to perfection by the practice of years.

He who esteems such a work easy, or even possible, has certainly a very moderate talent, since he has not even a suspicion of the high and the difficult; and it may be fairly maintained, that if Goethe had completed his "Faust" with only a deficiency of a few lines, such a youth would be unequal to supply the small gap.

I will not inquire whence the young men of our day acquire the notion that they are born with that which has hitherto been attained only by the study and experience of many years, but I think I may observe that this presumptuousness, now so common in Germany, which audaciously strides over all the steps of gradual culture, affords little hope of future masterpieces.

"The misfortune," said Goethe, "in the state is, that nobody can enjoy life in peace, but that everybody must govern; and in art, that nobody will enjoy what has been produced, but every one wants to reproduce on his own account. Again, no one thinks to be furthered in his own way by a work of poetry, but every one will do the same thing over again. There is, besides, no earnestness to approach the Whole, no willingness to do anything for the sake of the Whole; but each one tries to make his own Self observable, and to exhibit it as much as possible to the world. This false tendency is shown everywhere, and people imitate the modern musical virtuosi, who do not select those pieces which give the audience pure musical enjoyment, so much as those in which they can gain admiration by the dexterity they have acquired. Everywhere there is the individual who wants to show himself off to advantage, nowhere one honest effort to make oneself subservient to the Whole.

"Hence it is that men acquire a bungling mode of production, without knowing it. Children make verses, and go on till they fancy, as youths, they can do something, until at last, manhood gives them insight into the excellence that exists, and then they look back in despair on the years they have wasted on a false and highly futile effort. Nay, many never attain a knowledge of what is perfect, and of their own insufficiency, and go on doing things by halves to the end of their days.

"It is certain that if every one could early enough be made to feel how full the world is already of excellence, and how much must be done to produce anything worthy of being placed beside what has already been produced—of a hundred youths who are now poetizing, scarcely one would feel enough courage, perseverance, and talent to work quietly for the attainment of a similar mastery.

"Many young painters would never have taken their pencils in hand, if they could have felt, known, and understood early enough what really produced a master like Raphael."

The conversation turned upon false tendencies in general, and Goethe continued—

"Thus my tendency to practise painting was really a false one, for I had not natural talent from which anything of the sort could be developed. A certain sensibility to the surrounding landscapes was one of my qualities, and, consequently, my first attempts were really promising. The journey to Italy destroyed this pleasure in practice. A broad survey took its place, but the talent of love was lost, and as an artistical talent could neither technically nor æsthetically be developed, my efforts melted away into nothing.

"It is justly said," continued Goethe, "that the cultivation of all human powers in common is desirable, and also the chief end. But man is not born for this; every one must form himself as a particular being, seeking, however, to attain that general idea of which all mankind are constituents."*

I here thought of that passage in "Wilhelm Meister," where it is likewise said that all men, taken together, are requisite to constitute humanity, and that we are only so far worthy of esteem as we know how to appreciate.

I thought, too, of the "Wanderjahre," where Jarno advises each man to learn only one trade, and says that this is the time for one-sidedness, and that he is to be congratulated who understands this, and, in that spirit, works for himself and others.

Then comes the question, what occupation shall a

---

* *Den Begriff zu erlangen suchen, was alle zusammen sind.* The word "Begriff" (rendered not quite correctly "idea") is here used in the sense of the Hegelian school.—*Trans.*

man choose, that he may neither overstep his proper limits nor do too little?

He whose business it is to overlook *many* departments, to judge, to guide others, should endeavour to attain the best insight into many departments. Thus a prince or a future statesman cannot be too many-sided in his culture; for many-sidedness belongs to his craft.

The poet, too, should strive after manifold knowledge, for his subject is the whole world, which he has to handle and to express.

However, the poet should not try to be a painter, but content himself with reflecting the world in words, just as he allows the actor to bring it before our eyes by personally exhibiting himself.

Insight and *practical activity* are to be distinguished, and we ought to reflect that every art, when we reduce it to practice, is something very great and difficult, and that mastery in it requires a life.

Thus Goethe strove for insight into many things, but has practically confined himself to one thing only. Only one art has he practised, and that in a masterly style, viz., the art of writing German (*Deutsch zu schreiben*). That the matter which he uttered is of a many-sided nature, is another affair.

Culture is likewise to be distinguished from practical activity. Thus it belongs to the cultivation of the poet that his eye should be practised for the apprehension of external objects. And if Goethe calls his practical tendency to painting a false one, it was still of use in cultivating him as a poet.

"The objectivity of my poetry," said he, "may be

attributed to this great attention and discipline of the eye; and I ought highly to prize the knowledge which I have attained in this way."

But we must take care not to place the limits of our culture too far off.

"The investigators into nature," said Goethe, "are most in danger of this, because a general harmonious culture of the faculties is really required for the adequate observation of nature."

But, on the other hand, every one should strive to guard himself against one-sidedness and narrow views, with respect to the knowledge which is indispensable to his own department.

A poet who writes for the stage must have a knowledge of the stage, that he may weigh the means at his command, and know generally what is to be done, and what is to be left alone; the opera-composer, in like manner, should have some insight into poetry, that he may know how to distinguish the bad from the good, and not apply his art to something impracticable.

"Carl Maria von Weber," said Goethe, "should not have composed 'Euryanthe.' He should have seen at once that this was a bad material, of which nothing could be made. So much insight we have a right to expect of every composer, as belonging to his art."

Thus, too, the painter should be able to distinguish subjects: for it belongs to his department to know what he has to paint, and what to leave unpainted.

"But, when all is said," observed Goethe, "the greatest art is to limit and isolate oneself."

Accordingly, he has, ever since I have been with

him, constantly endeavoured to guard me against all distractions, and to concentrate me to a single department. If I showed an inclination to penetrate the secrets of natural science, he always advised me to let it alone, and confine myself to poetry for the present. If I wished to read a book which he thought would not advance me in my present pursuits, he always advised me to let it alone, saying that it was of no practical use to me.

"I myself," said he, one day, "have spent too much time on things which did not belong to my proper department. When I reflect what Lopez de Vega accomplished, the number of my poetical productions seems very small. I should have kept more to my own trade."

"If I had not busied myself so much with stones," said he, another time, "but had spent my time on something better, I might have won the finest ornament of diamonds."

For the same cause he esteems and praises his friend Meyer for having devoted his whole life exclusively to the study of art, and thus having obtained beyond a doubt the highest degree of penetration in his department.

"I also grew up with this tendency," said Goethe, "and passed almost half my life in the contemplation and study of works of art, but in a certain respect I am not on a par with Meyer. I, therefore, never venture to show him a new picture at once, but first see how far I can get on with it myself. When I think I am fully acquainted both with its beauties and defects, I show it to Meyer, who sees far more sharply into the matter, and who, in many respects, gives quite new lights. Thus I am ever convinced anew how much is needed to be thoroughly great in any *one* thing. In Meyer lies an insight into art belonging to thousands of years."

Why, then, it may be asked, if Goethe was so thoroughly persuaded that one man can only do one thing well, did he employ his life in such extremely various directions?

I answer, that, if Goethe now came into the world, and found the literary and scientific endeavours of his native country at the height which they have now, chiefly through him, attained, he certainly would find no occasion for such various tendencies, but would simply confine himself to a single department.

Thus, it was not only in his nature to look in every direction, and to make himself clear about earthly things, but it was needful for his time that he should speak out what he had observed.

On his appearance in the world, he came in for two large inheritances. *Error* and *insufficiency* fell to his lot that he might remove them, and required a labor in many directions as long as his life endured.

If the Newtonian theory had not appeared to Goethe as a great error, highly injurious to the human mind, is it to be supposed that he would have had the notion of writing a "theory of colours," and devoting the labour of years to such a merely collateral object? Certainly not. But it was his love of truth in conflict with error that induced him to make his pure light shine even into this darkness.

The same thing may be said of his doctrine of the

"Metamorphosis of Plants," through which we are indebted to him for a model of scientific treatment. Goethe would certainly never have thought of writing this work, if he had seen his contemporaries in the way towards such a goal.

Nay, the same thing may be said of his varied poetical efforts. It is a question whether Goethe would ever have written a novel, if a work like "Wilhelm Meister" had already been in the hands of his nation. It is a question whether in that case he would not have devoted himself exclusively to dramatic poetry.

What he would have effected and produced, if he had been confined to one direction, is not to be seen; but so much is certain, that if we look at the whole, no intelligent person will wish that Goethe had not produced everything to which it pleased his Creator to direct him.

(Sup.) Wednesday, April 27, 1825.

Towards the evening to Goethe, who had invited me to take a drive to the lower garden. "Before we go," said he, "I will give you a letter from Zelter, which I received yesterday, and wherein he touches upon the affairs of our theatre."

"'That you are not the man,' he writes, amongst other things, 'to found a drama for the people of Weimar I could have seen long ago. He who makes himself green, the goats will eat. Other high folks should take this into consideration, who would cork wine during its fermentation.

"'Friends, we have lived to see it; yes lived to see it.'"

Goethe looked at me, and we laughed. "Zelter is a capital fellow," said he; "but sometimes he does not quite understand me, and puts a false construction on my words.

"I have devoted my whole life to the people and their improvement, and why should I not also found a drama? But here in Weimar, in this small residence, which, as people jokingly say, has ten thousand poets and a few inhabitants, how can we talk about the people, much more a theatre for the people? Weimar will doubtless become, at some future time, a great city; but we must wait some centuries before the people of Weimar will form a mass sufficient to be able to found and support a drama."

The horses were now put to, and we drove to the lower garden. The evening was calm and mild, rather sultry, and large clouds appeared gathering in tempestuous masses. We walked up and down the dry gravel path, Goethe quietly by my side, apparently agitated by various thoughts. Meanwhile, I listened to the notes of the blackbird and thrush, who, upon the tops of the still leafless ash-trees, beyond the Ilm, sang against the gathering tempest.

Goethe cast his glances around, now towards the clouds, now upon the green which was bursting forth everywhere, on the sides of the path and on the meadows, as well as on the bushes and hedges. "A warm thunder-shower, which the evening promises," said he, "and spring will again appear in all her splendour and abundance."

In the mean time the clouds became more threatening, a low peal of thunder was heard, some drops of rain also fell, and Goethe thought it advisable to drive back into the town. "If you have no engagement," said he, as we alighted at his dwelling, " go up stairs, and spend an hour or so with me." This I did with great pleasure.

Zelter's letter still lay upon the table. "It is strange, very strange," said Goethe, "how easily one falls into a false position with respect to public opinion. I do not know that I ever joined in any way against the people; but it is now settled once for all, that I am no friend to the people. I am, indeed, no friend to the revolutionary mob, whose object is robbery, murder, and destruction, and who, behind the mask of public welfare, have their eyes only upon the meanest egotistical aims. I am no friend to such people, any more than I am a friend of a Louis XV. I hate every violent overthrow, because as much good is destroyed as is gained by it. I hate those who achieve it, as well as those who give cause for it. But am I therefore no friend to the people? Does any right-minded man think otherwise?

"You know how greatly I rejoice at every improvement, of which the future gives us some prospect. But, as I said, all violent transitions are revolting to my mind, for they are not conformable to nature.

"I am a friend to plants; I love the rose, as the most perfect flower which our German nature can produce; but I am not fool enough to desire that my garden should produce them now, at the end of April. I am satisfied if I now find the first green leaves, satisfied if I see how one leaf after another is formed upon the stem, from week to week; I am pleased when, in May, I perceive the buds, and am happy when, at last, in June, the rose itself appears in all its splendour and all its fragrance. If any one cannot wait, let him go to the hot-houses.

"It is farther said that I am a servant, a slave to princes; as if that were saying anything. Do I then serve a tyrant—a despot? Do I serve one who lives at the cost of the people, only for his own pleasures? Such princes and such times lie, God be praised, far behind us. I have been intimately connected with the Grand Duke for half a century, and have, during half a century, striven and worked with him; but I should speak falsely, if I were to say that I have known a single day, in which the Grand Duke has not thought of doing and executing something tending to the benefit of the land, and fitted to improve the condition of individuals. As for himself personally, what has he from his princely station, but toil and trouble? Is his dwelling, his apparel, or his table better appointed than that of any wealthy private man? Only go into our seaport towns, and you will find the kitchen and cellar of any considerable merchant better appointed than his.

"This autumn," continued Goethe, "we are going to celebrate the day, on which the Grand Duke will have governed for fifty years. But when I consider it rightly,—this government of his—what was it but a continual servitude? What has it been but a servitude in the attainment of great ends,—a servitude to the welfare of his people? If then I must perforce be the slave of a prince, it is at least my consolation, that I am still only the slave of one who is himself a slave to the common weal."

(Sup.) Friday, April 29, 1825.

The building of the new theatre up to this time, had advanced very rapidly; the foundation walls had already risen on every side, and gave promise of a very beautiful building.

But to-day, on going to the site of the building, I saw, to my horror, that the work was discontinued; and I heard it reported that another party, opposed to Goethe and Coudray's plan, had at last triumphed; that Coudray had retired from the direction of the building, and that another architect was going to finish it after a new design, and alter accordingly the foundation already laid.

I was deeply grieved at what I saw and heard; for I had rejoiced with many others, at the prospect of seeing a theatre arise in Weimar, executed according to Goethe's practical view of a judicious internal arrangement, and as far as beauty was concerned, in accordance with his cultivated taste.

But I also grieved for Goethe and Coudray, who must both, more or less, feel hurt by this event.

(Sup.) Sunday, May 1, 1825.

Dined with Goethe. It may be supposed that the alteration in the building of the theatre, was the first subject we talked upon. I had, as I said, feared that this most unexpected measure would deeply wound Goethe's feelings; but there was no sign of it. I found him in the mildest and most serene frame of mind, quite raised above all sensitive littleness.

"They have," said he, "assailed the Grand Duke on the side of expenditure, and the great saving of expense which will be effected by the change of plan for the building, and they have succeeded. I am quite content. A new theatre is, in the end, only a new funeral pile which some accident will, sooner or later, set on fire. I console myself with this. Besides, a trifle more or less is not worth mentioning. You will have a very tolerable house, if not exactly such a one as I wished and imagined. You will go to it, and I shall go to it too, and in the end, all will turn out well enough.

"The Grand Duke," said Goethe, "disclosed to me his opinion, that a theatre need not be of architectural magnificence, which could not be contradicted. He further said, that it was nothing but a house for the purpose of getting money. This view appears, at first sight, rather material; but rightly considered, it is not without a higher purport. For if a theatre is not only to pay its expenses, but is, besides, to make and save money, everything about it must be excellent. It must have the best management at its head; the actors must be of the best; and good pieces must continually be performed, that the attractive power required to draw a full house every evening may never cease. But that is saying a great deal in a few words—almost what is impossible."

"The Grand Duke's view," said I, "of making the theatre gain money, appears to be very practical, since it implies a necessity of remaining continually on a summit of excellence."

"Even Shakspeare and Moliere," returned Goethe,

"had no other view. Both of them wished, above all things, to make money by their theatres. In order to attain this, their principal aim, they necessarily strove that everything should be as good as possible, and that, besides good old plays, there should be some clever novelty to please and attract. The prohibition of 'Tartuffe' was a thunderbolt to Moliere; but not so much for the poet as for the director Moliere, who had to consider the welfare of an important troupe, and to find some means to procure bread for himself and his actors.

"Nothing," continued Goethe, "is more dangerous to the well-being of a theatre, than when the director is so placed, that a greater or less receipt at the treasury does not affect him personally, and he can live on in careless security, knowing that however the receipts at the treasury may fail in the course of the year, at the end of that time he will be able to indemnify himself from another source. It is a property of human nature soon to relax, when not impelled by personal advantage or disadvantage. Now, it is not desirable that a theatre, in such a town as Weimar, should support itself, and that no contribution from the Prince's treasury should be necessary. But still everything has its bounds and limits, and a thousand dollars yearly, more or less, is by no means a trifling matter, particularly as diminished receipts and deteriorations are dangers natural to a theatre; so that there is a loss not only of money, but also of honour.

"If I were the Grand Duke, I would in future, on any change in the management, once for all appoint a fixed sum for an annual contribution. I would strike the average of the contributions during the last ten years, and according to that, I would settle a sum sufficient to be regarded as a proper support. With this sum the house must be kept. But then I would go a step further, and say, that if the director and his *Regisseurs* contrived, by means of judicious and energetic management, to have an overplus in the treasury at the end of the year, this overplus should be shared, as a remuneration, between the director, the *Regisseurs*, and the principal members of the company. Then you would see what activity there would be, and how the establishment would awaken out of the drowsiness into which it must gradually fall.

"Our theatrical laws," continued Goethe, "contain various penalties; but there is no single law for the encouragement and reward of distinguished merit. This is a great defect. For if with every failure, I have a prospect of a deduction from my salary, I should also have the prospect of a reward, whenever I do more than can be properly expected of me. And it is by every one's doing more than can be hoped or expected of him, that a theatre rises."

Frau von Goethe, and Fräulein Ulrike now entered, both gracefully clothed in summer attire, on account of the beautiful weather. The conversation during dinner was light and cheerful. We spoke about various parties of pleasure during the past week, and also about similar plans for the following one.

"If we continue to have fine evenings," said Frau von Goethe, "I shall have great pleasure in giving a tea party in the park, where we can listen to the song of the nightingale. What do you say, dear father?"

"That would be very pleasant," returned Goethe. "And you, Eckermann," said Frau von Goethe, "how do you feel disposed? May one invite you?" "But Ottilia," rejoined Fraulein Ulrike, "how can you invite the doctor? He will not come; and if he does come, he sits as if upon thorns, and one can see that his mind is elsewhere, and that the sooner he is gone the better he would like it." "To speak the plain truth," returned I, "I would certainly rather ramble about the fields with Doolan. Tea, tea-parties, and tea-conversation, are so contrary to my nature, that I feel uncomfortable even when I think of them." "But, Eckermann," said Frau von Goethe, "at a tea-party in the park, you are in the open air, and quite in your element." "On the contrary," said I, "when I am so near nature, that I scent all her fragrance, and yet cannot thoroughly enjoy it, it is to me as unendurable, as it would be to a duck to be brought near to the water, and yet prevented from plunging into it." "You might say, too," remarked Goethe, laughing, "that you would feel like a horse, who, on raising his head in the stable, sees other horses running wild upon an extensive plain before his eyes. He scents the delights and freedom of fresh nature, but cannot partake of them. Let Eckermann alone; he is as he is, and you cannot alter him. But tell me, my good friend, how do you employ yourself with that Doolan of yours, in the open fields, these long fine afternoons?" "We look out for some retired grove," said I, "and shoot with bows and arrows."

"Humph!" said Goethe, "that may be a pretty amusement." "It is a glorious method," said I, "to get rid of the ills of winter." "But how in the world," said Goethe, "did you get bows and arrows here in Weimar?" "As for the arrows," returned I, "I brought a model with me, on my return from my expedition into Brabant in 1814. Shooting with bows and arrows is there universal. There is no town, however small, that has not an archery society. They take their station in some public-house, like our skittle-ground, and generally assemble late in the afternoon, when I have often watched them with great pleasure. What well-grown men were there, and what picturesque attitudes when they bent the bow! How was their strength displayed, and what excellent marksmen they were! They generally shot from a distance of sixty or eighty steps, at a paper mark upon a moist clay wall; they shot quickly one after another, and left the arrows sticking in. And it was not seldom that out of fifteen arrows, five struck the centre, which was about the size of a dollar, while the rest were very near it. When all had shot, each of them went and drew his arrow out of the soft wall, and the game went on afresh. I was then so enraptured with this archery, that I thought it would be a great thing to introduce it into Germany, and I was so stupid as to deem it possible. I often bargained for a bow; but there were none to be had under twenty franks, and how could a poor Jäger like myself scrape together so much money? I therefore confined myself to an arrow, as the most important and most elaborate article; and bought one at a manufactory at Brussels for a frank, which I brought home, together with a drawing, as my only prize of victory."

"That is just like you," said Goethe. "But do not think that you can make anything natural and beautiful popular. A long time, and a confounded deal of work will be requisite at any rate. But I can easily imagine that this Brabant archery, is very beautiful. Our German amusements in the skittle-ground appear rough and ordinary, in comparison with it, and savour strongly of the Philistine."*

"The beauty of archery," returned I, "is that it displays the body symmetrically, and exercises the powers in equal proportion. There is the left arm, which holds the bow, stiff, strong, and firm; there is the right, which draws the string with the arrow, and must be no less powerful. At the same time both the feet and the thighs are planted strongly, to form a firm basis for the upper part of the body. The eye directed to the aim, and the muscles of the neck are all in full tension and activity; and then the feeling of joy, when the arrow darts whizzing from the bow, and pierces the desired mark! I know no bodily exercise that can be at all compared to it."

"It would be very well suited to our gymnastic institutions," answered Goethe. "And I should not wonder if, in twenty years, we were to have skilful archers by the thousands in Germany. Generally speaking, much is not to be done with a full grown generation, in physical or in mental pursuits, in mat-

* "Philister," the academical slang corresponding to the English "snob."
—*Trans.*

ters of taste or of character. Be clever enough to begin with the schools, and you may succeed."

"But our German teachers of gymnastics," returned I, "do not understand the use of bows and arrows."

"Well," said Goethe, "several gymnastic societies might combine, and a skilful archer might be brought from Flanders or Brabant. Or they might send some fine, well-grown young gymnasts to Brabant, that they might be trained to good archers, and learn how to carve bows and make arrows. These young men might enter the German gymnastic institutions as travelling teachers, who would sojourn for a time, now with one society, and now with another."

"I have," continued Goethe, "no objection to German gymnastic exercises. On the contrary, I was sorry that so much politics crept into them, so that the authorities were obliged to restrain them, or even to forbid and abolish them. By this means we have thrown away the good with the bad.* But I hope that the gymnastic institutions will be revived; for our German youths need them, especially the students, who, with a great deal of mental and intellectual exertion, are without any physical equilibrium, and therefore without any necessary power of action. But tell me something more about your bow and arrow. Then you have really brought an arrow with you from Brabant? I should like to see it."

"It has been los long ago," returned I. "But I remembered it so well, that I succeeded in replacing it, and

* Literally, "thrown away the child with the bath" (das kind mit dem Bade verschüttet)—a German proverbial expression.—*Trans.*

indeed by a dozen instead of one. It was not, however, so easy as I expected, and I made many fruitless attempts and many failures, but by that very means I learned a great deal. The first thing to be attended to was the shaft; I had to see that it was straight, and would not warp in a short time; then that it was light and strong enough not to split in striking against a hard substance. I made experiments with the wood of the poplar, then of the pine, and then of the birch; but they were all deficient in one quality or another, and were not such as they ought to be. I then made experiments with the wood of the lime-tree from a slender straight stem, and I found exactly what I wished for and had sought. Such a shaft was light, straight and strong, on account of its fine fibres. The next thing to be done was to furnish the lower end with a tip of horn; but it soon became evident that all horn was not fit for the purpose, and that it must be cut out of the kernel, in order that it might not split, on being shot against any hard substance. But the most difficult part was yet to do, namely, the feathering of the arrow. How I bungled, and what failures I made, before I succeeded in bringing it to any perfection!"

"The feathers are not let into the shaft, but glued on, are they not?" said Goethe.

"They are glued on," returned I; "but this must be so strongly and so neatly done, that they shall appear as if they were a part of the shaft, and had grown out of it. It is not a matter of indifference what glue one uses. I have found that isinglass, steeped in water for some hours, and then with some spirit added, dissolved to a jelly over a gentle charcoal fire, makes the best glue. Neither are all feathers serviceable alike. The feathers drawn from the wings of all great birds are indeed good, but I have found the red feathers from the wings of the peacock, the large feathers of the turkey-cock, and particularly the strong and splendid ones of the eagle and bustard, the best of any."

"I hear all this with great interest," said Goethe. "One who did not know you, would scarcely believe that your tendencies were so lively. But tell me now, how came you by a bow?"

"I made some myself," returned I. "But here also I bungled dreadfully at first. I consulted cabinet-makers and cartwrights. I tried all the kinds of wood in this place, and at last arrived at excellent results. In the choice of woods, I had to take care that the bow should bend easily, that it should spring back strongly and quickly, and that its elasticity should last. I made my first experiment with ash, with a branchless stem of about ten years' growth, and of the thickness of a moderate-sized arm. But in working, I came to the heart, which was not good for my purpose, as the wood about it was of too coarse a grain. I was advised to take a stem which would be strong enough to *schlachten* into four parts."

"*Schlachten*," asked Goethe, "what is that?"

"It is a technical term used by cartwrights," returned I, "and means the same as *spalten* (to split), so that a wedge is driven quite through the stem, from one end to the other. Now if the stem grows straight, I mean if the fibres rise in a straight line, the pieces obtained by splitting will be straight and fit for a bow. But if the stem be curved, the pieces will have a curved, crooked direction, and be unfit for a bow, since the wedge follows the fibres."

"But what would be the result of sawing such a stem into four parts? One could thus obtain straight pieces in every case."

"One might," returned I, "cut through a stem in which the fibres were twisted, and this would make the parts of no use for a bow."

"I understand," said Goethe; "a bow in which the fibres were cut through would break. But go on further; this subject interests me."

"I therefore made," said I, "my second bow with a piece of split ash. There were no fibres divided at the back, the bow was strong and firm; but I discovered this fault that it was hard, instead of easy to bend." "You have taken a piece of a seedling ash," said the cartwright, "which is always a very stiff wood; but take one of the tough sort, and you will find it better. On this occasion, I learned that there is a great difference in ash, and that in all kinds of wood, a great deal depends upon the place and soil on which they grow. I learned that the wood of the Ettersberg is of little value as timber, that, on the contrary, the wood in the neighbourhood of Nohra possesses remarkable strength, on account of which the carriers of Weimar have great confidence in the cart-fittings made at Nohra. In my subsequent experiments, I made the discovery that all wood which grows upon the northern side of a declivity is stronger, and of more even fibres than that which grows on the southern side. This is comprehensible. For a young tree which grows on the shady north side of a cliff, must seek light and sun from above; on which account, longing for the sun, it continually struggles upwards, and draws the fibres in a perpendicular direction. Besides, a shady situation is favourable to the formation of a finer fibre, which is very strikingly apparent in those trees which grow in such a situation, that their south side is constantly exposed to the sun, whilst their north side is always in the shade. If such a stem lay sawn in pieces before us, we should remark that the point of the heart was by no means in the centre, but very much on one side. And this eccentricity of the heart arises from the circumstance that the yearly rings of the south side become, through the constant influence of the sun, developed more strongly, and are therefore broader than those on the shady north side. Hence, cabinet-makers and cartwrights, when they require a strong fine wood, choose in preference the more finely developed north side of a stem, which they call the winter side, and in which they have great confidence."

"You can imagine," said Goethe, "that your observations are very interesting to me, who have, for half my life, occupied myself with the growth of plants and trees. But continue your relation. You probably made then a bow from a tough ash?"

"I did so," returned I, "and I took a well split piece from the winter side, in which I found a tolerably fine fibre. The bow was also easy to bend, and very elastic. But after it had been in use some months, a very considerable curve showed itself, and it was evident that the elasticity did not continue. I then made experiments with the stem of a young oak, which was moreover a perfectly good wood; but I soon found the same fault in this. I then tried the stem of a walnut tree, which was better; and at last the stem of a fine-leafed maple—a *Masholder*, as it is called, which was the best, and which left nothing to desire."

"I know the wood," returned Goethe; "it is often found in hedges. I can imagine that it is good. But I have seldom found a young stem without knots; and to make a bow, do you not require wood quite free from them?"

"A young stem," returned I, "is indeed not without knots; but when one rears it to a tree, the knots are taken off, or if it grow in a thicket, they disappear in time of their own accord. Now, if a stem is about two or three inches in diameter, when the knots are removed, and if it is allowed to increase yearly, and to form new wood on the outside, at the expiration of fifty or eighty years, the knotty inner part will be encased in about six inches of sound wood, free from knots. Such a stem will present a very smooth exterior; but one cannot tell what imperfections it has within. We shall, therefore, at all events, be safe with a plank sawn from such a stem, if we keep to the outside, and cut a few inches from that piece which is immediately under the bark, that is to say the *splint* and what follows, as this is always the youngest and toughest wood, and the most suitable for a bow."

"I thought," said Goethe, "that the wood for a

bow should not be sawn, but must be split, or as you call it *Geschlachet.*"

"Certainly, when it can be split," returned I. "Ash, oak, and walnut may be split, because they are woods of a coarse fibre. But not the *Masholder.* For it is a wood of such a fine interwoven fibre, that it will not divide according to the course of the fibres, but splits quite against the natural grain. The wood of the *Masholder* must therefore be divided with the saw, and that without endangering the strength of the bow."

"Humph! humph!" said Goethe. "You have acquired considerable knowledge through your bow mania. And it is that lively kind of knowledge which is attained only in a practical way. But that is the advantage of a passionate liking for any pursuit, that it carries one to the very bottom of the subject. Besides, seeking and blundering are good, for it is by seeking and blundering that we learn. And, indeed, one learns not merely the thing itself, but everything connected with it. What should I have known of plants and colours, if my theory had been handed down to me ready made, and I had learned it by heart? But from the very circumstance, that I was obliged to seek and find everything for myself, and occasionally to make mistakes, I can say that I know something of both these subjects, and more than stands on paper. But tell me something more about your bow. I have seen some Scotch ones, which were quite straight to the point, and others the points of which were curved. Which do you consider the best?"

"I consider," returned I, "that the elasticity is much greater, when the ends of the bow are curved backwards. At first I made them straight, because I did not understand how to bend the ends. But when I had learned how to do it, I bent the ends, and I find that the bow not only has a more beautiful appearance, but also that it acquires more power."

"The curves are made by heat, are they not?" said Goethe.

"Yes; by moist heat," returned I. "When the bow is so far finished that the elasticity is equally distributed, and that it is nowhere stronger or weaker than it ought to be, I place one end of it in boiling water, about six or eight inches deep, and let it boil for about an hour. I then screw this softened end, while it is hot, between two small blocks, the inner surface of which has the form of the curve that I wish to give to my bow. In this state of pressure, I let it remain at least a day and a night, that it may be perfectly dry, and I then proceed with the other end in the same manner. Points so treated are as indestructible as if they had grown in such a curve."

"What do you think?" said Goethe, with a mysterious laugh. "I believe I have something for you, which will not be unacceptable. Suppose we went down together, and I were to put a genuine Baschkir bow* in your hands."

"A Baschkir bow!" exclaimed I, full of animation, "and a genuine one?"

"Yes, mad fellow, a genuine one," said Goethe. "Come along." We went down into the garden.

* The Baschkiren are a Tatar race subject to Russia.—*Trans.*

Goethe opened the under chamber of a small outhouse, the tables and walls of which appeared crammed with rarities and curiosities of every description. I cast only a transient glance at these treasures; my eyes sought the bow. "Here it is," said Goethe, "as he took it from a corner, out of a heap of all sorts of strange implements. I see it is in the same condition as when it was presented to me in the year 1814, by a Baschkir chief. Now, what do you say?"

I was delighted to hold the precious weapon in my hands. It appeared quite uninjured, and even the string appeared perfectly serviceable. I tried it in my hands, and found that it was still tolerably elastic. "It is a good bow," said I. "The form especially pleases me, and for the future it shall serve me as a model."

"Of what wood is it made, do you think?"

"It is, as you see, so covered with birch bark," replied I, "that very little of the wood is visible, and only the curved ends remain exposed. Even these are so embrowned by time, that one cannot well distinguish what the wood is. At the first glance, it looks like young oak, and then again like nut tree. I think that it is nut tree, or a wood that resembles it. Maple or masholder it is not. It is a wood of coarser fibre; besides, I observe signs of its having been split (*geschlachtet*)."

"Suppose you were to try it now," said Goethe. "Here you have an arrow. But be cautious with the iron point, it may be poisoned."

We went again into the garden, and I bent the bow. "Now, where will you shoot?" said Goethe.

"Into the air at first, I think," said I. "Go on, then," said Goethe. I shot up towards the sunny clouds in the blue sky. The arrow supported itself well, then turned round, came whizzing downwards, and stuck into the ground. "Now let me try," said Goethe. I was pleased that he, too, was going to shoot. I gave him the bow, and fetched the arrrow.

Goethe placed the notch of the arrow upon the string, and held the bow right, but was some time before he could manage it properly. He now aimed upwards, and drew the string. There he stood like an Apollo, with imperishable youth of soul, although old in body. The arrow only attained a very moderate height, and then fell to the ground. I ran and fetched the arrow. "Once more," said Goethe. He now took aim along the gravel path of the garden. The arrow supported itself about thirty paces tolerably well, then fell, and whizzed along upon the ground. Goethe pleased me beyond measure, by thus shooting with the bow and arrow. I thought of the verses,—

> "Does old age leave me in the lurch?
> Am I again a child?"

I brought him back the arrow. He begged me to shoot once in a horizontal direction, and gave me for a mark, a spot in the window-shutter of his workroom. I shot. The arrow was not far from the mark; but penetrated so deep into the soft wood, that I could not get it out again. "Let it stick there," said Goethe, "it shall serve me for some days as a remembrance of our sport."

We walked up and down the garden, enjoying the

fine weather; we then sat upon a bench with our backs against the young leaves of a thick hedge. We spoke about the bow of Ulysses, about the heroes of Homer, then about the Greek tragic poets, and lastly about the widely diffused opinion, that Euripides caused the decline of the Greek drama. Goethe was, by no means, of this opinion.

"Altogether," said he, "I am opposed to the view, that any single man can cause the decline of an art. Much, which it is not so easy to set forth, must co-operate to this end. The decline of the tragic art of the Greeks could no more have been caused by Euripides, than could that of sculpture by any great sculptor who lived in the time of Phidias, but was inferior to him. For when an epoch is great, it proceeds in the path of improvement, and an inferior production is without results. But what a great epoch was the time of Euripides! It was the time, not of a retrograde, but of a progressive taste. Sculpture had not yet reached its highest point, and painting was still in its infancy.

"If the pieces of Euripides, compared to those of Sophocles, had great faults, it was not necessary that succeeding poets should imitate these faults, and be spoilt by them. But if they had great merits, so that some of them were even preferable to plays of Sophocles, why did not succeeding poets strive to imitate their merits; and why did they not thus become at least as great as Euripides himself?

"But if after the three celebrated tragic poets, there appeared no equally great fourth, fifth, or sixth,—this is, indeed, a matter difficult to explain; nevertheless, we may have our own conjectures, and approach the truth in some degree.

" Man is a simple being. And however rich, varied, and unfathomable he may be, the cycle of his situations is soon run through.

"If the same circumstances had occurred, as with us poor Germans, for whom Lessing has written two or three, I myself three or four, and Schiller five or six passable plays, there might easily have been room for a fourth, fifth, and sixth tragic poet.

"But with the Greeks and the abundance of their productions,—for each of the three great poets has written a hundred, or nearly a hundred pieces, and the tragical subjects of Homer, and the heroic traditions, were some of them treated three or four times,—with such abundance of existing works, I say, one can well imagine that by degrees, subjects were exhausted, and that any poet who followed the three great ones, would be puzzled how to proceed.

"And, indeed, for what purpose should he write? Was there not, after all, enough for a time? And were not the productions of Æschylus, Sophocles, and Euripides, of that kind and of that depth, that they might be heard again and again without being esteemed trite, or put on one side? Even the few noble fragments which have come down to us, are so comprehensive and of such deep significance, that we poor Europeans have already busied ourselves with them for centuries, and shall find nutriment and work in them for centuries still."

Thursday, May 12, 1825.

Goethe spoke with much enthusiasm of Menander.

"I know no one, after Sophocles," said he, "whom I love so well. He is thoroughly pure, noble, great, and cheerful, and his grace is unattainable. It is certainly to be lamented that we possess so little of him, but that little is invaluable, and highly instructive to gifted men.

"The great point is, that he from whom we would learn should be congenial to our nature. Now, Calderon, for instance, great as he is, and much as I admire him, has exerted no influence over me for good or for ill. But he would have been dangerous to Schiller—he would have led him astray; and hence it is fortunate that Calderon was not generally known in Germany till after Schiller's death. Calderon is infinitely great in the technical and theatrical; Schiller, on the contrary, far more sound, earnest, and great in his intention, and it would have been a pity if he had lost any of these virtues, without, after all, attaining the greatness of Calderon in other respects."

We spoke of Moliere. "Moliere," said Goethe, "is so great, that one is astonished anew every time one reads him. He is a man by himself—his pieces border on tragedy; they are apprehensive; and no one has the courage to imitate them. His 'Miser,' where the vice destroys all the natural piety between father and son, is especially great, and in a high sense tragic. But when, in a German paraphrase, the son is changed into a relation, the whole is weakened, and loses its significance. They feared to show the vice in its true nature, as he did; but what is tragic there, or indeed anywhere, except what is intolerable?

"I read some pieces of Moliere's every year, just

as, from time to time, I contemplate the engravings after the great Italian masters. For we little men are not able to retain the greatness of such things within ourselves; we must therefore return to them from time to time, and renew our impressions.

"People are always talking about originality; but what do they mean? As soon as we are born, the world begins to work upon us, and this goes on to the end. And, after all, what can we call our own except energy, strength, and will? If I could give an account of all that I owe to great predecessors and contemporaries, there would be but a small balance in my favour.

"However, the time of life in which we are subjected to a new and important personal influence is, by no means, a matter of indifference. That Lessing, Winckelmann, and Kant were older than I, and that the first two acted upon my youth, the latter on my advanced age,—this circumstance was for me very important. Again, that Schiller was so much younger than I, and engaged in his freshest strivings, just as I began to be weary of the world,—just, too, as the brothers von Humboldt and Schlegel were beginning their career under my eye,—was of the greatest importance. I derived from it unspeakable advantages."

After these remarks respecting the influence which important persons had had upon him, the conversation turned on the influence which he had exerted over others; and I mentioned Bürger, whose case appeared to me problematical, inasmuch as his purely natural tendency showed no trace of influence on the part of Goethe.

"Bürger," said Goethe, "had an affinity to me as a talent; but the tree of his moral culture had its root in a wholly different soil, and took a wholly different direction. Each man proceeds as he has begun, in the ascending line of his culture. A man who, in his thirtieth year, could write such a poem as 'Frau Schnips,' had obviously taken a path which deviated a little from mine. He had also, by his really great talents, won for himself a public which he perfectly satisfied; and he had no need of troubling himself about a contemporary who did not affect him at all.

"Everywhere, we learn only from those whom we love. There is a favourable disposition towards me in the young talents who are now growing up, but I very rarely found it among my contemporaries. Nay, I can scarcely name one man, of any weight, who was perfectly satisfied with me. Even with 'Werther,' people found so much fault, that if I had erased every passage that was censured, scarcely a line of the whole book would have been left. However, all the censure did me no harm, for these subjective judgments of individuals, important as they may be, are at least rectified by the masses. He who does not expect a million of readers should not write a line.

"For twenty years, the public has been disputing which is the greatest, Schiller or I; and it ought to be glad that it has got a couple of fellows about whom it *can* dispute."

(Sup.) Monday, June 5, 1825.*

Goethe related to me that Preller had been with him, and had taken leave, as he is going to spend some years in Italy.

"As a parting word," said Goethe, "I counselled him not to allow himself to be distracted, but to confine himself particularly to Poussin and Claude Lorraine, and, above all, to study the works of these two great men, that he might plainly see how they regarded nature, and used her for the expression of their artistical views and feelings.

"Preller is an important talent, and I have no fear for him. He appears to me, besides, of a very earnest character. I am almost certain that he will rather incline to Poussin than to Claude Lorraine; still I have particularly recommended him to study the latter—and not without reason; for it is with the cultivation of an artist as with the cultivation of every other talent. Our strong points, to a certain extent, develope themselves; but those germs of our nature which are not in daily exercise, and are therefore less powerful, need particular care, in order that they may become strong likewise.

"So may a young singer, as I have often said, possess certain natural tones which are very excellent, and which leave nothing to desire; while other tones in his voice may be found less strong, clear, and full. But even these he must by constant exercise seek to bring to equal perfection with the others.

* In the original this is dated 1826, but from its position in the volume it may be conjectured that this is a misprint.—*Trans.*

"I am certain that Preller will one day succeed admirably in the solemn, the grand, and perhaps also the wild. Whether he will be equally happy in the cheerful, the graceful, and the lovely, is another question; and therefore have I especially recommended to him Claude Lorraine, in order that, by study, he may acquire that which does not lie in the actual tendency of his nature.

"There is one thing more to which I called his attention. I have seen many of his studies from nature: they were excellent, and executed with great energy and life; but they were all isolated objects, of which little can afterwards be made when one comes to inventions of one's own. I have now advised him never for the future to delineate an isolated object, such as single trees, single heaps of stones, or single cottages, but always to add a back ground and some surrounding objects.

"And for the following reasons. In nature we never see anything isolated, but every thing in connection with something else which is before it, beside it, under it, and over it. A single object, I grant, may strike us as particularly picturesque: it is not, however, the object alone which produces this effect, but it is the connection in which we see it, with that which is beside, behind, and above it, all of which contributes to that effect.

"Thus during a walk I may meet with an oak, the picturesque effect of which surprises me. But if I represent it alone, it will perhaps no longer appear to me as it did, because that is wanting which contributed to and enhanced the picturesque effect in nature.

Thus, too, a wood may appear beautiful through the influence of one particular sky, one particular light, and one particular situation of the sun. But if I omit all these in my drawing, it will perhaps appear without any force, and as something indifferent to which the proper charm is wanting.

"Further; there is in nature nothing beautiful which is not produced (*motivirt*) as *true* in conformity with the laws of nature. In order that that truth of nature may also appear true in the picture, it must be accounted for by the introduction of the influential circumstances.

"I find by a brook well-formed stones, the parts of which, exposed to the air, are in a picturesque manner covered with green moss. Now it is not alone the moisture of the water which has caused this formation of moss; but perhaps a northerly aspect, or the shade of the trees and bushes, have co-operated in this formation at this part of the brook. If I omit these influential causes in my picture, it will be without truth, and without the proper convincing power.

"Thus the situation of a tree, the kind of soil beneath it, and other trees behind and beside it, have a great influence on its formation. An oak which stands exposed to the wind on the western summit of a rocky hill, will acquire quite a different form from that of one which grows below on the moist ground of a sheltered valley. Both may be beautiful in their kind, but they will have a very different character, and can, therefore, in an artistically conceived landscape, only be used for such a situation as they occupied in nature. And, therefore, the delineation of surrounding objects, by which any particular situation is expressed, is of high importance to the artist. On the other hand, it would be foolish to attempt to represent all those prosaic casualties which have had as little influence upon the form of the principal objects, as upon its picturesque effect for the moment.

"I have imparted the substance of all these little hints to Preller, and I am certain that they will take root and thrive in him—as a born genius."

Saturday, June 11, 1825.

To-day Goethe talked much at dinner about Major Parry's book on Lord Byron. He gave it unqualified praise, and remarked that Lord Byron in this account appeared a far more complete character, and far more clear as to himself and his views, than in anything which had been written about him.

"Major Parry," continued Goethe, "must be an elevated—nay, a noble man, so fully to have conceived, and so perfectly to have described his friend. One passage in his book has pleased me particularly;—it is worthy of an old Greek—of a Plutarch. 'The noble lord,' says Parry, 'was destitute of all those virtues which adorn the *bourgeois* class, and which he was prevented from attaining by his birth, education, and mode of life. Now all his unfavourable judges are from the middle class, and these censoriously pity him, because they miss in him that which they have reason to prize in themselves. The good folks do not reflect that for his own high station he possessed virtues of which they can form no conception.' How do you like that?" said Goethe: "we do not hear so good a thing every day."

"I am glad," said I, "to see publicly expressed a view by which all the puny censors and detractors of a man higher than themselves must be at once disabled and cast down."

We then spoke of subjects of universal history in relation to poetry, and as to how far the history of one nation may be more favorable to the poet than that of another.

"The poet," said Goethe, "should seize the Particular, and he should, if there be anything sound in it, thus represent the Universal. The English history is excellent for poetry, because it is something genuine, healthy, and therefore universal, which repeats itself over and over again. The French history, on the contrary, is not for poetry, as it represents an era that cannot come again. The literature of the French, so far as it is founded on that era, stands as something of merely particular interest, which must grow old with time.

"The present era of French literature," said Goethe afterwards, "cannot be judged fairly. The German influence causes a great fermentation there, and we probably shall not know for twenty years what the result will be."

We then talked of the æsthetic writers, who labour to express the nature of poetry and the poet in abstract definitions, without arriving at any clear result.

"What need of much definition?" said Goethe. "Lively feeling of situations, and power to express them, make the poet."

Wednesday, October 15, 1825.

I found Goethe in a very elevated mood this evening, and had the pleasure of hearing from him many significant remarks. We talked about the state of the newest literature, when Goethe expressed himself as follows :—

" Deficiency of character in individual investigators and writers is," he said, " the source of all the evils of our newest literature.

" In criticism, especially, this defect produces mischief to the world, for it either diffuses the false instead of the true, or by a pitiful truth deprives us of something great, that would be better.

" Till lately, the world believed in the heroism of a Lucretia,—of a Mucius Scævola,—and suffered itself, by this belief, to be warmed and inspired. But now comes your historical criticism, and says that those persons never lived, but are to be regarded as fables and fictions, divined by the great mind of the Romans. What are we to do with so pitiful a truth ? If the Romans were great enough to invent such stories, we should at least be great enough to believe them.

" Till lately, I was always pleased with a great fact in the thirteenth century, when the Emperor Frederic the Second was at variance with the Pope, and the north of Germany was open to all sorts of hostile attacks. Asiatic hordes had actually penetrated as far as Silesia, when the Duke of Liegnitz terrified them by one great defeat. They then turned to Moravia, but were here defeated by Count Sternberg. These valiant men had on this account been living in my heart as the great saviours of the German nation. But now comes historical criticism, and says that these heroes sacrificed themselves quite uselessly, as the Asiatic army was already recalled, and would have returned of its own accord. Thus is a great national fact crippled and destroyed, which seems to me most abominable."

After these remarks on historical critics, Goethe spoke of another class of seekers and literary men.

"I could never," said he, " have known so well how paltry men are, and how little they care for really high aims, if I had not tested them by my scientific researches. Thus I saw that most men only care for science so far as they get a living by it, and that they worship even error when it affords them a subsistence.

"In *belles lettres* it is no better. There, too, high aims and genuine love for the true and sound, and for their diffusion, are very rare phenomena. One man cherishes and tolerates another, because he is by him cherished and tolerated in return. True greatness is hateful to them; they would fain drive it from the world, so that only such as they might be of importance in it. Such are the masses; and the prominent individuals are not better.

" ———'s great talents and world-embracing learning might have done much for his country. But his want of character has deprived the world of such great results, and himself of the esteem of the country.

"We want a man like Lessing. For how was he great, except in character,—in firmness? There are many men as clever and as cultivated, but where is such character?

"Many are full of *esprit* and knowledge, but they are also full of vanity; and that they may shine as wits before the short-sighted multitude, they have no shame or delicacy—nothing is sacred to them.

"Madame de Genlis was therefore perfectly right when she declaimed against the freedoms and profanities of Voltaire. Clever as they all may be, the world has derived no profit from them; they afford a foundation for nothing. Nay, they have been of the greatest injury, since they have confused men, and robbed them of their needful support.

"After all, what do we know, and how far can we go with all our wit?

"Man is born not to solve the problems of the universe, but to find out where the problem begins, and then to restrain himself within the limits of the comprehensible.

"His faculties are not sufficient to measure the actions of the universe; and an attempt to explain the outer world by reason is, with his narrow point of view, but a vain endeavour. The reason of man and the reason of the Deity are two very different things.

"If we grant freedom to man, there is an end to the omniscience of God; for if the Divinity knows how I shall act, I must act so perforce. I give this merely as a sign how little we know, and to show that it is not good to meddle with divine mysteries.

"Moreover, we should only utter higher maxims so far as they can benefit the world. The rest we should keep within ourselves, and they will diffuse over our actions a lustre like the mild radiance of a hidden sun."

Sunday, December 25, 1825.

I went to Goethe this evening at six o'clock. I found him alone, and passed with him some delightful hours.

"My mind," said he, "has of late been burdened by many things. So much good has been flowing in to me on all sides, that the mere ceremony of returning thanks has prevented me from having any practical life. The privileges respecting the publication of my works have been gradually coming in from the different courts; and as the position was different in each case, each required a different answer. Then came the proposals of innumerable booksellers, which also had to be considered, acted upon, and answered. Then my Jubilee has brought me such thousand-fold attentions, that I have not yet got through with my letters of acknowledgment. I cannot be content with hollow generalities, but wish to say something appropriate to every one. Now I am gradually becoming free, and feel again disposed for conversation.

"I have of late made an observation, which I will impart to you.

"Everything we do has a result. But that which is right and prudent does not always lead to good, nor the contrary to what is bad; frequently the reverse takes place. Some time since, I made a mistake in one of these transactions with booksellers, and was sorry that I had done so. But now circumstances have so altered, that, if I had not made that very mistake, I should have made a greater one. Such instances occur frequently in life, and hence we see men of the world, who know this, going to work with great freedom and boldness."

I was struck by this remark, which was new to me.

I then turned the conversation to some of his works, and we came to the elegy " Alexis and Dora."

" In this poem," said Goethe, " people have blamed the strong, passionate conclusion, and would have liked the elegy to end gently and peacefully, without that outbreak of jealousy; but I could not see that they were right. Jealousy is so manifestly an ingredient of the affair, that the poem would be incomplete if it were not introduced at all. I myself knew a young man who, in the midst of his impassioned love for an easily-won maiden, cried out, ' But would she not act to another as she has acted to me?'"

I agreed entirely with Goethe, and then mentioned the peculiar situations in this elegy, where, with so few strokes and in so narrow a space, all is so well delineated, that we think we see the whole life and domestic environment of the persons engaged in the action. "What you have described," said I, "appears as true as if you had worked from actual experience."

" I am glad it seems so to you," said Goethe. " There are, however, few men who have imagination for the truth of reality; most prefer strange countries and circumstances, of which they know nothing, and by which their imagination may be cultivated, oddly enough.

" Then there are others who cling altogether to reality, and, as they wholly want the poetic spirit, are too severe in their requisitions. For instance, in this elegy, some would have had me give Alexis a servant to carry his bundle, never thinking that all that was poetic and idyllic in the situation would thus have been destroyed."

From "Alexis and Dora," the conversation then turned to "Wilhelm Meister," "There are odd critics in this world," said Goethe; "they blamed me for letting the hero of this novel live so much in bad company; but by this very circumstance, that I considered this so called bad company as a vase, into which I could put everything I had to say about good society, I gained a poetical body, and a varied one into the bargain. Had I, on the contrary, delineated good society by the so called good society, nobody would have read the book.

"In the seeming trivialities of 'Wilhelm Meister,' there is always something higher at bottom, and nothing is required but eyes and knowledge of the world, and power of comprehension to perceive the great in the small. For those who are without such qualities, let it suffice to receive the picture of life as real life."

Goethe then showed me a very interesting English work, which illustrated all Shakspeare in copper plates. Each page embraced, in six small designs, one piece with some verses written beneath, so that the leading idea, and the most important situations of each work were brought before the eyes. All these immortal tragedies and comedies thus passed before the mind like processions of masks.

"It is even terrifying," said Goethe, "to look

through these little pictures. Thus are we first made to feel the infinite wealth and grandeur of Shakspeare. There is no *motive* in human life which he has not exhibited and expressed! And all with what ease and freedom!

"But we cannot talk about Shakspeare; everything is inadequate. I have touched upon the subject in my 'Wilhelm Meister,' but that is not saying much. He is not a theatrical poet; he never thought of the stage; it was far too narrow for his great mind; nay, the whole visible world was too narrow."

"He is even too rich and too powerful. A productive *nature** ought not to read more than one of his dramas in a year, if it would not be wrecked entirely. I did well to get rid of him by writing 'Goetz,' and 'Egmont,'† and Byron did well by not having too much respect and admiration for him, but going his own way. How many excellent Germans have been ruined by him and Calderon!

"Shakspeare gives us golden apples in silver dishes. We get, indeed, the silver dishes by studying his works; but, unfortunately, we have only potatoes to put into them."

I laughed, and was delighted with this admirable simile.

Goethe then read me a letter from Zelter, describing a representation of Macbeth at Berlin, where the music

---

* Vide p. 185, where a remark is made on the word *nature*, as applied to a person.—*Trans.*

† These plays were intended to be in the Shakspearian style, and Goethe means that by writing them he freed himself from Shakspeare, just as by writing 'Werther' he freed himself from thoughts of suicide.—*Trans.*

could not keep pace with the grand spirit and character of the piece, as Zelter set forth by various intimations. By Goethe's reading, the letter gained its full effect, and he often paused to admire with me, the point of some single passage,

"'Macbeth,' said Goethe, "is Shakspeare's best acting play, the one in which he shows most understanding with respect to the stage. But would you see his mind unfettered, read 'Troilus and Cressida,' where he treats the materials of the 'Iliad' in his own fashion."

The conversation turned upon Byron,—the disadvantage to which he appears, when placed beside the innocent cheerfulness of Shakspeare, and the frequent and generally not unjust blame which he drew upon himself by his manifold works of negation.

"If Lord Byron," said Goethe, "had had an opportunity of working off all the opposition in his character, by a number of strong parliamentary speeches, he would have been much more pure as a poet. But, as he scarcely ever spoke in parliament, he kept within himself all his feelings against his nation, and to free himself from them, he had no other means than to express them in poetical form. I could, therefore, call a great part of Byron's works of negation 'suppressed parliamentary speeches,' and think this would be no bad name for them."

We then mentioned one of our most modern German poets, who had lately gained a great name, and whose negative tendency was likewise disapproved. "We cannot deny," said Goethe, "that he has many brilliant qualities, but he is wanting in—*love*. He loves his readers and his fellow-poets as little as he loves himself, and thus we may apply to him the maxim of the apostle—'Though I speak with the tongues of men and angels, and have not love (charity), I am become as sounding brass and a tinkling cymbal.' I have lately read the poems of ———, and cannot deny his great talent. But, as I said, he is deficient in *love*, and thus he will never produce the effect which he ought. He will be feared, and will be the idol of those who would like to be as negative as himself, but have not his talent."

CONVERSATIONS OF GOETHE.

1826.

1826.

Sunday Evening, January 29, 1826.

THE most celebrated German improvisatore, Dr. Wolff of Hamburg, has been here several days, and has already given public proof of his rare talent. On Friday evening, he gave a brilliant display to a numerous audience, and in the presence of the court of Weimar. On the same evening, he received from Goethe an invitation to come to him the next day at noon.

I talked with him yesterday evening, after he had improvised before Goethe. He was much delighted, and declared that this hour would make an epoch in his life; for Goethe, by a few words, had opened to him a wholly new path, and when he had found fault with him, had hit the right nail on the head.

This evening, when I was at Goethe's, the conversation turned immediately on Wolff. " Dr. Wolff is very happy," said I, " that your excellency has given him good counsel."

" I was perfectly frank with him," said Goethe, " and if my words have made an impression on him and incited him, that is a very good sign. He is a decided talent without doubt, but he has the general sickness of the present day—subjectivity—and of that I would fain heal him. I gave him a task to try him:—'Describe to me,' said I, 'your return to Hamburg.' He was ready at once, and began immediately to speak in melodious verses. I could not but admire him, yet I could not praise him. It was not a return to Hamburg that he described, but merely the emotions on the return of a son to his parents, relations, and friends; and his poem would have served just as well for a return to Merseburg or Jena, as for a return to Hamburg. Yet what a remarkable, peculiar city is Hamburg! and what a rich field was offered him for the most minute description, if he had known or ventured to take hold of the subject properly!"

I remarked that this subjective tendency was the fault of the public, which decidedly applauds all sentimentality.

"Perhaps so," said Goethe; "but the public is still more pleased if you give it something better. I am certain that, if with Wolff's talent at improvisation, one could faithfully describe the life of great cities, such as Rome, Naples, Vienna, Hamburg, or London, and that in such a lively manner, that one's hearers would believe they saw with their own eyes, everybody would be enchanted. If he breaks through to the objective, he is saved, the stuff is in him; for he is not without imagination. Only he must make up his mind at once, and strive to grasp it."

"I fear," said I, "that this will be harder than we imagine, since it demands entire regeneration of his mode of thought. Even if he succeeds, he will, at all events, come to a momentary stand-still with his production, and long practice will be required to make the objective become a second nature."

"The step I grant is very great," said Goethe; "but he must take courage, and make his resolution at once. It is in such matters, like the dread of water in bathing,—we must jump in at once, and the element is ours.

"If a person learns to sing," continued Goethe, "all the notes which are within his natural compass are easy to him, while those which lie beyond the compass are at first extremely difficult. But to be a vocalist, he must conquer them, for he must have them all at command. Just so with the poet;—he deserves not the name while he only speaks out his few subjective feelings; but as soon as he can appropriate to himself, and express the world, he is a poet. Then he is inexhaustible, and can be always new, while a subjective nature has soon talked out his little internal material, and is at last ruined by mannerism. People always talk of the study of the ancients; but what does that mean, except that it says, turn your attention to the real world, and try to express it, for that is what the ancients did when they were alive."

Goethe arose and walked to and fro, while I remained seated at the table, as he likes to see me. He stood a moment at the stove, and then, like one who has reflected, came to me, and with his finger on his lips, said,

"I will now tell you something which you will often find confirmed in your experience. All eras in a state of decline and dissolution are subjective; on the other hand, all progressive eras have an objective tendency. Our present time is retrograde, for it is subjective: we see this not merely in poetry, but also in painting, and much besides. Every healthy effort, on the contrary, is directed from the inward to the outward world, as you will see in all great eras, which have been really in a state of progression, and all of an objective nature."

These remarks led to a most interesting conversation, in which especial mention was made of the great period of the fifteenth and sixteenth centuries.

The conversation now turned upon the theatre, and the weak, sentimental, gloomy character of modern productions.

"Moliére is my strength and consolation at present," said I; "I have translated his 'Avare,' and am now busy with his 'Médicin malgré lui.' Moliére is indeed a great, a genuine (*reiner*) man."

"Yes," said Goethe, "a genuine man; that is the proper term. There is nothing distorted about him. He ruled the manners of his day, while, on the contrary, our Iffland and Kotzebue allowed themselves to be ruled by theirs, and were limited and confined in them. Moliére chastised men by drawing them just as they were."

"I would give something," said I, "to see his plays acted in all their purity! Yet such things are much too strong and natural for the public, so far as I am acquainted with it. Is not this over-refinement to be attributed to the so-called ideal literature of certain authors?"

"No," said Goethe, "it has its source in society

itself. What business have our young girls at the theatre? They do not belong to it—they belong to the convent; and the theatre is only for men and women, who know something of human affairs. When Moliére wrote, girls were in the convent, and he was not forced to think about them. But now we cannot get rid of these young girls, and pieces which are weak, and therefore *proper*, will continue to be produced. Be wise and stay away, as I do. I was really interested in the theatre only so long as I could have a practical influence upon it. It was my delight to bring the establishment to a high degree of perfection; and when there was a performance, my interest was not so much in the pieces as in observing whether the actors played as they ought. The faults I wished to point out I sent in writing to the *Regisseur*, and was sure they would be avoided on the next representation. Now I can no longer have any practical influence in the theatre, I feel no calling to enter it; I should be forced to endure defects without being able to amend them; and that would not suit me. And with the reading of plays, it is no better. The young German poets are eternally sending me tragedies; but what am I to do with them? I have never read German plays except with the view of seeing whether I could act them; in every other respect they were indifferent to me. What am I to do now, in my present situation, with the pieces of these young people? I can gain nothing for myself by reading how things ought *not* to be done; and I cannot assist the young poets in a matter which is already finished. If, instead of their printed plays, they would send me the plan of a play, I could at least say, 'Do it,' or 'Leave it alone,' or 'Do it this way,' or 'Do it that;' and in this there might be some use.

"The whole mischief proceeds from this, that poetical culture is so widely diffused in Germany that nobody now ever makes a bad verse. The young poets who send me their works are not inferior to their predecessors, and, since they see these praised so highly, they cannot understand why they are not praised also. And yet we cannot encourage them, when talents of the sort exist by hundreds; and we ought not to favour superfluities while so much that is useful remains to be done. Were there a single one who towered above all the rest, it would be well, for the world can only be served by the extraordinary."

Thursday, February 16, 1826.

I went, at seven this evening, to Goethe, whom I found alone in his room. I sat down by him at the table, and told him that yesterday I had seen, at the inn, the Duke of Wellington, who was passing through on his way to St. Petersburg. "Indeed!" said Goethe, with animation; "what was he like? —tell me all about him. Does he look like his portrait?"

"Yes," said I; "but better, with more of marked character. If you ever look at his face, all the portraits are nought. One need only see him once never to forget him, such an impression does he make. His eyes are brown, and of the serenest brilliancy; one feels the effect of his glance; his mouth speaks, even when it is closed; he looks a man who has had many thoughts, and has lived through the greatest deeds, who now can handle the world serenely and calmly, and whom nothing more can disturb. He seemed to me as hard and as tempered as a Damascus blade. By his appearance, he is far advanced in the fifties; is upright, slim, and not very tall or stout. I saw him getting into his carriage to depart. There was something uncommonly cordial in his salutation as he passed through the crowd, and, with a very slight bow, touched his hat with his finger." Goethe listened to my description with visible interest. "You have seen one hero more," said he, "and that is saying something."

We then talked of Napoleon, and I lamented that I had never seen him.

"Truly," said Goethe, "that also was worth the trouble. What a compendium of the world!" "Did he look like something?" asked I. "He *was* something," replied Goethe; "and he looked what he was —that was all."

I had brought with me for Goethe a very remarkable poem, of which I had spoken to him some evenings before,—a poem of his own, written so long since that he had quite forgotten it. It was printed in the beginning of the year 1776, in " Die Sichtbaren" (the Visible), a periodical published at the time in Frankfort, and had been brought to Weimar by an old servant of Goethe's, through whom it had fallen into my hands. Undoubtedly it is the earliest known poem of Goethe's. The subject was the " Descent of Christ into Hell;" and it was remarkable to observe the readiness of the young author with his religious images. The purpose of the poem might have suited Klopstock; but the execution was quite of a different character; it was stronger, freer, and more easy, and had greater energy and better arrangement. The extraordinary ardour reminded one of a period of youth, full of impetuosity and power. Through a want of subject matter, it constantly reverted to the same point, and was of undue length.

I placed before Goethe the yellow, worn-out paper, and as soon as he saw it he remembered his poem. "It is possible," said he, "that Fräulein von Klettenberg induced me to write it: the heading shows that it was written by desire, and I know not any other friend who could have desired such a subject. I was then in want of materials, and was rejoiced when I got any thing that I could sing. Lately, a poem of that period fell into my hands, which I wrote in the English language, and in which I complained of the dearth of poetic subjects. We Germans are really ill off in that respect; our earliest history lies too much in obscurity, and the later is without general native interest, through the want of one ruling dynasty. Klopstock tried Arminius, but the subject lies too far off; nobody feels any connection with it; no one knows what to make of it, and accordingly it has never been popular, or produced any result. I made a happy hit with my "Goetz von Berlichingen;" that was, at any rate, bone of my bone, and flesh of my flesh, and something could be done with it.

"For 'Werther' and 'Faust' I was, on the contrary, obliged to draw upon my own bosom, for that which was handed down to me did not go far. I made devils and witches but once; I was glad when I had consumed my northern inheritance, and turned to the tables of the Greeks. Had I earlier known how many excellent things have been in existence for hundreds and thousands of years, I should not have written a line, but should have done something else."

Easter-day, March 26, 1826.

To-day, at dinner, Goethe was in one of his pleasantest moods. He had received something he highly valued, Lord Byron's manuscript of the dedication to his "Sardanapalus." He showed it to us after dinner, at the same time teazing his daughter to give him back Byron's letter from Genoa. "You see, my dear child," said he, "I have now everything collected which relates to my connection with Byron; even this valuable paper comes to me to-day in a remarkable manner, and now nothing is wanting but that letter."

However, the amiable admirer of Byron would not restore the letter. "You gave it to me once, dear father," said she, "and I shall not give it back; and if you wish, as is fit, that like should be with like, you had better give me the precious paper of to-day, and I will keep them all together." This was still more repugnant to Goethe, and the playful contest lasted for some time, when it merged into general lively conversation.

After we had risen from table, and the ladies had gone up-stairs, I remained with Goethe alone. He brought from his work-room a red portfolio, which he took to the window, and showed me its contents.

"Look," said he, "here I have everything together which relates to my connection with Lord Byron. Here is his letter from Leghorn; this is a copy of his dedication; this is my poem; and here is what I wrote for 'Medwin's Conversations;' now, I only want the letter from Genoa, and she will not give it me."

Goethe then told me of a friendly request, which had this day been made to him from England, with reference to Lord Byron, and which had excited him in a very pleasant manner. His mind was just now quite full of Byron, and he said a thousand interesting things about him, his works, and his talents.

"The English," said he, among other things, "may think of Byron as they please; but this is certain, that they can show no poet who is to be compared to him. He is different from all the others, and, for the most part, greater."

Monday, May 15, 1826.

I talked with Goethe to-day about St. Schütze, of whom he spoke very kindly. "When I was ill a few weeks since," said he, "I read his 'Heitere Stunden' (Cheerful Hours) with great pleasure. If Schütze had lived in England, he would have made an epoch; for, with his gift of observing and depicting, nothing was wanting but the sight of life on a large scale."

Thursday, June 1, 1826.

Goethe spoke of the "Globe." * "The contributors," said he, "are men of the world, cheerful, clear in their views, bold to the last degree. In their censure they are polished and *galant;* whereas our

* The celebrated French paper.—*Trans.*

German literati always think they must hate those who do not think like themselves. I consider the 'Globe' one of our most interesting periodicals, and could not do without it."

Wednesday, July 26, 1826.

This evening, I had the pleasure of hearing Goethe say a great deal about the theatre.

I told him that one of my friends intended to arrange Lord Byron's "Two Foscari" for the stage. Goethe doubted his success.

"It is indeed a temptation," he said. "When a piece makes a deep impression on us in reading, we think it will do the same upon the stage, and that we could obtain such a result with little trouble. But this is by no means the case. A piece that is not originally, by the intent and skill of the poet, written for the boards, will not succeed; but whatever is done to it, will always remain something unmanageable. What trouble have I taken with my 'Goetz von Berlichingen!' yet it will not go right as an acting play, but is too long; and I have been forced to divide it into two parts, of which the last is indeed theatrically effective, while the first is to be looked upon as a mere introduction. If the first part were given only once as an introduction, and then the second repeatedly, it might succeed. It is the same with 'Wallenstein:' 'The Piccolomini' does not bear repetition, but 'Wallenstein's Death' is always seen with delight."

I asked how a piece must be constructed so as to be fit for the theatre.

"It must be symbolical," replied Goethe; "that is to say, each incident must be significant in itself, and lead to another still more important. The 'Tartuffe' of Moliére is, in this respect, a great example. Only think what an introduction is the first scene! From the very beginning everything is highly significant, and leads us to expect something still more important which is to come. The beginning of Lessing's 'Minna von Barnhelm' is also admirable; but that of the 'Tartuffe' comes only once into the world: it is the greatest and best thing that exists of the kind."

We then came to the pieces of Calderon.

"In Calderon," said Goethe, "you find the same perfect adaptation to the theatre. His pieces are throughout fit for the boards; there is not a touch in them which is not directed towards the required effect. Calderon is a genius who had also the finest understanding."

"It is singular," said I, "that the dramas of Shakspeare are not theatrical pieces, properly so called, since he wrote them all for his theatre."

"Shakspeare," replied Goethe, "wrote those pieces direct from his own nature. Then, too, his age, and the existing arrangements of the stage, made no demands upon him; people were forced to put up with whatever he gave them. But if Shakspeare had written for the court of Madrid, or for the theatre of Louis XIV., he would probably have adapted himself to a severer theatrical form. This, however, is by no means to be regretted, for what Shakspeare has lost as a theatrical poet he has gained as a poet in general.

Shakspeare is a great psychologist, and we learn from his pieces the secrets of human nature."*

We then talked of the difficulties in managing a theatre.

"The knotty point," said Goethe, "is so to deal with contingencies that we are not tempted to deviate from our higher maxims. Among the higher maxims is this: to keep a good *repertoire* of excellent tragedies, operas, and comedies, to which we can adhere, and which may be regarded as permanent. Among contingencies, I reckon a new piece about which the public is anxious, a 'starring' character (*Gastrolle*), and so forth. We must not be led astray by things of this kind, but always return to our *repertoire*. Our time is so rich in really good pieces, that nothing is easier to a *connoisseur* than to form a good *repertoire*; but nothing is more difficult than to maintain one.

"When Schiller and I superintended the theatre, we had the great advantage of playing through the summer at Lauchstedt. There we had a select audience, who would have nothing but what was excellent; so we always returned to Weimar thoroughly practised in the best plays, and could repeat all our summer performances in the winter. Besides, the Weimar public had confidence in our management, and, even in the case of things they could not appreciate, they were convinced that we acted in accordance with some higher view.

"When the nineties began," continued Goethe, "the proper period of my interest in the theatre was

---

* Wie den Menschen zu Muthe ist. The above is only an approximation. —*Trans.*

already past, and I wrote nothing for the stage, but wished to devote myself to epic poetry. Schiller revived my extinct interest, and, for the sake of his works, I again took part in the theatre. At the time of my 'Clavigo,' I could easily have written a dozen theatrical pieces. I had no want of subjects, and production was easy to me. I might have written a piece every week, and I am sorry I did not."

Wednesday, November 8, 1826.

To-day, Goethe spoke again of Lord Byron with admiration. "I have," said he, "read once more his 'Deformed Transformed,' and must say, that to me his talent appears greater than ever. His devil was suggested by my Mephistophiles; but it is no imitation —it is thoroughly new and original, close, genuine, and spirited. There are no weak passages,—not a place where you could put the head of a pin, where you do not find invention and thought. Were it not for his hypochondriacal negative turn, he would be as great as Shakspeare and the ancients." I expressed surprise.

"Yes," said Goethe, "you may believe me. I have studied him anew, and am confirmed in this opinion."

In a conversation some time ago, Goethe had remarked that Byron had too much *empeiria*.* I did not well understand what he meant; but I forbore to ask, and thought of the matter in silence. However, I got nothing by reflection, and found that I must wait

---

* The import of this Greek word for "experience," and its cognate word "empiric," has nothing in common with the notion of "quackery." The general meaning is, that Byron is too *worldly*.—*Trans.*

till my improved culture, or some happy circumstance, should unlock the secret for me. Such a one occurred when an excellent representation of "Macbeth" at the theatre produced a strong effect upon me, and on the day afterwards I took up Byron's works to read his "Beppo." Now, I felt I could not relish this poem after "Macbeth;" and the more I read, the more I became enlightened as to Goethe's meaning.

In "Macbeth," a spirit had impressed me, whose grandeur, power, and sublimity could have proceeded from none but Shakspeare. There was the innate quality of a high and deep nature, which raises the individual who possesses it above all mankind, and thus makes him a great poet. Whatever has been given to this piece by knowledge of the world or experience, was subordinate to the poetic spirit, and served only to make this speak out and predominate. The great poet ruled us and lifted us up to his own point of view.

While reading "Beppo," on the contrary, I felt the predominance of a nefarious empirical world, with which the mind which introduced it to us had, in a certain measure, associated itself. I no more found the great and pure thoughts of a highly-gifted poet, but, by frequent intercourse with the world, the poet's mode of thought seemed to have acquired the same stamp. He seemed to be on the same level with all intellectual men of the world of the higher class, being only distinguished from them by his great talent for representation, so that he might be regarded as their mouthpiece.

So I felt, in reading "Beppo," that Lord Byron had too much *empeiria*, not because he brought too much real life before us, but because his higher poetic nature seemed to be silent, or even expelled by an empiric mode of thought.

Wednesday, November 29, 1826.

I had now also read Lord Byron's "Deformed Transformed," and talked with Goethe about it after dinner.

"Am I not right?" said he; "the first scenes are great—poetically great. The remainder, when the subject wanders to the siege of Rome, I will not call poetical, but it must be averred that it is very pointed* (*geistreich*)."

"To the highest degree," said I; "but there is no art in being pointed when one respects nothing."

Goethe laughed. "You are not quite wrong," said he. "We must, indeed, confess that the poet says more than ought to be said. He tells us the truth, but it is disagreeable, and we should like him better if he held his peace. There are things in the world which the poet should rather conceal than disclose; but this openness lies in Byron's character, and you would annihilate him if you made him other than he is."

"Yes," said I, "he is in the highest degree pointed. How excellent, for instance, is this passage,—

'The devil speaks truth much oftener than he's deemed;
He hath an ignorant audience?'"

"That is as good and as free as one of my Mephistophiles' sayings."

"Since we are talking of Mephistophiles," continued Goethe, "I will show you something which Coudray has brought me from Paris. What do you think of it?"

---

* "Pointed" is only an approximation,—the word here means "full of *esprit*."—*Trans.*

He laid before me a lithograph, representing the scene where Faust and Mephistophiles, on their way to free Margaret from prison, are rushing by the gallows at night on two horses. Faust rides a black horse, which gallops with all its might, and seems, as well as his rider, afraid of the spectres under the gallows. They ride so fast that Faust can scarcely keep his seat; the current of air has blown off his cap, which, fastened by straps about his neck, flies far behind him. He has turned his fearful inquiring face to Mephistophilès, and is listening to his words. Mephistophiles, on the contrary, sits quiet and undisturbed, like a being of a higher order. He rides no living horse, for he loves not what is living; indeed, he does not need it, for his will moves him with the swiftness he requires. He has a horse merely because he must look as if he were riding, and it has been quite enough for him to find a beast that is a mere bag of bones, from the first field he has come to. It is of a bright colour, and seems to be phosphorescent amid the darkness of night. It is neither bridled nor saddled, but goes without such appendages. The supernatural rider sits easily and negligently, with his face turned towards Faust, in conversation. The opposing element of air does not exist for him; neither he nor his horse feel anything of it. Not a hair of either is stirred.

We expressed much pleasure at this ingenious composition. "I must aver," said Goethe, "that I myself did not think it out so perfectly. Here is another. What say you to this?"

I saw a representation of the wild drinking scene in

Auerbach's cellar, at the all-important moment when the wine sparkles up into flames, and the brutality of the drinkers is shown in the most varied ways. All is passion and movement; Mephistophiles alone maintains his usual composure. The wild cursing and screaming, and the drawn knife of the man who stands next him, are to him nothing. He has seated himself on a corner of the table, dangling his legs. His upraised finger is enough to subdue flame and passion.

The more one looked at this excellent design, the greater seemed the intelligence of the artist, who made no figure like another, but in each one expressed some different part of the action.

"M. Delacroix," said Goethe, "is a man of great talent, who found in 'Faust' his proper aliment. The French censure his wildness, but it suits him well here. He will, I hope, go through all 'Faust,' and I anticipate a special pleasure from the witches' kitchen and the scenes on the Brocken. We can see that he has a good knowledge of life, for which a city like Paris has given him the best opportunity."

I observed that these designs greatly conduce to the comprehension of a poem.

"Undoubtedly," said Goethe; "for the more perfect imagination of such an artist constrains us to think the situations as beautiful as he conceived them himself. And if I must confess that M. Delacroix has, in some scenes, surpassed my own notions, how much more will the reader find all in full life, and surpassing his imagination."

Monday, December 11, 1826.

I found Goethe in a very happy mood. "Alexander von Humboldt has been some hours with me this morning," said he, coming to meet me with great vivacity; "what a man he is! Long as I have known him, he ever surprises me anew. One may say he has not his equal in knowledge and living wisdom. Then he has a many-sidedness such as I have found nowhere else. On whatever point you approach him, he is at home, and lavishes upon us his intellectual treasures. He is like a fountain with many pipes, under which you need only hold a vessel, and from which refreshing and inexhaustible streams are ever flowing. He will stay here some days; and I already feel that it will be with me as if I had lived for years."

Wednesday, December 13, 1826.

At table, the ladies praised a portrait by a young painter. "What is most surprising," they added, "he has learned everything by himself." This could be seen particularly in the hands, which were not correctly and artistically drawn. "We see," said Goethe, "that the young man has talent; however, you should not praise, but rather blame him, for learning everything by himself. A man of talent is not born to be left to himself, but to devote himself to art and good masters, who will make something out of him. I have lately read a letter from Mozart, where, in reply to a Baron who had sent him his composition, he writes somewhat in this fashion,—

"'You dillettanti must be blamed for two faults, since two you generally have; either you have no thoughts of your own, and take those of others, or, if you have thoughts of your own, you do not know what to do with them.'

"Is not this capital? and does not this fine remark, which Mozart makes about music, apply to all other arts?"

Goethe continued: "Leonardo da Vinci says, 'If your son has not sense enough to bring out what he draws by a bold shadowing, so that we can grasp it with our hands, he has no talent.'

"Further, Leonardo da Vinci says, 'If your son is a perfect master of perspective and anatomy, send him to a good master.'

"And now," said Goethe, "our young artists scarcely understand either when they leave their masters. So much have times altered."

"Our young painters," continued Goethe, "lack heart and intellect. Their inventions express nothing and effect nothing: they paint swords which do not cut, and arrows which do not hit; and I often think, in spite of myself, that all intellect has vanished from the world."

"And yet," I replied, "we should naturally think that the great military events of latter years would have stirred the intellect."

"They have stirred the will more than the intellect," said Goethe, "and the poetical intellect more than the artistical, while all *naïveté* and sensuousness are lost. Without these two great requisites how can a painter produce anything in which we can take any pleasure."

I said that I had lately, in his "Italian Travels," read of a picture by Correggio, which represents a "weaning," and in which the Infant Christ in Mary's lap stands in doubt between his mother's breast and a pear held before him, and does not know which of the two to choose.

"Aye," said Goethe, "there is a little picture for you! There are mind, *naïveté*, sensuousness, all together. The sacred subject is endowed with an universally human interest, and stands as a symbol for a period of life we must all pass through. Such a picture is immortal, because it grasps backwards at the earliest times of humanity, and forwards at the latest. On the contrary, if Christ were painted suffering the little children to come unto him, it would be a picture that expressed nothing—at any rate, nothing of importance.

"For above fifty years," continued Goethe, "I have watched German painting—nay, not merely watched it, but endeavoured to exert some influence on it, and now I can say so much, that as the matter now stands, little is to be expected. Some great talent must come, which will at once appropriate to itself all that is good in the period, and thus surpass every one. The means are at hand, and the way is pointed out. We have now the works of Phidias before our eyes, whereas in our youth nothing of the sort was to be thought of. As I have just said, nothing is wanting but a great talent, and this I hope will come; perhaps it is already in its cradle, and you will live to see its brilliancy."

Wednesday, December 20, 1826.

I told Goethe after dinner, that I had made a discovery which afforded me much pleasure. I had observed in a burning taper that the lower transparent part of the flame exhibits a phenomenon analogous to that of the blue sky, since in both we see darkness through a lighted but dense medium.

I asked Goethe whether he knew this phenomenon of the taper, and had mentioned it in his "Theory of Colours."

"Certainly," said he. He then took down a volume of "the Theory of Colours," and read me the paragraphs in which I found described all that I had seen. "I am glad," said he, "that you have been struck with this phenomenon, without learning it from my 'Theory,' for you have now comprehended it, and may say that you possess it. Moreover, you have thus gained a point of view from which you can proceed to the other phenomena. I will show you a new one now."

It was about four o'clock: the sky was clouded over, and twilight was beginning. Goethe lighted a candle, and went with it to a table near the window. He then set it on a white sheet of paper, and placed a small stick so that the light of the candle threw a shadow from the stick towards the daylight. "Now," said Goethe, "what do you say of this shadow?" "The shadow is blue," replied I. "There you get your blue again," said Goethe. "But what do you see on the other side of the stick towards the taper?" "Another shadow." "But of what colour." "The shadow is a reddish yellow," I replied; "but whence proceeds this double phenomenon?" "There is a point for you," said Goethe: "see if you can work it out. A solution is to be found, but it is difficult. Do not look at my 'Theory of Colours' until you have given up all hopes of finding it out yourself." I made this promise with great delight.

"The phenomenon of the lower part of the taper," said Goethe, "where a transparent flame stands before darkness and produces a blue colour, I will now show you on a larger scale." He took a spoon and poured into it some spirit, which he set on fire. Thus a transparent flame was again produced, through which the darkness appeared blue. If I held the burning spirit against the darkness, the blue increased in intensity; but if I held it against the light, the blue became fainter or vanished altogether.

I was delighted with this phenomenon. "Yes," said Goethe, "this is the grandeur of nature, that she is so simple, and that she always repeats her greatest phenomena on a small scale. The law by which the sky is blue, may likewise be observed in the lower part of a burning taper, in burning spirits, and also in the bright smoke which rises from a village with dark mountains in the back ground."

"But how do the disciples of Newton explain this extremely simple phenomenon?" "That you must not know," answered Goethe. "Their explanation is too stupid, and a good head-piece is incredibly damaged when it meddles with stupidities. Do not trouble yourself about the Newtonians, but be satisfied with the pure doctrine, and you will find it quite enough for you."

"An occupation with that which is wrong," said I, "is perhaps in this case as unpleasant and as injurious as taking up a bad tragedy to illustrate it in all its parts, and to expose it in its nudity."

" The case is precisely the same," said Goethe, " and we should not meddle with anything of the sort without actual necessity. I receive mathematics as the most sublime and useful science, so long as they are applied in their proper place; but I cannot commend the misuse of them in matters which do not belong to their sphere, and in which, noble science as they are, they seem to be mere nonsense. As if, forsooth! things only exist when they can be mathematically demonstrated. It would be foolish for a man not to believe in his mistress's love because she could not prove it to him mathematically. She can mathematically prove her dowry, but not her love. The mathematicians did not find out the metamorphosis of plants. I have achieved this discovery without mathematics, and the mathematicians were forced to put up with it. To understand the phenomena of colour nothing is required but unbiassed observation and a sound head, but these are scarcer than folks imagine."

" How do the French and English of the present day stand with respect to the theory of colour?" asked I. " Each of the two nations," replied Goethe, " has its advantages and disadvantages. With the English, it is a good quality, that they make every thing practical, but they are pedants. The French have good brains, but with them everything must be positive, and if it is not so they make it so. However, with respect to the theory of colours, they are in a good way, and one of their best men comes near the truth. He says that colours are inherent in the things themselves; for as there is in nature an acidulating principle, so also is there a colouring principle. This view, I admit, does not explain the phenomena, but it places the object within the sphere of nature, and frees it from the load of mathematics."

The Berlin papers were brought in, and Goethe sat down to read them. He handed one of them to me, and I found in the theatrical intelligence, that at the opera house and the theatre royal they gave just as bad pieces as they gave here. "How should it be otherwise?" said Goethe. "There is no doubt that with the help of good English, French, and Spanish pieces, a repertoire can be formed sufficiently abundant to furnish a good piece every evening. But what need is felt by the nation always to see good pieces? The time in which Æschylus, Sophocles, and Euripides lived was different. Then there was mind enough to desire only what was really greatest and best. But in our miserable times, where is felt a need for the best? where are the organs to appreciate it?

"And then," continued Goethe, "people will have something new. In Berlin or Paris, the public is always the same. A quantity of new pieces are written and brought out in Paris, and you must endure five or six thoroughly bad ones before you are compensated by a single good one. The only expedient to keep up a German theatre at the present time, is that of 'starring' (*Gastrollen*). If I had the direction of the theatre now, the whole winter should be provided with excellent 'stars.' Thus, not only would all the good pieces be represented once more, but the interest of the audience would be led more from the pieces to the acting; a power of comparing and judging would be acquired; the public would gain in penetration, and the superior acting of a distinguished star would maintain our own actors in a state of excitement and emulation. As I said before, keep on with your starring, and you will be astonished at the benefit that will accrue both to the theatre and the public. I foresee a time when a clever man, who understands the matter, will take four theatres at once, and provide them with stars by turns. And I am sure he will keep his ground better than if he only had one."

Wednesday, December 27, 1826.

I had been sedulously reflecting at home, on the phenomenon of the blue and yellow shadows, and although this long remained a riddle to me, a light gleamed upon me after constant meditation, and I was gradually convinced that I understood the phenomenon.

To-day at dinner, I told Goethe that I had solved the riddle. " That is saying a great deal," said Goethe, "you shall show me after dinner." " I would rather write my solution down," returned I, "for I want the right words for a verbal explanation." "You may write it down afterwards, but to-day you shall solve the problem before my eyes, and demonstrate it with your own mouth, that I may see whether you are in the right way."

After dinner, when it was still quite light, Goethe said to me, " Can you make the experiment now?" "No," said I. " Why not?" asked Goethe. " It is too light," I replied. " We must have a little dusk, in order that the candle may throw a decided shade, but not so much that daylight cannot fall upon this shadow." "Humph!" said Goethe, "that is not wrong."

The dusk of the evening at last set in, and I told Goethe that this was the time. He lighted the wax taper, and gave me a sheet of white paper and a stick. "Now, go on with your experiment and demonstration," said he.

I placed the taper on the table near the window, laid the sheet of paper near it, and when I placed the stick in the middle of the paper, between daylight and candle-light, the phenomenon was there in all its beauty. The shadow towards the candle was a decided yellow, and the one towards the window, a perfect blue.

"Now," said Goethe, "how is the blue shadow produced?" "Before I explain this," said I, "I will lay down the fundamental law, from which I deduce both phenomena. Light and darkness are not colours, but they are the two extremes between which, and by the modification of which, all colours are produced. Next to the extremes of light and darkness, arise the two colours yellow and blue. The yellow borders on light, inasmuch as it is produced by seeing light through a dimmed transparency; the blue borders on darkness, inasmuch as it is produced by seeing darkness through an illuminated transparency. If we now come to our phenomena," I continued, "we see that the stick, through the strength of the taper light, casts a decided shadow. This shadow would appear as so much black darkness if I closed the shutters and shut out the light of day; but here the daylight enters freely by the window, and forms an illuminated medium, through which I see the darkness of the shadow; and thus, in conformity with our law, the blue colour is produced."

Goethe laughed. "Well, that would be the blue, would it?" said he; "but how do you explain the yellow shadow?" "From the law of the dimmed light," I replied. "The burning taper throws upon the white paper a light which has already a slightly yellowish tinge. The daylight, however, is strong enough to throw a weak shadow, which, as far as it extends, dims the light; and thus, in conformity with our law, the yellow colour is produced. If I lessen the dimness by bringing the shadow as nearly as possible to the candle, a pure clear yellow is produced; but if I increase the dimness by removing the shadow as far as possible from the candle, the yellow is heightened to a reddish yellow, or even to a red."

Goethe again laughed, and looked very mysterious. "Now," said he, "am I right? You have observed your phenomenon well, and have described it very prettily," replied Goethe, "but you have not explained it. Your explanation is ingenious, but it is not the right one."

"Help me, then," said I, "and solve the riddle, for I am extremely impatient." "You shall learn the solution," replied Goethe, "but not to-day and not in this manner. I will next show you another phenomenon, which will bring the law plainly before your eyes. You are near the mark, and cannot proceed further in this direction. When you have once comprehended the new law, you will be transplanted into quite another region. Come some day and dine with me an hour earlier, when the sky is clear, and I will show you a plainer phenomenon, by which you will at once comprehend the law which lies at the foundation of this one. I am very glad," he continued, "that you take this interest in colours; it will prove a source of infinite delight."

When I left Goethe in the evening, I could not get the thought of the phenomenon out of my head, and it occupied my very dreams; but even thus I did not gain a clearer view, and did not advance one step nearer towards the solution of the enigma.

"I am going on, though slowly, with my papers on Natural Science," said Goethe to me lately; "not because I think that I can materially advance science, but on account of the many pleasant associations I maintain by it. Of all occupations, that with nature is the most innocent. As for any connection or correspondence in æsthetical matters, that is not to be thought of. They now want to know what town on the Rhine is meant in my 'Hermann and Dorothea,' as if it were not better to choose according to one's fancy. They want truth—they want actuality; and thus poetry is destroyed."

CONVERSATIONS OF GOETHE.

1827.

1827.

Wednesday, January 3, 1827.

AT dinner, we talked over Canning's excellent speech for Portugal. "Some people," said Goethe, "call this speech coarse; but these people know not what they want—they have a morbid desire to be *frondeurs* against all greatness. It is no opposition, it is mere '*frondation;*' they must have something great, that they may hate it. When Napoleon was alive they hated him, and he served as a good conduit-pipe. When it was all over with him, they grumbled (*frondirten*) at the Holy Alliance, and yet nothing greater or more beneficial for mankind was ever devised. Now it is Canning's turn. His speech for Portugal is the result of a grand consciousness. He feels very well the extent of his power and the dignity of his position; and he is right to speak as he feels. This the Sans Culottes cannot understand; and what to us seems sublime, seems to them coarse. The grand disturbs them; they are not so constituted as to respect it, and cannot endure it."

Thursday evening, January 4, 1827.

Goethe praised highly the poems of Victor Hugo.

"He is," said he, "a man of decided talent, on whom German literature has had an influence. His poetic youth has, unfortunately, been disturbed by the pedantry of the classic school; but now he has the 'Globe' on his side, and is thus sure of his game. I am inclined to compare him with Manzoni. He has much objectivity, and seems to me quite as important as MM. De Lamartine and De la Vigne. On closely observing him, I see the source of this and other fresh talent of the same sort. They all come from Chateaubriand, who has really a distinguished rhetorico-poetical talent. That you may see how Victor Hugo writes, only read this poem upon Napoleon—*Les Deux Isles.*"

Goethe gave me the book, and went to the stove. I read the poem. "Has he not excellent images," said Goethe, "and has not he managed his subject with great freedom?" He came back to me. "Only look at this passage—how fine it is!" He read the passage about the storm-cloud, from which the lightning darts upward and strikes the hero. "That is fine; for the image is correct: as you will find in the mountains, where we often have the storm beneath us, and where the lightning darts upwards."

"I praise this in the French," said I, "that their poetry never deserts the firm ground of reality. We can translate their poems into prose, without losing anything essential."

"That," said Goethe, "is because the French poets have knowledge, while our German simpletons think they would lose their talent, if they laboured for knowledge; although, in fact, all talent must derive its nutriment from knowledge, and thus only is enabled to use its strength. But let them pass; we cannot help them, and real talent soon finds its way. The many young poets who are now carrying on their trade have no real talent; they only show an impotence which has been excited into productiveness by the high state of German literature.

"That the French," continued Goethe, "have passed from their pedantry into a freer manner is not surprising. Even before the revolution, Diderot, and minds like his, sought to break open this path. The revolution itself, and the reign of Napoleon, have been favourable to the cause; for if the years of war allowed no real poetical interest to spring up, and were consequently for the moment unfavourable to the Muses, yet a multitude of free intellects were formed in this period, who now, in times of peace, attain reflection, and come forward as talents of importance."

I asked Goethe whether the classical party had been opposed to the excellent Béranger. "The *genre* of Béranger's poetry," said Goethe, "is old and traditional, and people were accustomed to it. However, he has been in many respects more free than his predecessors, and has therefore been attacked by the pedantic party."

The conversation turned upon painting, and on the mischief of the antiquity-worshipping school. "You do not pretend to be a connoisseur," said Goethe; "but I will show you a picture, in which, though it has been painted by one of the best living German artists, you will at the first glance be struck by the most glaring offences against the primary laws of art.

You will see that details are nicely done, but you will be dissatisfied with the whole, and will not know what to make of it; and this not because the painter has not sufficient talent, but because his mind, which should have directed his talent, is darkened, like that of all the other bigots to antiquity; so that he ignores the perfect masters, and, going back to their imperfect predecessors, takes them for his patterns.

"Raphael and his contemporaries broke through a limited mannerism, to nature and freedom. And now our artists, instead of being thankful, using these advantages, and proceeding on the good way, return to the state of limitation.

"This is too bad, and it is hard to understand such darkening of the intellect. And since in this course they find no support in art itself, they seek one from religion and faction—without these two they could not sustain themselves in their weakness.

"There is," continued Goethe, "through all art a filiation. If you see a great master, you will always find that he used what was good in his predecessors, and that it was this which made him great. Men like Raphael do not spring out of the ground. They took root in the antique, and the best which had been done before them. Had they not used the advantages of their time, there would be little to say about them."

The conversation now turned upon old German poetry: I mentioned Flemming. "Flemming," said Goethe, "is a very fair talent, a little prosaic and citizen-like, and of no practical use nowadays. It is strange," he continued, "that with all I have done, there is not one of my poems that would suit the

Lutheran hymn-book." I laughed and assented, while I said to myself that in this odd expression there was more than could be seen at the first glance.

Sunday evening, January 12, 1827.

I found a musical party at Goethe's. The performers were the Eberwein family, and some members of the orchestra. Among the few hearers were General Superintendent Röhr, Hofrath Vogel, and some ladies. Goethe had wished to hear a quartet by a celebrated young composer, and this was played first. Karl Eberwein, a boy twelve years old, played the piano entirely to Goethe's great satisfaction, and indeed admirably, so that the quartet was in every respect well performed.

" It is a strange state," said Goethe, " to which the great improvements in the technical and mechanical part of the art have brought our newest composers. Their productions are no longer music; they go beyond the level of human feelings, and one can give them no response from the mind and heart. How do *you* feel? I hear with my ears only."

I replied that I fared no better.

" Yet the Allegro," said he, " had character; that ceaseless whirling and twirling brought before my mind the witches' dance on the Blocksberg, and thus I had a picture to illustrate this odd music."

After a pause, during which the party discoursed and took refreshments, Goethe asked Madame Eberwein to sing some songs. She sang the beautiful song, " Um Mitternacht," with Zelter's music, which made the deepest impression.

"That song," said Goethe, " remains beautiful, however often it is heard! There is something eternal, indestructible, in the melody!"

The "Erlkönig" obtained great applause; and the aria, "Ich hab's gesagt der guten Mutter," made every one remark that the music so happily fitted the words, that no one could even conceive it otherwise. Goethe himself was in the highest degree pleased.

By way of conclusion to this pleasant evening, Madame Eberwein, at Goethe's request, sang some songs from his " Divan," with her husband's music. The passage, " Jussuf's Reize möcht' ich borgen," pleased Goethe especially. " Eberwein," he said, " sometimes surpasses himself." He then asked for the song, " Ach um deine feuchten Schwingen," which was also of a kind to excite the deepest emotions.

After the party had left, I remained some moments alone with Goethe. " I have," said he, " this evening made the remark that these songs in the 'Divan' have no further connection with me. Both the oriental and impassioned elements have ceased to live in me. I have left them behind, like a cast-off snake-skin on my path. The song, 'Um Mitternacht,' on the contrary, has not lost its connection with me; it is a living part of me, and goes on living with me still.

" Oftentimes, my own productions seem wholly strange to me. To-day, I read a passage in French, and thought as I read—'This man speaks cleverly enough—you would not have said it otherwise:' when I look at it closely, I find it is a passage translated from my own writings!"

Monday evening, January 15, 1827.

After the completion of the "Helena," Goethe had employed himself last summer with the continuation of the "Wanderjahre." He often talked to me about the progress of this work.

"In order the better to use the materials I possess," said he to me one day, "I have taken the first part entirely to pieces, and intend, by mingling the old with the new, to make two parts. I have ordered everything that is printed to be copied entire. The places where I have new matter to introduce are marked, and when my secretary comes to such a mark, I dictate what is wanting, and thus compel myself never to let my work stop."

Another day he said to me, "All the printed part of the 'Wanderjahre' is now completely copied. The places where I am to introduce new matter are filled with blue paper, so that I have always before my eyes what is yet to be done. As I go on at present, the blue spots gradually vanish, to my great delight."

Some weeks ago, I had heard from his secretary that he was at work on a new *novel*. I therefore abstained from evening visits, and satisfied myself with seeing him once a week at dinner. The novel had now been finished for some time, and this evening he showed me the first sheets. I was delighted, and read as far as the important passage where all stand round the dead tiger, and the messenger brings the intelligence that the lion has laid himself in the sun by the ruins.

While reading, I could not but admire the extraordinary clearness with which all objects, down to the very smallest locality, were brought before the eyes. The going out to hunt, the old ruins of the castle, the fair, the way through the fields to the ruins, were all so distinctly painted, that one could not conceive them otherwise than as the poet intended. At the same time, all was written with such circumspection and mastery of subject, that one could never anticipate what was coming, or see a line further than one read.

"Your excellency," said I, "must have worked after a very defined plan."

"Yes, indeed," replied Goethe; "I was going to treat the subject thirty years ago, and have carried it in my head ever since. The work went on oddly enough. At that time, immediately after 'Hermann and Dorothea,' I meant to treat it in an epic form and in hexameters, and had drawn up a complete outline with this view. But when I now took up the subject again, not being able to find my old outline, I was obliged to make a new one, and that suitable to the altered form I intended to give the subject. Now my work is ended, the old outline is again found, and I am glad I did not have it earlier; for it would only have confused me. The action and the progress of development were, indeed, unaltered, but the details were entirely different; it had been conceived with a view to an epic treatment in hexameters, and would not therefore have been applicable to this prose form."

The conversation then turned upon the contents.

"That is a beautiful situation," said I, "where Honorio, opposite to the princess, stands over the dead tiger, when the lamenting woman with her boy comes up, and the prince, too, with his retinue of huntsmen, hastens to join this singular group; it would make an excellent picture, and I should like to see it painted."

" Yes," said Goethe, " that would be a fine picture. Yet, perhaps," continued he, after some reflection, " the subject is almost too rich, and the figures are too many, so that it would be very difficult for the artist to group them, and distribute the light and shade. That earlier moment, where Honorio kneels on the tiger, and the princess is opposite to him on horseback, I have imagined as a picture, and that might be done."

I felt that Goethe was right, and added that this moment contained in fact the gist of the whole situation.

I also remarked that this novel had a character quite distinct from those of the " Wanderjahre," inasmuch as everything represented the external world—everything was real.

" True," said Goethe, " you will find in it scarcely anything of the inward world, and in my other things there is almost too much."

" I am now curious to learn," said I, " how the lion will be conquered; I almost guess that this will take place in quite a different manner, but *how* I cannot conceive." " It would not be right for you to guess it," said Goethe, " and I will not reveal the secret to-day. On Thursday evening I will give you the conclusion. Till then, the lion shall lie in the sun."

I turned the conversation to the second part of " Faust," especially the classical Walpurgis night, which existed as yet only as a sketch, and which

Goethe had told me he meant to print in that form. I had ventured to advise him not to do so; for I found that if it were once printed, it would be always left in this unfinished state. Goethe must have thought that over in the meantime, for he now told me that he had resolved not to print the sketch.

"I am very glad of it," said I; "for now I shall hope to see you complete it."

"It might be done in three months," said he; "but when am I to get time for it? The day has too many claims on me; it is difficult to isolate myself sufficiently. This morning, the hereditary Grand Duke was with me; to-morrow at noon, the Grand Duchess proposes visiting me. I must prize such visits as a high favour; they embellish my life, but they occupy my mind. I am obliged to think what I have new to offer to such dignified personages, and how I can worthily entertain them."

"And yet," said I, "you finished 'Helena,' last winter, when you were no less disturbed than now."

"Why," he replied, "one goes on, and must go on; but it is difficult."

"'Tis well," said I, "that your outline is so completely made out."

"The outline is indeed complete," said Goethe, "but the most difficult part is yet to be done; and in the execution of parts, everything depends too much on luck. The classic Walpurgis night must be written in rhyme, and yet the whole must have an antique character. It is not easy to find a suitable sort of verse;—and then the dialogue!"

"Is not that also in the plan?" said I.

"The *what* is there," replied Goethe, "but not the *how*. Then, only think what is to be said on that mad night! Faust's speech to Proserpine, when he would move her to give him Helena—what a speech should that be, when Proserpine herself is moved to tears! All this is not easy to do, and depends much on good luck, nay, almost entirely on the mood and strength at the moment."

Wednesday, January 17, 1827.

Lately, during Goethe's occasional indisposition, we had dined in his work-room, which looks out on the garden. To-day, the cloth was again laid in what is called the Urbino-chamber, which I looked upon as a good omen. When I entered, I found Goethe and his son: both welcomed me in their *naïve*, affectionate manner; Goethe himself was in his happiest mood, as I could perceive by the animation of his face.

Through the open door of the next room, I saw Chancellor von Müller stooping over a large engraving; he soon came in to us, and I was glad to greet him as a pleasant companion at table. Frau von Goethe was still absent, but we sat down to table without her. The engraving was talked about with admiration, and Goethe said that it was a work of the celebrated Parisian Gérard, who had lately sent it to him as a present. "Go you at once," added he, "and take a peep before the soup comes in."

I followed his wish and my own inclination, and was delighted both with the sight of the admirable work and with the inscription of the artist, by which he dedicates it to Goethe as a proof of his esteem. I could not look long; Frau von Goethe came in, and I hastened back to my place.

"Is not that something great?" said Goethe. "You may study it days and weeks before you can find out all its rich thoughts and perfections."

We were very lively at table. The Chancellor produced a letter by an important man at Paris, who had held a difficult post as ambassador here in the time of the French occupation, and had from that period kept up a friendly communication with Weimar. He mentioned the Grand Duke and Goethe, and congratulated Weimar for being able to maintain so intimate an alliance between genius and the highest power.

Frau von Goethe gave a highly graceful tone to the conversation. The discourse was upon certain purchases; and she teazed young Goethe, who would not give in.

"We must not spoil fair ladies too much," said Goethe; "they are so ready to break all bounds. Even at Elba, Napoleon received milliners' bills, which he had to pay; yet, in such matters, he would as easily do too little as too much. One day, at the Tuileries, a *marchand de modes* offered, in his presence, some valuable goods to his consort. As Napoleon showed no disposition to buy anything, the man gave him to understand that he was doing but little in this way for his wife. Napoleon did not answer a word, but looked upon the man with such a look, that he packed up his things at once, and never showed his face again."

"Did he do this when consul?" asked Frau von Goethe.

"Probably when emperor," replied Goethe, "for otherwise his look would not have been so formidable. I cannot but laugh at the man, who was pierced through by the glance, and who saw himself already beheaded or shot."

We were in the liveliest mood, and continued to talk of Napoleon.

"I wish," said young Goethe, "that I had good pictures or engravings of all Napoleon's deeds, to decorate a large room."

"The room must be very large," said Goethe, "and even then it would not hold the pictures, so great are the deeds."

The Chancellor turned the conversation on Luden's "History of the Germans;" and I had reason to admire the dexterity and penetration which young Goethe displayed in deducing all which the reviewers had found to blame in the book from the time in which it was written, and the national views and feelings which had animated the author. We arrived at the result that the wars of Napoleon first explained to us those of Cæsar. "Previously," said Goethe, "Cæsar's book was really not much more than an exercise for classical schools."

From the old German time, the conversation turned upon the Gothic. We spoke of a bookcase which had a Gothic character, and from this were led to discuss the late fashion of arranging entire apartments in the old German and Gothic style, and thus living under the influences of a bygone time.

"In a house," said Goethe, "where there are so many rooms that some are entered only three or four times a year, such a fancy may pass; and I think it a pretty notion of Madame Pankoucke at Paris that she has a Chinese apartment. But I cannot praise the man who fits out the rooms in which he lives with these strange, old-fashioned objects. It is a sort of masquerade, which can, in the long run, do no good in any respect, but must, on the contrary, have an unfavourable influence on the man who adopts it. Such a fashion is in contradiction to the age in which we live, and will only confirm the empty and hollow way of thinking and feeling in which it originates. It is well enough, on a merry winter's evening, to go to a masquerade as a Turk; but what should we think of a man who wore such a mask all the year round? We should think either that he was crazy, or in a fair way to become so before long."

We found Goethe's remarks on this highly practical subject very convincing, and as the reproof did not even lightly touch any of us, we received the truth with the pleasantest feelings.

The conversation now turned upon the theatre, and Goethe rallied me for having, last Monday evening, sacrificed it to him. " He has now been here three years," said he, turning to the others, " and this is the first evening that he has given up the theatre for my sake. I ought to think a great deal of it. I had invited him, and he had promised to come, but yet I doubted whether he would keep his word, especially as it struck half-past six and he was not here. Indeed, I should have rejoiced if he had not come; for then I could have said: this is a crazy fellow, who loves the theatre better than his dearest friends, and whom nothing can turn aside from his obstinate partiality. But did I not make it up to you? have I not shown you fine things?" By these words Goethe alluded to the new novel.

We talked of Schiller's "Fiesco," which was acted last Saturday. "I saw it for the first time," said I, "and have been much occupied with thinking whether those extremely rough scenes could not be softened; but I find very little could be done to them without spoiling the character of the whole."

"You are right—it cannot be done," replied Goethe. "Schiller often talked with me on the matter; for he himself could not endure his first plays, and would never allow them to be acted while we had the direction of the theatre. At last we were in want of pieces, and would willingly have gained those three powerful firstlings for our *repertoire*. But we found it impossible; all the parts were too closely interwoven one with another; so that Schiller himself despaired of accomplishing the plan, and found himself constrained to give it up, and leave the pieces just as they were."

"'Tis a pity," said I; "for, notwithstanding all their roughness, I love them a thousand times better than the weak, forced, and unnatural pieces of some of the best of our later tragic poets. A grand intellect and character is felt in everything of Schiller's."

"Yes," said Goethe, "Schiller might do what he would, he could not make anything which would not come out far greater than the best things of these later people. Even when he cut his nails, he showed he was greater than these gentlemen." We laughed at this striking metaphor.

"But I have known persons," continued he, "who could never be content with those first dramas of Schiller. One summer, at a bathing place, I was walking through a very secluded, narrow path, which led to a mill. There Prince ——— met me, and as at the same moment some mules laden with meal-sacks came up to us, we were obliged to get out of the way and enter a small house. Here, in a narrow room, we fell, after the fashion of that prince, into deep discussion about things divine and human; we also came to Schiller's 'Robbers,' when the prince expressed himself thus: 'If I had been the Deity on the point of creating the world, and had foreseen, at the moment, that Schiller's 'Robbers' would have been written in it, I would have left the world uncreated.'" We could not help laughing. "What do you say to that?" said Goethe; "that is a dislike which goes pretty far, and which one can scarcely understand."

"There is nothing of this dislike," I observed, "in our young people, especially our students. The most excellent and matured pieces by Schiller and others may be performed, and we shall see but few young people and students in the theatre; but if Schiller's 'Robbers' or Schiller's 'Fiesco' is given, the house is almost filled by students alone."

"So it was," said Goethe, "fifty years ago, and so it will probably be fifty years hence. Do not let us imagine that the world will so much advance in culture and good taste that young people will pass over the ruder epoch. What a young man has written, is always best enjoyed by young people. Even if the world progresses generally, youth will always begin at the beginning, and the epochs of the world's cultivation will be repeated in the individual. This has ceased to irritate me, and a long time ago I made a verse in this fashion:

> Still let the bonfire blaze away,
> Let pleasure never know decay;
> Old brooms to stumps are always worn,
> And youngsters every day are born.

"I need only look out of the window to see, in the brooms that sweep the street, and the children who run about, a visible symbol of the world, that is always wearing out and always becoming young again. Children's games and the diversions of youth are preserved from century to century; for, absurd as these may appear to a more mature age, children are always children, and are at all times alike. Hence we ought not to put down the midsummer bonfires, or spoil the pleasure which the little dears take in them."

With this and the like cheerful conversation the hours at table passed swiftly by. We younger people then went into the upper room, while the Chancellor remained with Goethe.

Thursday evening, January 18, 1827.

Goethe had promised me the rest of the novel this evening. I went to him at half-past six, and found him alone in his comfortable work-room. I sat down with him at table, and after we had talked over the immediate events of the day, Goethe arose and gave me the wished for last sheets. "There you may read the conclusion," said he. I began, while Goethe walked up and down the room, and occasionally stood at the stove. As usual, I read softly to myself.

The sheets of the last evening had ended where the

lion is lying in the sun outside the wall of the old ruin, at the foot of an aged beech, and preparations are made to subdue him. The prince is going to send the hunters after him, but the stranger begs him to spare his lion, being confident that he can bring him back into his cage by milder means. This child, said he, will accomplish his work by pleasant words and the sweet tones of his flute. The prince consents, and after he has arranged the necessary measures of precaution, rides back into the town with his men. Honorio, with a number of hunters, occupies the defile, that, in case the lion comes down, he may scare him back by kindling a fire. The mother and the child, led by the warder of the castle, ascend the ruin, on the other side of which the lion is lying by the outer wall.

The design is to lure the mighty animal into the spacious castle-yard. The mother and the warder conceal themselves above in the half-ruined hall, while the child goes alone after the lion through the dark opening in the wall of the court-yard. An anxious pause arises. They do not know what has become of the child—his flute gives no sound. The warder reproaches himself that he did not go also, but the mother is calm.

At last the sounds of the flute are again heard. They approach nearer and nearer. The child returns to the castle-yard by the opening in the wall, and the lion, now docile, follows him with heavy step. They go once round the yard. Then the child sits down in a sunny spot, while the lion settles himself peacefully beside him, and lays one of his heavy paws in his lap.

A thorn has entered it; the child draws it out, and, taking his silken kerchief from his neck, binds the paw. The mother and the warder, who have witnessed the whole scene from the hall above, are transported with delight. The lion is tamed and in safety, and, as the child alternately with the sounds of his flute sings his charming pious songs to soothe the monster, he concludes the whole novel by singing the following verses :—

> Holy angels thus take heed
> Of the good and docile child,
> Aiding ev'ry worthy deed,
> Checking ev'ry impulse wild.
> Pious thoughts and melody
> Both together work for good,
> Luring to the infant's knee
> E'en the tyrant of the wood.*

I had not read without emotion the concluding incident. Still I did not know what to say. I was astonished but not satisfied. It seemed to me

---

* Those who know the difficulty of the original will not be too severe on the above translation. The words as they stand in Cotta's editions of Goethe, are as follows:—

> Und so geht mit guten Kindern
> Sel'ger Engel gern zu Rath,
> Böses Willen zu verhindern,
> Zu befördern schöne That.
> So beschwören fest zu bannen
> Lieben Sohn ans zarte Knie
> Ihn des Waldes Hochtyrannen
> Frommer Sinn und Melodie.

Unless the most forced construction be adopted, these lines seem to me quite inexplicable. But in the passage as quoted by Eckermann, "liebem" stands in the place of "lieben," and this reading, which I suspect to be the right one, gives a sense to which my version approximates.—*Trans.*

that the conclusion was too simple,* too ideal, too lyrical; and that at least some of the other figures should have reappeared, and, by winding up the whole, have given more breadth to the termination. Goethe observed that I had a doubt in my mind, and endeavoured to set me right. "If," said he, "I had again brought in some of the other figures at the end, the conclusion would have been prosaic. What could they do and say, when everything is done already. The prince and his men have ridden into the town, where his assistance is needed. Honorio, as soon as he learns that the lion is secured, will follow with his hunters, and the man will soon come from the town with his iron cage and put the lion into it. All these things are foreseen, and therefore should not be detailed. If they were, we should become prosaic. But an ideal, nay a lyrical conclusion, was necessary; for after the pathetic speech of the man, which in itself is poetical prose, a further elevation is required, and I was obliged to have recourse to lyrical poetry, nay, even to a song.

"To find a simile to this novel," continued Goethe, "imagine a green plant shooting up from its root, thrusting forth strong green leaves from the sides of its sturdy stem, and at last terminating in a flower. The flower is unexpected and startling, but come it must—nay, the whole foliage has existed only for the sake of that flower, and would be worthless without it."

At these words I breathed lightly. The scales

* In the sense of a group being *simple*. The German word is "einsam" (solitary).—*Trans.*

seemed to fall from my eyes, and a feeling of the excellence of this marvellous composition began to stir within me.

Goethe continued,—" The purpose of this novel was to show how the unmanageable and the invincible is often better restrained by love and pious feeling than by force. And this beautiful aim, which is set forth by the child and the lion, charmed me on to the completion of the work. This is the ideal—this is the flower. The green foliage of the extremely real introduction is only there for the sake of this ideal, and only worth anything on account of it. For what is the real in itself? We take delight in it when it is represented with truth—nay, it may give us a clearer knowledge of certain things, but the proper gain to our higher nature lies alone in the ideal, which proceeds from the heart of the poet."

I palpably felt how right Goethe was, for the conclusion of his novel still acted upon me, and had produced in me a tone of piety such as I had not known for a long time. How pure and intense, thought I to myself, must be the feelings of the poet, that he can write anything so beautiful at his advanced age. I did not refrain from expressing myself on this point to Goethe, and from congratulating myself that this production, which was unique in itself, had now a visible existence.

" I am glad," said Goethe, " that you are satisfied with it; and I am also glad on my own account, that I have got rid of a subject which I carried about with me for thirty years. Schiller and Humboldt, to whom I formerly communicated my plan, dissuaded me from going on with it, because they could see nothing in it, and because the poet alone knows what charms he is capable of giving to his subject. One should therefore never ask any body if one means to write anything. If Schiller had asked me about his 'Wallenstein' before he had written it, I should surely have advised him against it; for I could never have dreamed that, from such a subject, so excellent a drama could be made. Schiller was opposed to that treatment of my subject in hexameters, to which I was inclined immediately after my 'Herman and Dorothea,' and advised Ottava Rima. You see, however, that I have succeeded, but with prose; for much depended on an accurate description of the locality, and in this I should have been constrained by a verse of the sort recommended. Besides the very real character at the beginning, and the very ideal character at the conclusion of the novel, tell best in prose; while the little songs have a pretty effect, which could not be produced either by hexameters or by Ottava Rima."

The single tales and novels of the "Wanderjahre" were talked of; and it was observed that each was distinguished from the others by peculiar character and tone. "The reason of this," said Goethe, "I will explain. I went to work like a painter, who, with certain subjects, shuns certain colours, and makes others predominate. Thus for a morning landscape, he puts a great deal of blue on his palette, and but little yellow. But, if he is to paint an evening scene, he takes a great deal of yellow, and almost omits the blue. I proceeded in the same way with my different literary productions, and this is the cause of their varied character."

I thought within myself that this was a very wise maxim, and was pleased that Goethe had uttered it.

I then, especially with reference to this last novel, admired the detail with which the scenery was described.

"I have," said Goethe, "never observed Nature with a view to poetical production; but, because my early drawing of landscapes, and my later studies in natural science, led me to a constant, close observation of natural objects, I have gradually learned Nature by heart even to the minutest details, so that, when I need anything as a poet, it is at my command; and I cannot easily sin against truth. Schiller had not this observation of Nature. The localities of Switzerland, which he used in 'William Tell,' were all related to him by me; but he had such a wonderful mind, that even on hearsay, he could make something that possessed reality."

The conversation now turned wholly on Schiller, and Goethe proceeded thus :—

"Schiller's proper productive talent lay in the ideal; and it may be said he has not his equal in German or any other literature. He has almost everything that Lord Byron has; but Lord Byron is his superior in knowledge of the world. I wish Schiller had lived to know Lord Byron's works, and wonder what he would have said to so congenial a mind. Did Byron publish anything during Schiller's life?"

I could not say with certainty. Goethe took down the "Conversations Lexicon," and read the article on Byron, making many hasty remarks as he proceeded. It appeared that Byron had published nothing before

1807, and that therefore Schiller could have seen nothing of his.

"Through all Schiller's works," continued Goethe, "goes the idea of freedom; though this idea assumed a new shape as Schiller advanced in his culture and became another man. In his youth it was physical freedom which occupied him, and influenced his poems; in his later life it was ideal freedom.

"Freedom is an odd thing, and every man has enough of it, if he can only satisfy himself. What avails a superfluity of freedom which we cannot use? Look at this chamber and the next, in which, through the open door, you see my bed. Neither of them is large; and they are rendered still narrower by necessary furniture, books, manuscripts, and works of art; but they are enough for me. I have lived in them all the winter, scarcely entering my front rooms. What have I done with my spacious house, and the liberty of going from one room to another, when I have not found it requisite to make use of them.

"If a man has freedom enough to live healthy, and work at his craft, he has enough; and so much all can easily obtain. Then all of us are only free under certain conditions, which we must fulfil. The citizen is as free as the nobleman, when he restrains himself within the limits which God appointed by placing him in that rank. The nobleman is as free as the prince; for, if he will but observe a few ceremonies at court, he may feel himself his equal. Freedom consists not in refusing to recognize anything above us, but in respecting something which is above us; for, by respecting it, we raise ourselves to it, and by our very acknowledgment, make manifest that we bear within ourselves what is higher, and are worthy to be on a level with it.

"I have, on my journeys, often met merchants from the north of Germany, who fancied they were my equals, if they rudely seated themselves next me at table. They were, by this method, nothing of the kind; but they would have been so, if they had known how to value and treat me.

"That this physical freedom gave Schiller so much trouble in his youthful years, was caused partly by the nature of his mind, but still more by the restraint which he endured at the military school. In later days, when he had enough physical freedom, he passed over to the ideal; and I would almost say that this idea killed him, since it led him to make demands on his physical nature which were too much for his strength.

"The Grand Duke fixed on Schiller, when he was established here, an income of one thousand dollars yearly, and offered to give him twice as much in case he should be hindered by sickness from working. Schiller declined this last offer, and never availed himself of it. 'I have talent,' said he, 'and must help myself.' But as his family enlarged of late years, he was obliged, for a livelihood, to write two dramas annually; and to accomplish this, he forced himself to write days and weeks when he was not well. He would have his talent obey him at any hour. He never drank much; he was very temperate; but, in such hours of bodily weakness, he was obliged to stimulate his powers by the use of spirituous liquors. This habit impaired his health, and was likewise injurious to his productions. The faults which some wiseacres find in his works I deduce from this source. All the passages which they say are not what they ought to be, I would call pathological passages; for he wrote them on those days when he had not strength to find the right and true motives. I have every respect for the categorical imperative. I know how much good may proceed from it; but one must not carry it too far, for then this idea of ideal freedom certainly leads to no good."

Amid these interesting remarks, and similar discourse on Lord Byron and the celebrated German authors, of whom Schiller had said, that he liked Kotzebue best, for he, at any rate, produced something, the hours of evening passed swiftly along, and Goethe gave me the novel, that I might study it quietly at home.

Sunday evening, January 21, 1827.

I went at half-past seven this evening to Goethe, and staid with him about an hour. He showed me a volume of new French poems, by Mademoiselle Gay, and spoke of them with great praise.

" The French," said he, " push their way, and it is well worth while to look after them. I have lately been striving hard to form a notion of the present state of French literature; and if I succeed I shall express my opinion of it. It is very interesting to observe that those elements are now, for the first time, at work with them which we went through long ago.

" A mediocre talent is, indeed, always biassed by its age, and must be fed by the elements of the age. With the French it is the same as with us, down to the most modern pietism, only that with them this appears more *galant* and *spirituel.*"

" What says your excellency to Beranger, and the author of ' Clara Gazul?' "

" Those I except," said Goethe; " they are great geniuses, who have a foundation in themselves, and keep free from the mode of thinking which belongs to their time."

" I am glad to hear you say this," said I, " for I have had a similar feeling about them both."

The conversation turned from French to German literature. " I will show you something," said Goethe, " that will be interesting to you. Give me one of those two volumes which lie before you. Solger is known to you."

" Certainly," said I; " I am very fond of him, I have his translation of Sophocles, and both this and the preface gave me long since a high opinion of him."

" You know he has been dead several years," said Goethe; " and now a collection of the writings and letters he left is published. He is not so happy in his philosophical inquiries, which he has given us in the form of the Platonic dialogues; but his letters are excellent. In one of them, he writes to Tieck upon the *Wahlverwandtschaften* (elective affinities), and I wish to read it to you; for it would not be easy to say anything better about that novel."

Goethe read me these excellent remarks, and we talked them over point by point, admiring the dignified character of the views, and the logical sequence of the reasoning. Although Solger admitted that the facts of the " Wahlverwandtschaften" had their germ in the nature of all the characters, he nevertheless blamed that of Edward.

"I do not quarrel with him," said Goethe, "because he cannot endure Edward. I myself cannot endure him, but was obliged to make him such a man in order to bring out my fact. He is, besides, very true to nature; for you find many people in the higher ranks, with whom, quite like him, obstinacy takes the place of character.

"High above all, Solger placed the Architect; because, while all the other persons of the novel show themselves loving and weak, he alone remains strong and free; and the beauty of his nature consists not so much in this, that he does not fall into the errors of the other characters—but in this, that the poet has made him so noble that he *could* not fall into them."

We were pleased with this remark.

"That is really very fine," said Goethe.

"I have," said I, "felt the importance and amiability of the Architect's character; but I never remarked that he was so very excellent, just because by his very nature he could not fall into those bewilderments of love."

"No wonder," said Goethe, "for I myself never thought of it when I was creating him; yet Solger is right—this certainly is his character.

"These remarks," continued he, "were written as early as the year 1809. I should then have been much cheered to have heard so kind a word about the 'Wahlverwandtschaften,' for at that time, and afterwards, not many pleasant remarks were vouchsafed me about that novel.

"I see from these letters that Solger was much attached to me: in one of them, he complains that I have returned no answer about the 'Sophocles' which he sent me. Good Heavens! how am I placed. It is not to be wondered at. I have known great lords, to whom many presents were sent. These had certain formulas and phrases with which they answered everything; and thus they wrote letters to hundreds, all alike, and all mere phrases. This I never could do. If I could not say to each man something distinct and appropriate to the occasion, I preferred not writing to him at all. I esteemed superficial phrases unworthy, and thus I have failed to answer many an excellent man to whom I would willingly have written. You see yourself how it is with me, and what messages and despatches daily flow in upon me from every quarter, and you must confess that more than one man's life would be required to answer all these, in ever so careless a way. But I am sorry about Solger; he was an admirable being, and deserved, better than many, a friendly answer."

I turned the conversation to the novel, which I had now frequently read and studied at home. "All the first part," said I, "is only an introduction, but nothing is set forth beyond what is necessary; and this necessary preliminary is executed with such grace, that we cannot fancy it is only for the sake of something else, but would give it a value of its own."

"I am glad that you feel this," said Goethe, "but I must do something yet. According to the laws of a good introduction, the proprietors of the animals must make their appearance in it. When the princess and the uncle ride by the booth, the people must come out and entreat the princess to honour it with a visit."

"Assuredly you are right," said I; "for, since all the rest is indicated in the introduction, these people must be so likewise; and it is perfectly natural that, with their devotion to their treasury, they would not let the princess pass unassailed."

"You see," said Goethe, "that in a work of this kind, even when it is finished as a whole, there is still something to be done with the details."

Goethe then told me of a foreigner who had lately visited him, and had talked of translating several of his works.

"He is a good man," said Goethe, "but, as to literature, he shows himself a mere dilettante; for he does not yet know German at all, and is already talking of the translations he will make, and of the portraits which he will prefix to them.

"That is the very nature of the dilettanti, that they have no idea of the difficulties which lie in a subject, and always wish to undertake something for which they have no capacity."

Thursday evening, January 29, 1827.

At seven o'clock I went with the manuscript of the novel and a copy of Beranger to Goethe. I found M. Soret in conversation with him upon modern French literature. I listened with interest, and it was observed that the modern writers had learned a great deal from De Lille, as far as good versification was concerned. Since M. Soret, as a born Genevese, did not speak German fluently, while Goethe talks French tolerably well, the conversation was carried on in that language, and only became German when I put in a word. I took my "Beranger" out of my pocket, and gave it to Goethe, who wished to read his admirable songs again. M. Soret thought the portrait prefixed to the poems was not a good likeness. Goethe was much pleased to have this beautiful copy in his hands.

"These songs," said he, "may be looked upon as perfect, and as the best things in their kind, especially when you observe the burden, without which they would be almost too earnest, too pointed, and too epigrammatic, for songs. Beranger reminds me ever of Horace and Hafiz, who stood in the same way above their times, satirically and playfully setting forth the corruption of manners. Beranger has the same relation to his cotemporaries; but as he belongs to the lower class, the licentious and vulgar are not very hateful to him, and he treats them with a sort of partiality."

Many similar remarks were made upon Beranger, and other modern French writers, till M. Soret went to court, and I remained alone with Goethe.

A sealed packet lay upon the table. Goethe laid his hand upon it. "This," said he, "is 'Helena,' which is going to Cotta to be printed."

I felt, at these words, more than I could say; I felt the importance of the moment. For, as it is with a newly-built vessel which first goes to sea, and with respect to which we know not what destinies it must encounter, so is it likewise with the intellectual creation of a great master which first goes forth into the world to exercise its influence through many ages, and to produce and to undergo manifold destinies.

"I have," said Goethe, "till now, been always finding little things to add or to touch up; but I must finish now, and I am glad that it is going to the post, and that I shall be at liberty to turn to some other object. Let it meet its proper destiny. My comfort is, that the general culture of Germany stands at an incredibly high point; so that I need not fear that such a production will long remain misunderstood and without effect."

"There is a whole antiquity in it," said I.

"Yes," said Goethe, "the philologists will find work."

"I have no fear," said I, "about the antique part; for there we have the most minute detail, the most thorough development of individuals, and each personage says just what he should. But the modern romantic part is very difficult, for half the history of the world lies behind it; the material is so rich that it can only be lightly indicated, and heavy demands are made upon the reader."

"Yet," said Goethe, "it all appeals to the senses, and on the stage would satisfy the eye: more I did not intend. Let the crowd of spectators take pleasure in the spectacle; the higher import will not escape the initiated, as has been the case with the 'Magic Flute,' and other things beside."

"It will produce a most unusual effect on the stage," said I, "that a piece should begin as a tragedy and end as an opera. But something is required to represent the grandeur of these persons, and to express the sublime language and verse."

"The first part," said Goethe, "requires the first tragic artists, and the operatic part must be sustained by the first vocalists, male and female. That of Helena ought to be played, not by one, but by two great female artists; for we seldom find that a fine vocalist has sufficient talent as a tragic actress."

"The whole," said I, "will furnish an occasion for great splendour of scenery and costume, and I cannot deny that I look forward with pleasure to its representation on the stage. If we could only get a good composer."

"It should be one," said Goethe, "who, like Meyerbeer, has lived long in Italy, so that he combines his German nature with the Italian style and manner. However, that will be found somehow or other; I only rejoice that I am rid of it. Of the notion that the chorus does not descend into the lower world, but rather disperses itself among the elements on the cheerful surface of the earth, I am not a little proud."

"It is a new sort of immortality," said I.

"Now," continued Goethe, "how do you go on with the novel?"

"I have brought it with me," said I. "After reading it again, I find that your Excellency must not make the intended alteration. It produces a good effect that the people first appear by the slain tiger as completely new beings, with their outlandish costume and manners, and announce themselves as the owners of the beasts. If you made them first appear in the introduction, this effect would be completely weakened, if not destroyed."

"You are right," said Goethe; "I must leave it as it is; unquestionably, you are right. It must have been my design, when first I planned the tale, not to bring the people in sooner, otherwise I should not have left them out. The intended alteration was a requisition on the part of the understanding, which would certainly have led me into a fault. This is a remarkable case in æsthetics, that a rule must be departed from if faults are to be avoided."

We talked over the title which should be given to the novel. Many were proposed; some suited the beginning, others the end, but none seemed exactly suitable to the whole.

"I'll tell you what," said Goethe, "we will call it 'The Novel (Die Novelle);' for what is a novel but a peculiar and as yet unheard-of event? This is the proper meaning of this name; and much which in Germany passes as a novel is no novel at all, but a mere narrative, or whatever else you like to call it. In that original sense of an unheard-of event, even the 'Wahlverwandtschaften' may be called a 'novel.'"

"If we consider rightly," said I, "a poem has always originated without a title, and is that which it is without a title; so that we may imagine the title is not really essential to the matter."

"It is not," said Goethe; "the ancient poems had no titles; but this is a custom of the moderns, from whom also the poems of the ancients obtained titles at a later period. However, this custom is the result of a necessity to name things, and distinguish them from each other, when a literature becomes extensive."

"Here," said Goethe, "you have something new;—read it."

With these words, he handed over to me a translation by Herr Gerhard of a Servian poem. I read it with great pleasure, for the poem was very beautiful, and the translation so simple and clear that one was never disturbed in the contemplation of the object. It was entitled "the Prison-Key." I say nothing of the course of the action, except that the conclusion seemed to me abrupt, and rather unsatisfactory.

"That," said Goethe, "is the beauty of it; for it thus leaves a sting in the heart, and the imagination of the reader is excited to devise every possible case which can follow. The conclusion leaves untold the material for a whole tragedy, but of a kind that has often been done already. On the contrary, that which is set forth in the poem is really new and beautiful, and the poet acted very wisely in delineating this alone, and leaving the rest to the reader. I would willingly insert the poem in 'Kunst und Alterthum,' but it is too long: on the other hand, I have asked Herr Gerard to give me these three in rhyme, which I shall print in the next number. What do you say to this? Only listen."

Goethe read first the song of the old man who loves a young maiden, then the women's drinking song, and finally that animated one beginning "Dance for us, Theodore." He read them admirably, each in a different tone and manner, so that it would not be easy to hear anything more perfect.

We praised Herr Gerhard for having, in each instance, chosen the most appropriate versification and burden, and for having executed all in such an easy and perfect manner, that we could not easily conceive anything better done. "There you see," said Goethe, "what technical practice does for such a talent as Gerhard's; and it is fortunate for him that he has no actual literary profession, but one that daily takes him into practical life. He has, moreover, travelled much in England and other countries; and thus, with his sense for the actual, he has many advantages over our learned young poets.

"If he confines himself to making good translations, he is not likely to produce anything bad; but original inventions demand a great deal, and are difficult matters."

Some reflections were here made upon the productions of our newest young poets, and it was remarked that scarce one of them had come out with good prose. "That is very easily explained," said Goethe: "to write prose, one must have something to say; but he who has nothing to say can still make verses and rhymes, where one word suggests the other, and at last something comes out, which in fact is nothing, but looks as if it were something."

Wednesday, January 31, 1827.

Dined with Goethe. "Within the last few days, since I saw you," said he, "I have read many and various things; especially a Chinese novel, which occupies me still, and seems to me very remarkable."

"Chinese novel!" said I; "that must look strange enough."

"Not so much as you might think," said Goethe; "the Chinamen think, act, and feel almost exactly like us; and we soon find that we are perfectly like them, excepting that all they do is more clear, more pure, and decorous, than with us.

"With them all is orderly, citizen-like, without great passion or poetic flight; and there is a strong resemblance to my 'Hermann and Dorothea,' as well as to the English novels of Richardson. They likewise differ from us, inasmuch as with them external nature is always associated with the human figures. You always hear the goldfish splashing in the pond, the birds are always singing on the bough, the day is always serene and sunny, the night is always clear. There is much talk about the moon, but it does not alter the landscape, its light is conceived to be as bright as day itself; and the interior of the houses is as neat and elegant as their pictures. For instance, 'I heard the lovely girls laughing, and when I got a sight of them, they were sitting on cane chairs.' There you have, at once, the prettiest situation; for cane chairs are necessarily associated with the greatest lightness and elegance. Then there is an infinite number of legends which are constantly introduced into the narrative, and are applied almost like proverbs; as, for instance, one of a girl, who was so light and graceful in the feet, that she could balance herself on a flower without breaking it; and then another, of a young man so virtuous and brave, that in his thirtieth year, he had the honour to talk with the Emperor; then there is another of two lovers who showed such great purity during a long acquaintance, that when they were on one occasion obliged to pass the night in the same chamber, they occupied the time with conversation, and did not approach one another.

"And in the same way, there are innumerable other legends, all turning upon what is moral and proper. It is by this severe moderation in everything that the Chinese Empire has sustained itself for thousands of years, and will endure hereafter.

"I find a highly remarkable contrast to this Chinese novel in the 'Chansons de Beranger,' which have, almost every one, some immoral licentious subject for their foundation, and which would be extremely odious to me if managed by a genius inferior to Beranger; he, however, has made them not only tolerable, but pleasing. Tell me yourself, is it not remarkable that the subjects of the Chinese poet should be so thoroughly moral, and those of the first French poet of the present day be exactly the contrary?"

"Such a talent as Beranger's," said I, "would find no field in moral subjects."

"You are right," said Goethe; "the very perversions of his time have revealed and developed his better nature."

"But," said I, "is this Chinese romance one of their best?"

"By no means," said Goethe; "the Chinese have thousands of them, and had already when our forefathers were still living in the woods.

"I am more and more convinced," he continued, "that poetry is the universal possession of mankind, revealing itself everywhere, and at all times, in hundreds and hundreds of men. One makes it a little better than another, and swims on the surface a little longer than another,—that is all. Herr von Matthisson must not think he is the man, nor must I think that I am the man; but each must say to himself, that the gift of poetry is by no means so very rare, and that nobody need think very much of himself because he has written a good poem.

"But, really, we Germans are very likely to fall too easily into this pedantic conceit, when we do not look beyond the narrow circle which surrounds us. I therefore like to look about me in foreign nations, and advise every one to do the same. National literature is now rather an unmeaning term; the epoch of World literature is at hand, and every one must strive to hasten its approach. But, while we thus value what is foreign, we must not bind ourselves to anything in particular, and regard it as a model. We must not give this value to the Chinese, or the Servian, or Calderon, or the Nibelungen; but if we really want a pattern, we must always return to the ancient Greeks, in whose works the beauty of mankind is constantly represented. All the rest we must look at only historically, appropriating to ourselves what is good, so far as it goes."

I was glad to hear Goethe talk at length on a subject of such importance. The bells of passing sledges allured us to the window, as we expected that the long procession which went out to Belvidere this morning would return about this time.

Goethe, meanwhile, continued his instructive conversation. We talked of Alexander Manzoni; and he told me that Count Reinhard, not long since, saw Manzoni at Paris, where, as a young author of celebrity, he had been well received in society, and that he was now living happily on his estate in the neighbourhood of Milan, with a young family and his mother.

"Manzoni," continued he, "wants nothing except to know what a good poet he is, and what rights belong to him as such. He has too much respect for history, and on this account is always adding notes to his pieces, in which he shows how faithful he has been to detail. Now, though his facts may be historical, his characters are not so, any more than my Thoas and Iphigenia. No poet has ever known the historical characters which he has painted; if he had, he could scarcely have made use of them. The poet must know what effects he wishes to produce, and regulate the nature of his characters accordingly. If I had tried to make Egmont as history represents him, the father of a dozen children, his light-minded proceedings would have appeared very absurd. I needed an Egmont more in harmony with his own actions and my poetic views; and this is, as Clara says, *my* Egmont.

"What would be the use of poets, if they only repeated the record of the historian. The poet must go further, and give us, if possible, something higher and better. All the characters of Sophocles bear something of that great poet's lofty soul; and it is the same with the characters of Shakspeare. This is as it ought to be. Nay, Shakspeare goes farther, and makes his Romans Englishmen; and there too he is right; for otherwise his nation would not have understood him.

"Here, again," continued Goethe, "the Greeks were so great, that they regarded fidelity to historic facts less than the treatment of them by the poet. We have, fortunately, a fine example in Philoctetes, which subject has been treated by all three of the great tragedians, and lastly and best by Sophocles. This poet's excellent play has, fortunately, come down to us entire, while of the Philoctetes of Æschylus and Euripides only fragments have been found, although sufficient to show how they have managed the subject. If time permitted, I would restore these pieces, as I did the Phäeton of Euripides; it would be to me no unpleasant or useless task.

"In this subject the problem was very simple, namely, to bring Philoctetes, with his bow, from the island of Lemnos. But the manner of doing this was the business of the poet, and here each could show the power of his invention, and one could excel another. Ulysses must fetch him; but shall he be known by Philoctetes or not? and if not, how shall he be disguised? Shall Ulysses go alone, or shall he have companions, and who shall they be? In Æschylus, there is no companion; in Euripides, it is Diomed; in Sophocles, the son of Achilles. Then, in what situation is Philoctetes to be found? Shall the island be inhabited or not? and, if inhabited, shall any sympathetic soul have taken compassion on him or not? And so with a hundred other things, which are all at the discretion of the poet, and in the selection and omission of which one may show his superiority in wisdom to another. Here is the grand point, and our present poets should do like the ancients. They should not be always asking whether a subject has been used before, and look to south and north for unheard-of adventures, which are often barbarous enough, and merely make an impression as incidents. But to make something of a simple subject by a masterly treatment requires intellect and great talent, and these we do not find."

Some passing sledges again allured us to the window; but it was not the expected train from Belvedere. We laughed and talked about trivial matters, and then I asked Goethe how the novel was going on.

"I have not touched it of late," said he; "but one incident more must yet take place in the introduction. The lion must roar as the princess passes the booth; upon which some good remarks may be made on the formidable nature of this mighty beast."

"That is a very happy thought," said I; "for thus you gain an introduction, which is not only good and essential in its place, but which gives a greater effect to all that follows. Hitherto the lion has appeared almost too gentle, inasmuch as he has shown no trace of ferocity; but by roaring he at least makes us suspect how formidable he is, and the effect is heightened when he gently follows the boy's flute."

"This mode of altering and improving," said Goethe, "where by continued invention the imperfect is heightened to the perfect, is the right one. But the re-making and carrying further what is already complete—as, for instance, Walter Scott has done with my 'Mignon,'* whom, in addition to her other qualities, he makes deaf and dumb—this mode of altering I cannot commend."

* This allusion is to Fenella in "Peveril of the Peak."

Thursday evening, February 1, 1827.

Goethe told me of a visit which the Crown Prince of Prussia had been making him in company with the Grand Duke. "The princes Charles and William of Prussia," said he, "were also with me this morning. The Crown Prince and Grand Duke stayed nearly three hours, and we talked about many things, which gave me a high opinion of the intellect, taste, knowledge, and way of thinking of these young princes."

Goethe had a volume of the "Theory of Colours" before him. "I still," said he, "owe you an answer with respect to the phenomenon of the coloured shadows; but as this presupposes a great deal, and is connected with much besides, I will not give you an explanation detached from the rest, but rather think it would be better if, on the evenings when we meet, we read through the whole 'Theory of Colours' together. Thus we shall always have a solid subject for discourse; and you yourself will have made the whole theory so much your own, that you will hardly know how you have come by it. What you have already learned begins to live and to be productive within you; and hence I foresee this science will soon be your own property. Now read the first section."

With these words Goethe laid the open book before me. I felt highly pleased with his good intentions towards me. I read the first paragraph respecting the physiological* colours.

"You see," said Goethe, "that there is nothing

* Eckermann says "psychologisch," but this is manifestly a misprint.—*Trans.*

without us that is not also within us, and that the eye, like the external world, has its colours. Since a great point in this science is the decided separation of the objective from the subjective, I have properly begun with the colours which belong to the eye, that in all our perceptions we may accurately distinguish whether a colour really exists externally to ourselves, or whether it is only a seeming colour which the eye itself has produced. I think that I have begun at the right end, by first disposing of the organ by means of which all our perceptions and observations must take place."

I read on as far as those interesting paragraphs where it is taught that the eye has need of change, since it never willingly dwells on the same colour, but always requires another, and that so urgently that it produces colours itself if it does not actually find them.

This remark led our conversation to a great law which pervades all nature, and on which all life and all the joy of life depend. "This," said Goethe, "is the case not only with all our other senses, but also with our higher spiritual nature; and it is because the eye is so eminent a sense, that this law of required change (*Gesetz des geforderten Wechsels*) is so striking and so especially clear with respect to colours. We have dances which please us in a high degree on account of the alternation of major and minor, while dances in only one of these modes weary us at once."

"The same law," said I, "seems to lie at the foundation of a good style, where we like to avoid a sound which we have just heard. Even on the stage a great deal might be done with this law, if it were well applied. Plays, especially tragedies, in which an uniform tone uninterrupted by change prevails, have always something wearisome about them; and if the orchestra plays melancholy depressing music during the *entr'actes* of a melancholy piece, we are tortured by an insupportable feeling, which we would escape by all possible means."

"Perhaps," said Goethe, "the lively scenes introduced into Shakspeare's plays rest upon this 'law of required change,' but it does not seem applicable to the higher tragedy of the Greeks, where, on the contrary, a certain fundamental tone pervades the whole."

"The Greek tragedy," said I, "is not of such a length as to be rendered wearisome by one pervading tone. Then there is an interchange of chorus and dialogue; and the sublime sense is of such a kind that it cannot become fatiguing, since a certain genuine reality, which is always of a cheerful nature, constantly lies at the foundation."

"You may be right," said Goethe; "and it would be well worth the trouble to investigate how far the Greek tragedy is subject to the general 'law of required change.' You see how all things are connected with each other, and how a law respecting the theory of colours can lead to an inquiry into Greek tragedy. We must only take care not to push such a law too far, and make it the foundation for much besides. We shall go more safely if we only apply it by analogy."

We talked of the manner in which Goethe had set forth his theory of colours, deducing the whole from great fundamental laws, and always referring to these the single phenomena; by which method he had made it very comprehensible and fitted for the intellect.

"This may be the case," said Goethe, "and you may praise me on that account; but, nevertheless, the method requires students who do not live amid distractions, and are capable of taking up the matter. Some very clever people have been imbued with my theory of colours; but, unfortunately, they do not adhere to the straight path, but before I am aware of it they turn aside, and follow an idea instead of keeping their eyes properly fixed on the object. Nevertheless, a good head-piece, when really seeking the truth, can always do a great deal."

We talked about the professors who, after they had found a better theory, still talked of that of Newton. "This is not to be wondered at," said Goethe; "such people continue in error because they are indebted to it for their existence. They would otherwise have to learn everything over again, and that would be very inconvenient." "But," said I, "how can their experiments prove the truth when the basis of their doctrine is false?" "They do *not* prove the truth," said Goethe, "nor is such the intention; the only point with these professors is to prove their own opinion. On this account, they conceal all those experiments which would reveal the truth, and show their doctrine was untenable. Then, with respect to the scholars—what do they care for the truth? They, like the rest, are perfectly satisfied if they can prate away about the subject empirically;—that is the whole matter. Men altogether are of a peculiar nature: as soon as a lake is frozen over, they flock to it by hundreds, and amuse themselves on the smooth surface; but which of them thinks of inquiring how deep it is, and what sort of fish are swimming about under the ice? Niebuhr has just discovered a very ancient commercial treaty between Rome and Carthage, from which it appears that all Livy's history respecting the early condition of the Roman people is a mere fable, and that Rome at a very early period was in a far higher state of civilization than Livy represents; but if you imagine that this treaty will occasion a great reform in the manner of teaching Roman history, you are mistaken. Think of the frozen lake. I have learned to know mankind: thus it is, and no otherwise."

"Nevertheless," said I, "you cannot repent of having written your theory of colours, since not only have you laid a firm foundation for this excellent science, but you have produced a model of scientific treatment, which can always be followed in the treatment of similar subjects."

"I do not repent it at all," said Goethe, "though I have expended half a life upon it. Perhaps I might have written half a dozen tragedies more, but that is all, and people enough will come after me to do that.

"After all, you are right; I think, the treatment of the subject is good, there is method in it. In the same manner, I have also written a musical theory, and my metamorphosis of plants is based on the same method of observation and deduction.

"With my metamorphosis of plants, I went on singularly enough. I came to it as Herschel came to his discoveries. Herschel was so poor that he could not purchase a telescope, but was obliged to make one for himself. In this his good fortune consisted; for the home-made telescope was better than any other, and with it he made his great discoveries. I came to botany by the empirical road. I now know well enough, that with respect to the formation of the sexes, the theory went so far into detail that I had not courage to grasp it. This impelled me to pursue the subject in my own way, and to find that which was common to all plants without distinction, and thus I discovered the law of metamorphosis.

"To pursue botany further in detail is not my purpose; this I leave to others who are my superiors in the matter. My only concern was to reduce the phenomena to a general fundamental law.

"Mineralogy has interested me only for two reasons; first, I valued it for its great practical utility, and then I thought to find a document elucidating the primary formation of the world, of which Werner's doctrine gave hopes. Since this science has been turned upside down by the death of that excellent man, I do not proceed further in it, but remain quiet with my own convictions.

"In the theory of colours, I have next to develop the formation of the rainbow. This is an extremely difficult problem, which, however, I hope to solve. On this account, I am glad to go through the theory of colours once more with you, since thus, especially with your interest for the subject, it becomes quite fresh again.

"I have," continued Goethe, "attempted natural science in nearly every department; but, nevertheless, my tendencies have always been confined to such objects as lay terrestrially around me, and could be immediately perceived by the senses. On this account, I have never occupied myself with astronomy, because here the senses are not sufficient, and one must have recourse to instruments, calculations, and mechanics, which require a whole life, and were not in my line.

"If I have done anything with respect to the subjects which lay in my way, I had this advantage, that my life fell in a time that was richer than any other in great natural discoveries. As a child, I became acquainted with Franklin's doctrine of electricity, the law of which he had just discovered. Thus through my whole life, down to the present hour, has one great discovery followed another, so that I was not only directed towards nature in my early years, but my interest in it has been maintained in it ever since.

"Advances such as I could never have foreseen are now made even on paths which I opened, and I feel like one who walks towards the morning dawn, and when the sun rises, is astonished at its brilliancy."

Among the Germans, Goethe here took occasion to mention the names of Carus, D'Alton, and Meyer of Königsberg, with admiration.

"If," continued Goethe, "when the truth was once found, people would not again pervert and obscure it, I should be satisfied; for mankind requires something positive, to be handed down from generation to generation, and it would be well if the positive were also the true. On this account, I should be glad if people came to a clear understanding in natural science, and then adhered to the truth, not *transcending* again after all had been done in the region of the comprehensible. But mankind cannot be at peace, and confusion always returns before one is aware of it.

"Thus they are now pulling to pieces the five books of Moses, and if an annihilating criticism is injurious in anything, it is so in matters of religion; for here everything depends upon faith, to which we cannot return when we have once lost it.

"In poetry, an annihilating criticism is not so injurious. Wolf has demolished Homer, but he has not been able to injure the poem; for this poem has a miraculous power like the heroes of Walhalla, who hew one another to pieces in the morning, but sit down to dinner with whole limbs at noon."

Goethe was in the best humour, and I was delighted to hear him talk once more on such important subjects. "We will quietly keep to the right way," said he, "and let others go as they please; that is, after all, the best plan."

Wednesday, February 7, 1827.

To-day Goethe spoke severely of certain critics, who were not satisfied with Lessing, and made unjust demands upon him. "When people," said he, "compare the pieces of Lessing with those of the ancients, and call them paltry and miserable, what do they mean? Rather pity the extraordinary man for being obliged to live in a pitiful time, which afforded him no better materials than are treated in his pieces; pity him, because in his 'Minna von Barnhelm,' he found nothing better to do than to meddle with the squabbles of Saxony and Prussia. His constant polemical turn, too, resulted from the badness of his time.

In 'Emilia Galeotti,' he vented his pique against princes; in 'Nathan,' against the priests."

Friday, February 16, 1827.

I told Goethe that I lately had been reading Winckelmann's work upon the imitation of Greek works of art, and I confessed that it often seemed to me that Winckelmann was not perfectly clear about his subject.

"You are quite right," said Goethe; "we sometimes find him merely groping about; but what is the great matter, his groping always leads to something. He is like Columbus, when he had not yet discovered the new world, yet had a presentiment of it in his mind. We learn nothing by reading him, but we *become* something.

"Now, Meyer has gone further, and has carried the knowledge of art to its highest point. His history of art is an immortal work; but he would not have become what he is, if, in his youth, he had not formed himself on Winckelmann, and walked in the path which Winckelmann pointed out.

"Thus you see once again what is done for a man by a great predecessor, and the advantage of making a proper use of him."

(Sup.) *Wednesday, February 21, 1827.*

Dined with Goethe. He spoke much, and with admiration, of Alexander von Humboldt, whose work on Cuba and Columbia he had begun to read, and whose views as to the project for making a passage through the Isthmus of Panama appeared to have a particular interest for him. "Humboldt," said Goethe, "has, with a great knowledge of his subject, given other points where, by making use of some streams which flow into the Gulf of Mexico, the end may be perhaps better attained than at Panama. All this is reserved for the future, and for an enterprising spirit. So much, however, is certain, that, if they succeed in cutting such a canal that ships of any burden and size can be navigated through it from the Mexican Gulf to the Pacific Ocean, innumerable benefits would result to the whole human race, civilized and uncivilized. But I should wonder if the United States were to let an opportunity escape of getting such a work into their own hands. It may be foreseen that this young state, with its decided predilection to the West, will, in thirty or forty years, have occupied and peopled the large tract of land beyond the Rocky Mountains. It may, furthermore, be foreseen that along the whole coast of the Pacific Ocean, where nature has already formed the most capacious and secure harbours, important commercial towns will gradually arise, for the furtherance of a great intercourse between China and the East Indies and the United States. In such a case, it would not only be desirable, but almost necessary, that a more rapid communication should be maintained between the eastern and western shores of North America, both by merchant-ships and men-of-war, than has hitherto been possible with the tedious, disagreeable, and expensive voyage round Cape Horn. I therefore repeat, that it is absolutely indispensable for the United States to effect a passage from the Mexican Gulf to the Pacific Ocean; and I am certain that they will do it.

"Would that I might live to see it!—but I shall not. I should like to see another thing,—a junction of the Danube and the Rhine. But this undertaking is so gigantic that I have doubts of its completion, particularly when I consider our German resources. And thirdly, and lastly, I should wish to see England in possession of a canal through the Isthmus of Suez. Would I could live to see these three great works! it would be well worth the trouble to last some fifty years more for the very purpose."

(Sup.) Thursday, March 1, 1827.

Dined with Goethe. He related to me that he had received a communication from Count Sternberg and Zauper, which had given him great pleasure. We then talked a great deal about the theory of colours, the subjective prismatic experiments, and the laws by which the rainbow is formed. He was pleased with my continually increasing interest in these difficult subjects.

(Sup.) Wednesday, March 21, 1827.

Goethe showed me a little book, by Hinrichs, on the nature of antique tragedy. "I have read it with great interest," said he. "Hinrichs has taken the Œdipus and Antigone of Sophocles as the foundation whereon to develop his views. It is very remarkable; and I will lend it to you that you may read it, and that we may be able to converse upon it. I am by no means of his opinion; but it is highly instructive to see how a man of such thoroughly philosophical culture regards a poetical work of art from the point of view peculiar to his school.* I will say no more to-day, that I may not influence your opinion. Only read it, and you will find that it suggests all kinds of thoughts."

(Sup.) Wednesday, March 28, 1827.

I brought back to Goethe the book by Hinrichs, which I had read attentively. I had also gone once more through all the plays of Sophocles, to be in complete possession of my subject.

"Now," said Goethe, "how did you like him? He attacks a matter well—does he not?"

"This book affected me very strangely," said I. "No other book has aroused so many thoughts in me as this; and yet there is none I have so often been disposed to contradict."

"That is exactly the point," said Goethe. "What we agree with leaves us inactive, but contradiction makes us productive."

"His intentions," said I, "appear to me in the highest degree laudable, and he by no means confines himself to the surface of things. But he so often loses himself in refinements and motives—and that in so subjective a manner—that he loses the true aspect of the subject in detail, as well as the survey of the whole; and in such a case one is obliged to do violence both to oneself and the theme to think as he does. Besides, I have often fancied that my organs were not fine enough to apprehend the unusual subtlety of his distinctions."

"If they were philosophically prepared like his," said Goethe, " it would be better. But, to speak

---

* That of Hegel.—*Trans.*

frankly, I am sorry that a man of undoubted innate power from the northern coast of Germany, like Hinrichs, should be so spoilt by the philosophy of Hegel as to lose all unbiassed and natural observation and thought, and gradually to get into an artificial and heavy style, both of thought and expression; so that we find passages in his book where our understanding comes to a stand-still, and we no longer know what we are reading"

"I have fared no better," said I. "Still I have rejoiced to meet with some passages, which have appeared to me perfectly clear and fitted for humanity in general; such, for instance, as his relation of the fable of Œdipus."

"Here," said Goethe, "he has been obliged to confine himself strictly to his subject. But there are in his book several passages in which the thought does not progress, but in which the obscure language constantly moves on the same spot and in the same circle, just like the 'Einmaleins'* of the witch in my 'Faust.' Give me the book again. Of his sixth lecture upon the chorus, I scarcely understood anything. What do you say, for instance, to this passage, which occurs near the end:—

"This realization (*i. e.* of popular life) is, as the true signification thereof,† on this account alone its

---

* This word, which signifies "multiplication table," refers to the arithmetical jargon uttered by the witch in her kitchen.—*Trans.*

† The word "derselben," in the passage as cited, seems to want an antecedent. The reader is requested not to be too critical with this almost unreadable passage, which Goethe only refers to as an instance of obscurity. —*Trans.*

true realization, which as a truth and certainty to itself, therefore constitutes the universally mental certainty, which certainly is at the same time the atoning certainty of the chorus, so that in this certainty alone, which has shown itself as the result of the combined movement of the tragic action, the chorus preserves its fitting relation to the universal popular consciousness, and in this capacity does not merely represent the people, but is that people according to its certainty."

" I think we have had enough of this. What must the English and French think of the language of our philosophers, when we Germans do not understand them ourselves." " And in spite of all this," said I, " we both agree that a noble purpose lies at the foundation of the book, and that it possesses the quality of awakening thoughts."

" His idea of the relation between family and state," said Goethe, " and the tragical conflicts that may arise from them is certainly good and suggestive; still I cannot allow that it is the only right one, or even the best for tragic art. We are indeed all members both of a family and of a state, and a tragical fate does not often befal us which does not wound us in both capacities. Still we might be very good tragical characters, if we were merely members of a family or merely members of a state; for, after all, the only point is to get a conflict which admits of no solution, and this may arise from an antagonistical position in any relation whatever, provided a person has a really natural foundation, and is himself really tragic. Thus Ajax falls a victim to the demon of wounded honour, and Hercules to the demon of jealousy. In neither of these cases is there the least conflict between family piety and political virtue; though this, according to Hinrichs, should be the element of Greek tragedy."

"One sees clearly," said I, "that in this theory he merely had Antigone in his mind. He also appears to have had before his eyes merely the character and mode of action of this heroine, as he makes the assertion that family piety appears most pure in woman, and especially in a sister; and that a sister can love only a brother with perfect purity, and without sexual feeling."

"I should think," returned Goethe, "that the love of sister for sister was still more pure and unsexual. As if we did not know that numerous cases have occurred in which the most sensual inclinations have existed between brother and sister, both knowingly and unknowingly!"

"You must have remarked generally," continued Goethe, "that Hinrichs, in considering Greek tragedy, sets out from the *idea;* and that he looks upon Sophocles as one who, in the invention and arrangement of his pieces, likewise set out from an idea, and regulated the sex and rank of his characters accordingly. But Sophocles, when he wrote his pieces, by no means started from an *idea;* on the contrary, he seized upon some ancient ready-made popular tradition in which a good idea existed, and then only thought of adapting it in the best and most effective manner for the theatre. The Atrides will not allow Ajax to be buried; but as in Antigone the sister struggles for the brother, so in the Ajax the brother struggles for the brother. That the sister takes charge of the unburied

Polyneices, and the brother takes charge of the fallen Ajax, is a contingent circumstance, and does not belong to the invention of the poet, but to the tradition, which the poet followed and was obliged to follow."

"What he says about Creon's conduct," replied I, "appears to be equally untenable. He tries to prove that, in prohibiting the burial of Polyneices, Creon acts from pure political virtue; and since Creon is not merely a man, but also a prince, he lays down the proposition, that, as a man represents the tragic power of the state, this man can be no other than he who is himself the personification of the state itself—namely, the prince; and that of all persons the man as prince must be just that person who displays the greatest political virtue."

"These are assertions which no one will believe," returned Goethe with a smile. "Besides, Creon by no means acts out of political virtue, but from hatred towards the dead. When Polyneices endeavoured to reconquer his paternal inheritance, from which he had been forcibly expelled, he did not commit such a monstrous crime against the state that his death was insufficient, and that the further punishment of the innocent corpse was required.

"An action should never be placed in the category of political virtue which is opposed to virtue in general. When Creon forbids the burial of Polyneices, and not only taints the air with the decaying corpse, but also affords an opportunity for the dogs and birds of prey to drag about pieces torn from the dead body, and thus to defile the altars—an action so offensive both to gods and men is by no means politically virtuous, but on the contrary a political crime. Besides, he has everybody in the play against him. He has the elders of the state, who form the chorus, against him; he has the people at large against him; he has Teiresias against him; he has his own family against him; but he hears not, and obstinately persists in his impiety, until he has brought to ruin all who belong to him, and is himself at last nothing but a shadow."

" And still," said I, " when one hears him speak, one cannot help believing that he is somewhat in the right."

" That is the very thing," said Goethe, " in which Sophocles is a master; and in which consists the very life of the dramatic in general. His characters all possess this gift of eloquence, and know how to explain the motives for their action so convincingly, that the hearer is almost always on the side of the last speaker.

" One can see that, in his youth, he enjoyed an excellent rhetorical education, by which he became trained to look for all the reasons and seeming reasons of things. Still, his great talent in this respect betrayed him into faults, as he sometimes went too far.

" There is a passage in Antigone which I always look upon as a blemish, and I would give a great deal for an apt philologist to prove that it is interpolated and spurious.

" After the heroine has, in the course of the piece, explained the noble motives for her action, and displayed the elevated purity of her soul, she at last, when she is led to death, brings forward a motive which is quite unworthy, and almost borders upon the comic.

"She says that, if she had been a mother, she would not have done, either for her dead children or for her dead husband, what she has done for her brother. For," says she, "if my husband died I could have had another, and if my children died I could have had others by my new husband. But with my brother, the case is different. I cannot have another brother; for since my mother and father are dead, there is no one to beget one.

"This is, at least, the bare sense of this passage, which in my opinion, when placed in the mouth of a heroine going to her death, disturbs the tragic tone, and appears to me very far-fetched,—to savor too much of dialectical calculation. As I said, I should like a philologist to show us that the passage is spurious."

We then conversed further upon Sophocles, remarking that in his pieces he always less considered a moral tendency than an apt treatment of the subject in hand, particularly with regard to theatrical effect.

"I do not object," said Goethe, "to a dramatic poet having a moral influence in view; but when the point is to bring his subject clearly and effectively before his audience, his moral purpose proves of little use, and he needs much more a faculty for delineation and a familiarity with the stage to know what to do and what to leave undone. If there be a moral in the subject, it will appear, and the poet has nothing to consider but the effective and artistic treatment of his subject. If a poet has as high a soul as Sophocles, his influence will always be moral, let him do what he will. Besides, he knew the stage, and understood his craft thoroughly."

"How well he knew the theatre," answered I, "and how much he had in view a theatrical effect, we see in his 'Philoctetes,' and the great resemblance which this piece bears to ' Œdipus, in Colonos,' both in the arrangement and the course of action.

"In both pieces we see the hero in a helpless condition; both are old and suffering from bodily infirmities. Œdipus has, at his side, his daughter as a guide and a prop; Philoctetes has his bow. The resemblance is carried still further. Both have been thrust aside in their afflictions; but when the oracle declares with respect to both of them, that the victory can be obtained with their aid alone, an endeavour is made to get them back again; Ulysses comes to Philoctetes, Creon to Œdipus. Both begin their discourse with cunning and honied words; but when these are of no avail they use violence, and we see Philoctetes deprived of his bow, and Œdipus of his daughter."

"Such acts of violence," said Goethe, "give an opportunity for excellent altercations, and such situations of helplessness excited the emotions of the audience, on which account the poet, whose object it was to produce an effect upon the public, liked to introduce them. In order to strengthen this effect in the Œdipus, Sophocles brings him in as a weak old man, when he still, according to all circumstances, must have been a man in the prime of life. But at this vigorous age, the poet could not have used him for his play; he would have produced no effect, and he therefore made him a weak, helpless old man."

"The resemblance to Philoctetes," continued I, "goes still further. The hero, in both pieces, does not act, but suffers. On the other hand, each of these passive heroes has two active characters against him. Œdipus has Creon and Polyneices, Philoctetes has Neoptolemus and Ulysses; two such opposing characters were necessary to discuss the subject on all sides, and to gain the necessary body and fulness for the piece."

"You might add," interposed Goethe, "that both pieces bear this further resemblance, that we see in both the extremely effective situation of a happy change, since one hero, in his disconsolate situation, has his beloved daughter restored to him, and the other, his no less beloved bow."

The happy conclusions of these two pieces are also similar; for both heroes are delivered from their sorrows: Œdipus is blissfully snatched away, and as for Philoctetes, we are forewarned by the oracle of his cure, before Troy, by Æsculapius.

"When we," continued Goethe, "for our modern purposes, wish to learn how to conduct ourselves upon the theatre, Moliére is the man to whom we should apply.

"Do you know his 'Malade Imaginaire?' There is a scene in it which, as often as I read the piece, appears to me the symbol of a perfect knowledge of the boards. I mean the scene where the 'Malade Imaginaire' asks his little daughter Louison, if there has not been a young man in the chamber of her eldest sister.

"Now, any other who did not understand his craft so well would have let the little Louison plainly tell the fact at once, and there would have been the end of the matter.

"But what various motives for delay are introduced by Moliére into this examination, for the sake of life and effect. He first makes the little Louison act as if she did not understand her father; then she denies that she knows anything; then, threatened with the rod, she falls down as if dead; then, when her father bursts out in despair, she springs up from her feigned swoon with roguish hilarity, and at last, little by little, she confesses all.

"My explanation can only give you a very meagre notion of the animation of the scene; but read this scene yourself till you become thoroughly impressed with its theatrical worth, and you will confess that there is more practical instruction contained in it than in all the theories in the world.

"I have known and loved Moliére," continued Goethe, "from my youth, and have learned from him during my whole life. I never fail to read some of his plays every year, that I may keep up a constant intercourse with what is excellent. It is not merely the perfectly artistic treatment which delights me; but particularly the amiable nature, the highly-formed mind, of the poet. There is in him a grace and a feeling for the decorous, and a tone of good society, which his innate beautiful nature could only attain by daily intercourse with the most eminent men of his age. Of Menander, I only know the few fragments; but these give me so high an idea of him, that I look upon this great Greek as the only man who could be compared to Moliére."

"I am happy," returned I, " to hear you speak so highly of Moliere. This sounds a little different from Herr von Schlegel! I have to-day, with great repugnance, swallowed what he says concerning Moliére in his lectures on dramatic poetry. He quite looks down upon him, as a vulgar buffoon, who has only seen good society at a distance, and whose business it was to invent all sorts of pleasantries for the amusement of his lord. In these low pleasantries, Schlegel admits he was most happy, but he stole the best of them. He was obliged to force himself into the higher school of comedy, and never succeeded in it."

"To a man like Schlegel," returned Goethe, "a genuine nature like Moliere's is a veritable eyesore; he feels that he has nothing in common with him, he cannot endure him. The 'Misanthrope,' which I read over and over again, as one of my most favourite pieces, is repugnant to him; he is forced to praise 'Tartuffe' a little, but he lets him down again as much as he can. Schlegel cannot forgive Moliére for ridiculing the affectation of learned ladies; he feels, probably as one of my friends has remarked, that he himself would have been ridiculed if he had lived with Moliere.

"It is not to be denied," continued Goethe, "that Schlegel knows a great deal, and one is almost terrified at his extraordinary attainments and his extensive reading. But this is not enough. All the learning in the world is still no judgment. His criticism is completely one-sided, because in all theatrical pieces he merely regards the skeleton of the plot and arrangement, and only points out small points of resemblance to great predecessors, without troubling himself in the least as to what the author brings forward of graceful life and the culture of a high soul. But of what use are all the arts of a talent, if we do not find in a theatrical piece an amiable or great personality of the author? This alone influences the cultivation of the people.

"I look upon the manner in which Schlegel has treated the French drama as a sort of recipe for the formation of a bad critic, who is wanting in every organ for the veneration of excellence, and who passes over a sound nature and a great character as if they were chaff and stubble."

"Shakspeare and Calderon, on the other hand," I replied, "he treats justly, and even with decided affection."

"Both," returned Goethe, "are of such a kind that one cannot say enough in praise of them, although I should not have wondered if Schlegel had scornfully let them down also. Thus he is also just to Æschylus and Sophocles; but this does not seem to arise so much from a lively conviction of their extraordinary merit as from the tradition among philologists to place them both very high; for, in fact, Schlegel's own little person is not sufficient to comprehend and appreciate such lofty natures. If this had been the case, he would have been just to Euripides too, and would have gone to work with him in a different manner. But he knows that philologists do not estimate him very highly, and he therefore feels no little delight that he is permitted, upon such high authority, to fall foul of this mighty ancient, and to schoolmaster him as much as he can. I do not deny that Euripides has his faults; but he was always a very respectable competitor with Sophocles and Æschylus. If he did not possess the great earnestness and the severe artistic completeness of his two predecessors, and as a dramatic poet treated things a little more leniently and humanely, he probably knew his Athenians well enough to be aware that the chord which he struck was the right one for his contemporaries. A poet whom Socrates called his friend, whom Aristotle lauded, whom Menander admired, and for whom Sophocles and the city of Athens put on mourning on hearing of his death, must certainly have been something. If a modern man like Schlegel must pick out faults in so great an ancient, he ought only to do it upon his knees."

(Sup.) Sunday, April 1, 1827.

In the evening with Goethe. I conversed with him upon the yesterday's performance of his "Iphigenia," in which Herr Krüger, from the Theatre Royal at Berlin, played Orestes with great applause.

"The piece," said Goethe, "has its difficulties. It is rich in internal but poor in external life: the point is to make the internal life come out. It is full of the most effective means, arising from the various horrors which form the foundation of the piece. The printed words are indeed only a faint reflex of the life which stirred within me during the invention; but the actor must bring us back to this first fire which animated the poet with respect to his subject. We wish to see the vigorous Greeks and heroes, with the fresh sea-breezes blowing upon them, who, oppressed and tormented by various ills and dangers, speak out strongly as their hearts prompt them. But we want none of those feeble, sentimental actors who have only just learned their part by rote, and still less do we want those who are not even perfect in their parts.

"I must confess that I have never succeeded in witnessing a perfect representation of my 'Iphigenia.' That was the reason why I did not go yesterday; for I suffer dreadfully when I have to do with these spectres who do not manifest themselves as they ought."

"You would probably have been satisfied with Orestes as Herr Krüger represented him," said I. "There was such perspicuity in his acting, that nothing could be more comprehensible or tangible than his part: it seemed to comprise everything; and I shall never forget his words and gestures.

"All that belongs to the higher intuition—to the vision in this part, was so brought forward by his bodily movements, and the varying tones of his voice, that one could fancy one saw it with one's own eyes. At the sight of this Orestes, Schiller would certainly not have missed the furies—they were behind him, they were around him.

"The important place where Orestes, awakening from his swoon, believes himself transported to the lower regions, succeeded so as to produce astonishment. We saw the rows of ancestors engaged in conversation: we saw Orestes join them, question them, and become one of their number. We felt ourselves transported into the midst of those blessed persons, so pure and deep was the feeling of the artist, and so great was his power of bringing the impalpable before our eyes."

"You are just the people to be worked upon," said Goethe laughing: "but go on. He appears then to have been really good, and his physical capabilities to have been great."

"His organ," said I, "was clear and melodious, besides being well practised, and therefore capable of the highest flexion and variety. He has at command physical strength and bodily activity in the execution of every difficulty. It seemed that, during his whole life, he had never neglected to cultivate and exercise his body in the most various ways."

"An actor," said Goethe, "should properly go to school to a sculptor and a painter; for, in order to represent a Greek hero, it is necessary for him to study carefully the antique sculptures which have come down to us, and to impress on his mind the natural grace of their sitting, standing, and going. But the merely bodily is not enough. He must also, by diligent study of the best ancient and modern authors, give a great cultivation to his mind. This will not only assist him to understand his part, but will also give a higher tone to his whole being and his whole deportment. But tell me more! What else did you see good in him?"

"It appeared to me," said I, "that he possessed great love for his subject. He had by diligent study made every detail clear to himself, so that he lived and moved in his hero with great freedom; and nothing remained which he had not made entirely his own. Thence arose a just expression and a just accentuation for every word; together with such certainty, that the prompter was for him a person quite superfluous."

"I am pleased with this," said Goethe; "this is as it ought to be. Nothing is more dreadful than when the actors are not masters of their parts, and at every new sentence must listen to the prompter. By this their acting becomes a mere nullity, without any life and power. When the actors are not perfect in their parts in a piece like my 'Iphigenia,' it is better not to play it; for the piece can have success only when all goes surely, rapidly, and with animation. However, I am glad that it went off so well with Krüger. Zelter recommended him to me, and I should have been annoyed if he had not turned out so well as he has. I will have a little joke with him, and will present him with a prettily bound copy of my 'Iphigenia,' with some verses inscribed in reference to his acting."

The conversation then turned upon the 'Antigone' of Sophocles, and the high moral tone prevailing in it; and, lastly, upon the question—how the moral element came into the world?

"Through God himself," returned Goethe, "like everything else. It is no product of human reflection, but a beautiful nature inherent and inborn. It is, more or less, inherent in mankind generally, but to a high degree in a few eminently gifted minds. These have, by great deeds or doctrines, manifested their divine nature; which, then, by the beauty of its appearance, won the love of men, and powerfully attracted them to reverence and emulation."

"A consciousness of the worth of the morally beautiful and good could be attained by experience and wisdom, inasmuch as the bad showed itself in its consequences as a destroyer of happiness, both in individuals and the whole body, while the noble and right seemed to produce and secure the happiness of one and all. Thus the morally beautiful could become a doctrine, and diffuse itself over whole nations as something plainly expressed."

"I have lately read somewhere," answered I, "the opinion that the Greek tragedy had made moral beauty a special object."

"Not so much morality," returned Goethe, "as pure humanity in its whole extent; especially in such positions where, by falling into contact with rude power, it could assume a tragic character. In this region, indeed, even the moral stood as a principal part of human nature.

"The morality of Antigone, besides, was not invented by Sophocles, but was contained in the subject, which Sophocles chose the more readily, as it united so much dramatic effect with moral beauty."

Goethe then spoke about the characters of Creon and Ismene, and on the necessity for these two persons for the development of the beautiful soul of the heroine.

"All that is noble," said he, "is in itself of a quiet nature, and appears to sleep until it is aroused and summoned forth by contrast. Such a contrast is Creon, who is brought in, partly on account of Antigone, in order that her noble nature and the right which is on her side may be brought out by him, partly on his own account, in order that his unhappy error may appear odious to us.

"But, as Sophocles meant to display the elevated soul of his heroine even before the deed, another contrast was requisite by which her character might be developed; and this is her sister Ismene. In this character, the poet has given us a beautiful standard of the commonplace, so that the greatness of Antigone, which is far above such a standard, is the more strikingly visible."

The conversation then turned upon dramatic authors in general, and upon the important influence which they exerted, and could exert, upon the great mass of the people.

"A great dramatic poet," said Goethe, "if he is at the same time productive, and is actuated by a strong noble purpose, which pervades all his works, may succeed in making the soul of his pieces become the soul of the people. I should think that this was something well worth the trouble. From Corneille proceeded an influence capable of forming heroes. This was something for Napoleon, who had need of an heroic people; on which account, he said of Corneille, that if he were still living, he would make a prince of him. A dramatic poet who knows his vocation, should therefore work incessantly at its higher development, in order that his influence on the people may be noble and beneficial.

"One should not study contemporaries and competitors, but the great men of antiquity, whose works have, for centuries, received equal homage and consideration. Indeed, a man of really superior endowments will feel the necessity of this, and it is just this need for an intercourse with great predecessors, which is the sign of a higher talent. Let us study Moliére, let us study Shakspeare, but above all things, the old Greeks, and always the Greeks."

"For highly endowed natures," remarked I, "the study of the authors of antiquity may be perfectly invaluable; but, in general, it appears to have little influence upon personal character. If this were the case, all philologists and theologians would be the most excellent of men. But this is by no means the case; and such connoisseurs of the ancient Greek and Latin authors are able people or pitiful creatures, according to the good or bad qualities which God has given them, or which they have inherited from their father and mother."

"There is nothing to be said against that," returned Goethe; "but it must not, therefore, be said, that the study of the authors of antiquity is entirely without effect upon the formation of character. A worthless man will always remain worthless, and a little mind will not, by daily intercourse with the great minds of antiquity, become one inch greater. But a noble man, in whose soul God has placed the capability for future greatness of character, and elevation of mind, will, by a knowledge of, and familiar intercourse with, the elevated natures of ancient Greeks and Romans, every day make a visible approximation to similar greatness."

(Sup.) Wednesday, April 11, 1827.

I went to day about one o'clock to Goethe, who

had invited me to take a drive with him before dinner. We took the road to Erfurt. The weather was very fine ; the corn-fields on both sides of the way refreshed the eye with the liveliest green. Goethe seemed in his feelings gay and young as the early spring, but in his words old in wisdom.

"I ever repeat it," he began, " the world could not exist, if it were not so simple. This wretched soil has been tilled a thousand years, yet its powers are always the same ; a little rain, a little sun, and each spring it grows green and so forth."

I could make no answer or addition to these words. Goethe allowed his eyes to wander over the verdant fields, and then, turning again to me, continued thus on other subjects :—

"I have been lately reading something odd,—the letters of Jacobi and his friends. This is a remarkable book, and you must read it; not to learn anything from it, but to take a glance into the state of education and literature at a time of which people now have no idea. We see men who are to a certain extent important, but no trace of a similar direction and a common interest ; each one as an isolated being goes his own way, without sympathizing at all in the exertions of others. They seem to me like billiard balls, which run blindly by one another on the green cover, without knowing anything of each other ; and which, if they come in contact, only recede so much the farther from one another."

I smiled at this excellent simile. I asked about the corresponding persons, and Goethe named them to me, with some special remark about each.

"Jacobi was really a born diplomatist, a handsome man of slender figure, elegant and noble mien—who, as an ambassador, would have been quite in his place. As a poet, a philosopher, he had deficiencies.

"His relation to me was peculiar. He loved me personally, without taking interest in my endeavours, or even approving of them: friendship was necessary to bind us together. But my connection with Schiller was very peculiar, because we found the strongest bond of union in our common efforts, and had no need of what is commonly called friendship."

I asked whether Lessing appeared in this correspondence.

"No," said he, "but Herder and Wieland do. Herder, however, did not enjoy such connections; he stood so high that this hollowness could not fail to weary him in the long run. Hamann, too, treated these people with marked superiority of mind.

"Wieland, as usual, appears in these letters quite cheerful and at home. Caring for no opinion in particular, he was adroit enough to enter into all. He was like a reed, moved hither and thither by the wind of opinion, yet always adhering firmly to its root.

"My personal relation to Wieland was always very pleasant, especially in those earlier days when he belonged to me alone. His little tales were written at my suggestion; but, when Herder came to Weimar, Wieland was false to me. Herder took him away from me, for this man's power of personal attraction was very great."

The carriage now began to return. We saw

towards the east many rain-clouds driving one into another.

"These clouds," said I, "threaten to descend in rain every moment. Do you think they could possibly dissipate, if the barometer rose?"

"Yes," said he, "they would be dispersed from the top downwards, and be spun off like a distaff at once. So strong is my faith in the barometer. Nay, I always say and maintain, that if, in the night of the great inundation of Petersburg, the barometer had risen, the waves would not have overflowed.

"My son believes that the moon influences the weather, and you perhaps think the same, and I do not blame you; the moon is so important an orb that we must ascribe to it a decided influence on our earth; but the change of the weather, the rise and fall of the barometer, are not affected by the changes of the moon; they are purely telluric.

"I compare the earth and her atmosphere to a great living being perpetually inhaling and exhaling. If she inhale, she draws the atmosphere to her, so that, coming near her surface, it is condensed to clouds and rain. This state I call water-affirmative (*Wasser-bejahung*). Should it continue an irregular length of time, the earth would be drowned. This the earth does not allow, but exhales again, and sends the watery vapours upwards, when they are dissipated through the whole space of the higher atmosphere, and become so rarified, that not only does the sun penetrate them with his brilliancy, but the eternal darkness of infinite space is seen through as a fresh blue. This state of the atmosphere I call the water-negative (*Wasser-verneinung*).

For as, under the contrary influence, not only water comes profusely from above, but also the moisture of the earth cannot be dried and dissipated,—so, on the contrary, in this state, not only no moisture comes from above, but the damp of the earth itself flies upwards; so that, if this should continue an irregular length of time, the earth, even if the sun did not shine, would be in danger of drying up."

Thus spoke Goethe on this important subject, and I listened to him with great attention.

"The thing is very simple, and I abide by what is simple and comprehensive, without being disturbed by occasional deviations. High barometer, dry weather, east wind; low barometer, wet weather, and west wind; this is the general rule by which I abide. Should wet clouds blow hither now and then, when the barometer is high, and the wind east, or, if we have a blue sky, with a west wind, this does not disturb me, or make me lose my faith in the general rule. I merely observe that many collateral influences exist, the nature of which we do not yet understand.

"I will tell you something, by which you may abide during your future life. There is in nature an accessible and inaccessible. Be careful to discriminate between the two, be circumspect, and proceed with reverence.

"We have already done something, if we only know this in a general way, though it is always difficult to see where the one begins and the other leaves off. He who does not know it torments himself, perhaps his life long, about the inaccessible, without ever coming near the truth. But he who knows it and is wise, will confine himself to the accessible; and, while he traverses this region in every direction, and confirms himself therein, will be able to win somewhat even from the inaccessible, though he must at last confess that many things can only be approached to a certain degree, and that nature has ever something problematical in reserve, which man's faculties are insufficient to fathom."

During this discourse we had returned into the town. Conversation turned upon unimportant subjects, so that those high views could still dwell for a while within me.

We had returned too early for dinner, and Goethe had time to show me a landscape, by Rubens, representing a summer's evening. On the left of the foreground, you saw field-labourers going homewards; in the midst of the picture, a flock of sheep followed their shepherd to the hamlet; a little farther back, on the right, stood a hay-cart, which people were busy in loading; while the horses, not yet put in, were grazing near; afar off, in the meadow and thickets, mares were grazing with their foals, and appearances indicated that they would remain there all night. Several villages and a town bordered the bright horizon of the picture, in which the ideas of activity and repose were expressed in the most graceful manner.

The whole seemed to me put together with such truth, and the details painted with such fidelity, that I said, Rubens must have copied the picture from nature.

"By no means," said Goethe, "so perfect a picture

has never been seen in nature; but we are indebted for its composition to the poetic mind of the painter. Still, the great Rubens had such an extraordinary memory, that he carried all nature in his head, and she was always at his command, in the minutest particulars. Thence comes this truth in the whole, and the details, so that we think it is a mere copy from nature. No such landscapes are painted now-a-days. That way of feeling and seeing nature no longer exists. Our painters are wanting in poetry.

"Then our young talents are left to themselves; they are without living masters, to initiate them into the mysteries of art. Something, indeed, may be learned from the dead, but this is rather a catching of details, than a penetration into the deep thoughts and method of a master."

Frau and Herr von Goethe came in, and we sat down to dinner. The lively topics of the day, such as the theatre, balls, and the court, were lightly discussed; but soon we came to more serious matters, and found ourselves deeply engaged in conversation on the religious doctrines of England.

"You ought, like me," said Goethe, "to have studied church history for fifty years, to understand how all this hangs together. On the other hand, it is highly remarkable to see with what doctrines the Mahometans commence the work of education. As a religious foundation, they confirm their youth in the conviction that nothing can happen to man, except what was long since decreed by an all-ruling divinity. With this they are prepared and satisfied for a whole life, and scarce need anything further.

"I will not inquire what is true or false, useful or pernicious, in this doctrine; but really something of this faith is held in us all, even without being taught. 'The ball on which my name is not written, cannot hit me,' says the soldier in the battle-field; and, without such a belief, how could he maintain such courage and cheerfulness in the most imminent perils? The Christian doctrine, 'No sparrow falls to the ground without the consent of our Father,' comes from the same source, intimating that there is a Providence, which keeps in its eye the smallest things, and without whose will and permission nothing can happen.

"Then the Mahometans begin their instruction in philosophy, with the doctrine that nothing exists of which the contrary may not be affirmed. Thus they practise the minds of youth, by giving them the task of detecting and expressing the opposite of every proposition; from which great adroitness in thinking and speaking is sure to arise.

"Certainly, after the contrary of any proposition has been maintained, doubt arises as to which is really true. But there is no permanence in doubt; it incites the mind to closer inquiry and experiment, from which, if rightly managed, certainty proceeds, and in this alone can man find thorough satisfaction.

"You see that nothing is wanting in this doctrine; that with all our systems, we have got no further; and that, generally speaking, no one can get further."

"You remind me of the Greeks," said I, "who made use of a similar mode of philosophical instruction, as is obvious from their tragedy, which, in its course of action, rests wholly upon contradiction, not one of the speakers ever maintaining any opinion of which the other cannot, with equal dexterity, maintain the contrary."

"You are perfectly right," said Goethe; "and that doubt is brought in which is awakened in the spectator or reader. Thus, at the end, we are brought to certainty by fate, which attaches itself to the moral, and espouses its cause."

We rose from table, and Goethe took me down with him into the garden, to continue our conversation.

"It is remarkable in Lessing," said I, "that in his theoretical writings, for instance, in the 'Laocoon,' he never leads us directly to results, but always takes us by the philosophical way of opinion, counter opinion, and doubt, before he lets us arrive at any sort of certainty. We rather see the operation of thinking and seeking, than obtain great views and great truths that can excite our own powers of thought, and make ourselves productive."

"You are right," said Goethe; "Lessing himself is reported to have said, that if God would give him truth, he would decline the gift, and prefer the labour of seeking it for himself.

"That philosophic system of the Mahometans is a good standard, which we can apply to ourselves and others, to ascertain the degree of mental progress which we have attained.

"Lessing, from his polemical nature, loved best the region of doubt and contradiction. Analysis is his province; and there his fine understanding aided him most nobly. You will find me wholly the reverse. I have always avoided contradictions, have striven to dispel the doubts within me, and have uttered only the results I have discovered."

I asked Goethe which of the new philosophers he thought the highest.

"Kant," said he, "beyond a doubt. He is the one whose doctrines still continue to work, and have penetrated most deeply into our German civilization. He has influenced even you, although you have never read him; now you need him no longer, for what he could give you, you possess already. If you wish, by and by, to read something of his, I recommend to you his 'Critique on the Power of Judgment,' in which he has written admirably upon rhetoric, tolerably upon poetry, but unsatisfactorily on plastic art."

"Has your Excellency ever had any personal connection with Kant?"

"No," he replied; "Kant never took any notice of me, though from my own nature I went a way like his own. I wrote my 'Metamorphosis of Plants' before I knew anything about Kant; and yet it is wholly in the spirit of his doctrine. The separation of subject from object, and further, the opinion that each creature exists for its own sake, and that corktrees do not grow merely that we may stop our bottles—this Kant shared with me, and I rejoiced to meet him on such ground. Afterwards I wrote my 'doctrine of experiment,'* which is to be regarded as

---

* The title of this paper, which appeared in 1793, and is contained in Goethe's works, is "Der Versuch als Vermittler von Object und Subject."
—*Trans.*

criticism upon subject and object, and a mediation of both.

"Schiller was always wont to advise me against the study of Kant's philosophy. He usually said Kant could give me nothing; but he himself studied Kant with great zeal; and I have studied him too, and not without profit."

While talking thus, we walked up and down the garden: the clouds had been gathering; and it began to rain, so that we were obliged to return to the house, where we continued our conversation for some time.

(Sup.) Wednesday, April 18, 1827.

Before dinner, I took a ride with Goethe some distance along the road to Erfurt.

We were met by all sorts of vehicles laden with wares for the fair at Leipsic; also a string of horses, amongst which were some very fine animals.

"I cannot help laughing at the æsthetical folks," said Goethe, "who torment themselves in endeavouring, by some abstract words, to reduce to a conception that inexpressible thing to which we give the name of beauty. Beauty is a primeval phenomenon, which itself never makes its appearance, but the reflection of which is visible in a thousand different utterances of the creative mind, and is as various as nature herself."

"I have often heard it said that nature is always beautiful," said I; "that she causes the artists to despair, because they are seldom capable of reaching her completely."

"I know well," returned Goethe, "that nature often reveals an unattainable charm; but I am by no means of opinion that she is beautiful in all her aspects. Her intentions are, indeed, always good; but not so the conditions which are required to make her manifest herself completely.

"Thus, the oak is a tree which may be very beautiful; but how many favourable circumstances must concur before nature can succeed in producing one truly beautiful! If an oak grow in the midst of a forest, encompassed with large neighbouring trunks, its tendency will always be upwards, towards free air and light; only small, weak branches will grow on its sides, and these will in the course of a century decay and fall off. But if it has at last succeeded in reaching the free air with its summit, it will then rest in its upward tendency, and begin to spread itself from its sides, and form a crown. But it is by this time already past its middle age: its many years of upward striving have consumed its freshest powers, and its present endeavour to put forth its strength by increasing in breadth will not now have its proper results. When full grown, it will be high, strong, and slender stemmed, but still without such a proportion between its crown and its stem as would render it beautiful.

"Again; if the oak grow in a moist, marshy place, and the earth is too nourishing, it will, with proper space, prematurely shoot forth many branches and twigs on all sides: but it will still want the opposing, retarding influences; it will not show itself gnarled, stubborn, and indented, and, seen from a distance, it will have the appearance of a weak tree of the lime species; and it will not be beautiful,—at least, not as an oak.

"If, lastly, it grow upon mountainous slopes, upon poor, stony soil, it will become excessively gnarled and knotty; but it will lack free development: it will become prematurely stunted, and will never attain such perfection that one can say of it, 'there is in that oak something which creates astonishment.'"

I rejoiced at these words. "I saw very beautiful oaks," said I, "when, some years ago, I made short tours from Göttingen into the valley of the Weser. I found them particularly magnificent in the neighbourhood of Höxter."

"A sandy soil, or one mixed with sand," continued Goethe, "where the oak is able to spread its strong roots in every direction, appears to be most favourable; and then it needs a situation where it has the necessary space to feel the effects on all sides of light, sun, rain, and wind. If it grows up snugly sheltered from wind and weather, it becomes nothing; but a century's struggle with the elements makes it strong and powerful, so that, at its full growth, its presence inspires us with astonishment and admiration."

"Cannot one, from these remarks of yours," returned I, "draw a conclusion, and say, 'a creature is beautiful when it has attained the summit of its natural development?'"

"Certainly," returned Goethe; "but still one must first explain what one means by the summit of its natural development."

"I would by that," returned I, "signify the period

of growth in which the character peculiar to any creature appears perfectly impressed on it."

"In that sense," said Goethe, "there would be nothing to object, especially if we add that, for such a perfect development of character, it is likewise requisite that the build of the different members of a creature should be conformable to its natural destination.

"In that case, a marriageable girl, whose natural destiny is to bear and suckle children, will not be beautiful without the proper breadth of the pelvis and the necessary fullness of the breasts. Still, an excess in these respects would not be beautiful, for that would go beyond conformity to an end.

"On this account, we might call some of the saddle-horses which we met a little time ago beautiful, even according to the fitness of their build. It is not merely the elegance, lightness, and gracefulness of their movements, but something more, of which a good horseman and judge of horses alone can speak, and of which we others merely receive the general impression."

"Might we not, on the other hand," said I, "call a cart-horse beautiful, like those strong specimens which we met a little time ago drawing the wagons of the Brabant carriers?"

"Certainly," said Goethe; "and why not? A painter would probably find a far more varied display of all kinds of beauties in the strongly-marked character and powerful development of bone, sinew, and muscle, in such an animal, than in the softer and more equal character of an elegant saddle-horse."

"The main point is," continued Goethe, "that the race is pure, and that man has not applied his mutilating hand. A horse with his mane and tail cut, a hound with cropped ears, a tree from which the strongest branches have been lopped and the rest cut into a spherical form, and, above all, a young girl whose youthful form has been spoiled and deformed by stays, are things from which good taste revolts, and which merely occupy a place in the Philistine's catechism of beauty."

During this and similar conversations, we had returned. We walked about a little in the garden of the house before dinner. The weather was very beautiful; the spring sun had begun to grow powerful, and to bring out all sorts of leaves and blossoms on bushes and hedges. Goethe was full of thought and hopes of a delightful summer.

At dinner we were very cheerful. Young Goethe had read his father's "Helena," and spoke upon it with much judgment and natural intelligence. He showed decided delight at the part conceived in the antique spirit, while we could see that he had not fully entered into the operatic, romantic half.

"You are right," said Goethe; "it is something peculiar. One cannot say that the rational is always beautiful; but the beautiful is always rational, or, at least, ought to be so. The antique part pleases you because it is comprehensible, because you can take a survey of the details, and approach my reason with your own. In the second half, all sorts of understanding and reason are likewise employed and expended; but it is difficult, and requires some study, before the reader can approach the meaning, and with his own reason discover the reason of the author."

Goethe then spoke with much praise and acknowledgement of the poems of Madame Tastu, with which he had been lately occupied.

When the rest had departed, and I also prepared to go, he begged of me to remain a little longer. He ordered a portfolio, with engravings and etchings by Dutch masters, to be brought in.

"I will treat you with something good, by way of dessert," said he. With these words, he placed before me a landscape by Rubens.

"You have," said he, "already seen this picture; but one cannot look often enough at anything really excellent;—besides, there is something very particular attached to this. Will you tell me what you see?"

"I begin from the distance," said I. "I see in the remotest background a very clear sky, as if after sunset. Then, still in the extreme distance, a village and a town, in the light of evening. In the middle of the picture there is a road, along which a flock of sheep is hastening to the village. At the right hand of the picture are several haystacks, and a wagon which appears well laden. Unharnessed* horses are grazing near. On one side, among the bushes, are several mares with their foals, which appear as if they were going to remain out of doors all night. Then, nearer to the foreground, there is a group of large trees;

---

* The original says "harnessed" (angeschirrt), but as this is evidently the same engraving as the one mentioned at p. 389, where the horses are described as "unharnessed" (abgespannt), I assume that "angeschirrt" is a misprint for "abgeschirrt."—*Trans.*

and lastly, quite in the foreground to the left, there are various labourers returning homewards."

"Good," said Goethe, "that is apparently all. But the principal point is still wanting. All these things, which we see represented, the flock of sheep, the wagon with hay, the horses, the returning labourers, —on which side are they lighted?"

"They receive light," said I, "from the side turned to us, and the shadow is thrown into the picture. The returning labourers in the foreground are especially in the light, which produces an excellent effect."

"But how has Rubens produced this beautiful effect?"

"By making these light figures appear on a dark ground," said I.

"But this dark ground," said Goethe, "whence does it arise!" "It is the powerful shadow," said I, "thrown by the group of trees towards the figures." "But how?" continued I, with surprise, "the figures cast their shadows into the picture; the group of trees, on the contrary, cast their's towards the spectator. We have, thus, light from two different sides, which is quite contrary to Nature."

"That is the point," returned Goethe, with a smile. "It is by this that Rubens proves himself great, and shows to the world that he, with a free spirit, stands *above* Nature, and treats her conformably to his high purposes. The double light is certainly a violent expedient, and you certainly say that it is contrary to Nature. But if it is contrary to Nature, I still say it is higher than Nature; I say it is the bold stroke of the master, by which he, in a genial manner, proclaims to the world, that art is not entirely subject to natural necessities, but has laws of its own.

"The artist," continued Goethe, " must, indeed, in his details faithfully and reverently copy nature; he must not, arbitrarily, change the structure of the bones, or the position of the muscles and sinews of an animal, so that the peculiar character is destroyed. This would be annihilating nature. But in the higher regions of artistical production, by which a picture really becomes a picture, he has freer play, and here he may have recourse to *fictions*, as Rubens has done with the double light in this landscape.

"The artist has a twofold relation to nature; he is at once her master and her slave. He is her slave, inasmuch as he must work with earthly things, in order to be understood; but he is her master, inasmuch as he subjects these earthly means to his higher intentions, and renders them subservient.

"The artist would speak to the world through an entirety; however, he does not find this entirety in nature; but it is the fruit of his own mind, or, if you like it, of the aspiration of a fructifying divine breath.

"If we observe this landscape by Rubens only slightly, everything appears as natural to us as if it had been copied exactly from nature. But this is not the case. So beautiful a picture has never been seen in nature, any more than a landscape by Poussin or Claude Lorraine, which appears very natural to us, but which we vainly seek in the actual world."

"Are there not," said I, " bold strokes of artistic

fiction, similar to this double light of Rubens, to be found in literature?"

"We need not go far," said Goethe, after some reflection; "I could show you a dozen of them in Shakspeare. Only take Macbeth. When the lady would animate her husband to the deed, she says,—

"I have given suck," &c.

Whether this be true or not does not appear; but the lady says it, and she must say it, in order to give emphasis to her speech. But in the course of the piece, when Macduff hears of the account of the destruction of his family, he exclaims in wild rage,—

"He has no children!"

These words of Macduff contradict those of Lady Macbeth; but this does not trouble Shakspeare. The grand point with him is the force of each speech; and as the lady, in order to give the highest emphasis to her words, must say 'I have given suck,' so, for the same purpose, Macduff must say 'he has no children.'

"Generally," continued Goethe, "we must not judge too exactly and narrowly of the pencil touches of a painter, or the words of a poet; we should rather contemplate and enjoy a work of art that has been produced in a bold and free spirit, and if possible with the same spirit.

"Thus it would be foolish, if, from the words of Macbeth,—

"Bring forth men children only!" &c.

the conclusions were drawn that the lady was a

young creature who had not yet borne any children. And it would be equally foolish if we were to go still further, and say that the lady must be represented on the stage as a very youthful person.

"Shakspeare by no means makes Macbeth say these words to show the youth of the lady; but these words, like those of Lady Macbeth and Macduff, which I quoted just now, are merely introduced for rhetorical purposes, and prove nothing more than that the poet always makes his character say whatever is proper, effective, and good in each *particular place*, without troubling himself to calculate whether these words may, perhaps, fall into apparent contradiction with some other passage.

"Shakspeare, in writing his pieces, could hardly have thought that they would appear in print, so as to be told over, and compared one with another; he had rather the stage in view when he wrote; he regarded his plays as a lively and moving scene, that would pass rapidly before the eyes and ears upon the stage, not as one that was to be held firmly, and carped at in detail. Hence, his only point was to be effective and significant for the moment."

(Sup.) Tuesday, April 24, 1827.

August Wilhelm von Schlegel is here. Before dinner, Goethe took a drive with him round the Webicht, and this evening gave a great tea party in honour of him, at which Schlegel's fellow-traveller, Doctor Lassen, was present. All in Weimar, of any rank and name, were invited, so that the press in Goethe's room was very great. Herr von Schlegel was quite surrounded by ladies, to whom he showed thin rolled-up strips with Indian idols, as well as the whole text of two great Indian poems, of which no one but himself and Doctor Lassen probably understood anything. Schlegel was dressed with extreme neatness, and had an extremely youthful and blooming appearance, so that some of the assembled guests were pleased to maintain that he appeared not unskilled in the use of cosmetic means.

Goethe drew me to the window. "Now, how does he please you?" "Not better than I expected," returned I. "He is truly, in many respects, no true man," continued Goethe; "but still, one must bear with him a little, on account of his extensive knowledge and great deserts."

(Sup.) Wednesday, April 25th, 1827.

Dined with Goethe and Dr. Lassen. Schlegel had once more gone to dine at the court. Here Lassen displayed great knowledge of Indian poetry, which seemed highly acceptable to Goethe, as he could thus complete his own very deficient knowledge of these things.

In the evening I again spent a few moments with Goethe. He related to me that Schlegel had been with him at twilight, and that they had carried on a very important conversation on historical and literary subjects, which had been very instructive to him. "Only," said he, "one must not expect grapes from thorns, or figs from thistles; for the rest, all is very excellent."

(Sup.) Thursday, May 3rd, 1827.

The highly successful translation of Goethe's dramatic works, by Stapfer, was noticed by Monsieur J. J. Ampere in the "Parisian Globe" of last year, in a manner no less excellent, and this affected Goethe so agreeably that he very often recurred to it, and expressed his great obligations to it.

"Ampère's point of view is a very high one," said he. "When German critics on similar occasions start from philosophy, and in the consideration and discussion of a poetical production proceed in a manner that what they intend as an elucidation is only intelligible to philosophers of their own school, while for other people it is far more obscure than the work upon which they intended to throw a light, M. Ampère, on the contrary, shows himself quite practical and popular. Like one who knows his profession thoroughly, he shows the relation between the production and the producer, and judges the different poetical productions as different fruits of different epochs of the poet's life.

"He has studied most profoundly the changing course of my earthly career, and of the condition of my mind, and has had the faculty of seeing what I have not expressed, and what, so to speak, could only be read between the lines. How truly has he remarked that, during the first ten years of my official and court life at Weimar, I scarcely did anything; that despair drove me to Italy; and that I there, with new delight in producing, seized upon the history of Tasso, in order to free myself, by the treatment of this agreeable subject, from the painful and troublesome impressions and recollections of my life at Weimar. He therefore very happily calls Tasso an elevated Werther.

"Then, concerning Faust, his remarks are no less clever, since he not only notes, as part of myself, the gloomy, discontented striving of the principal character, but also the scorn and the bitter irony of Mephistophiles."

In this, and a similar spirit of acknowledgment, Goethe often spoke of M. Ampere. We took a decided interest in him; we endeavoured to picture to ourselves his personal appearance, and, if we could not succeed in this, we at least agreed that he must be a man of middle age to understand the reciprocal action of life and poetry on each other. We were, therefore, extremely surprised when M. Ampère arrived in Weimar a few days ago, and proved to be a lively youth, some twenty years old; and we were no less surprised when, in the course of further intercourse, he told us that the whole of the contributors to the "Globe," whose wisdom, moderation, and high degree of cultivation we had often admired, were only young people like himself.

"I can well comprehend," said I, "that a person may be young and may still produce something of importance—like Merimee, for instance, who wrote excellent pieces in his twentieth year; but that any one at so early an age should have at his command such a comprehensive view, and such deep insight, as to attain such mature judgment as the gentlemen of the 'Globe,' is to me something entirely new."

"To you, in your Heath,"* returned Goethe, "it has not been so easy; and we others also, in Cen-

* This doubtless refers to the Heath country in which Eckermann was born.—*Trans.*

tral Germany, have been forced to buy our little wisdom dearly enough. Then we all lead a very isolated miserable sort of life! From the people, properly so called, we derive very little culture. Our talents and men of brains are scattered over the whole of Germany. One is in Vienna, another in Berlin, another in Königsberg, another in Bonn or Düsseldorf —all about a hundred miles apart from each other, so that personal contact and personal exchange of thought may be considered as rarities. I feel what this must be, when such men as Alexander von Humboldt come here, and in one single day lead me nearer to what I am seeking, and what I require to know, than I should have done for years in my own solitary way.

"But now conceive a city like Paris, where the highest talents of a great kingdom are all assembled in a single spot, and by daily intercourse, strife, and emulation, mutually instruct and advance each other; where the best works, both of nature and art, from all the kingdoms of the earth, are open to daily inspection;—conceive this metropolis of the world, I say, where every walk over a bridge or across a square recalls some mighty past, and where some historical event is connected with every corner of a street. In addition to all this, conceive not the Paris of a dull, spiritless time, but the Paris of the nineteenth century, in which, during three generations, such men as Moliére, Voltaire, Diderot, and the like, have kept up such a current of intellect as cannot be found twice in a single spot on the whole world, and you will comprehend that a man of talent like Ampère, who has grown up amid such abundance, can easily be something in his four-and-twentieth year."

"You said just now," said Goethe, "that you could well understand how any one in his twentieth year could write pieces as good as those of Mérimée. I have nothing to oppose to this; and I am, on the whole, quite of your opinion that good productiveness is easier than good judgment in a youthful man. But in Germany, one had better not, when so young as Mérimée, attempt to produce anything so mature as he has done in his pieces of 'Clara Gazul.' It is true, Schiller was very young when he wrote his 'Robbers,' his 'Love and Intrigue,' his 'Fiesco;' but, to speak the truth, all three pieces are rather the utterances of an extraordinary talent than signs of mature cultivation in the author. This, however, is not Schiller's fault, but rather the result of the state of culture of his nation, and the great difficulty which we all experience in assisting ourselves on our solitary way.

"On the other hand, take up Béranger. He is the son of poor parents, the descendant of a poor tailor; at one time a poor printer's apprentice, then placed in some office with a small salary: he has never been to a classical school or university; and yet his songs are so full of mature cultivation, so full of wit and the most refined irony, and there is such artistic perfection and masterly handling of the language, that he is the admiration, not only of France, but of all civilized Europe.

"But imagine this same Béranger—instead of being born in Paris, and brought up in this metropolis of the world — the son of a poor tailor in Jena or Weimar, and let him commence his career, in an equally miserable manner, in such small places, and ask yourself what fruit would have been produced by this same tree grown in such a soil and in such an atmosphere.

"Therefore, my good friend, I repeat that, if a talent is to be speedily and happily developed, the great point is that a great deal of intellect and sound culture should be current in a nation.

"We admire the tragedies of the ancient Greeks; but, to take a correct view of the case, we ought rather to admire the period and the nation in which their production was possible than the individual authors; for though these pieces differ a little from each other, and though one of these poets appears somewhat greater and more finished than the other, still, taking all things together, only one decided character runs through the whole.

"This is the character of grandeur, fitness, soundness, human perfection, elevated wisdom, sublime thought, pure, strong intuition, and whatever other qualities one might enumerate. But when we find all these qualities, not only in the dramatic works that have come down to us, but also in lyrical and epic works, in the philosophers, the orators, and the historians, and in an equally high degree in the works of plastic art that have come down to us, we must feel convinced that such qualities did not merely belong to individuals, but were the current property of the nation and the whole period.

"Now, take up Burns. How is he great, except

through the circumstance that the whole songs of his predecessors lived in the mouth of the people,—that they were, so to speak, sung at his cradle; that, as a boy, he grew up amongst them, and the high excellence of these models so pervaded him that he had therein a living basis on which he could proceed further? Again, why is he great, but from this, that his own songs at once found susceptible ears amongst his compatriots; that, sung by reapers and sheaf-binders, they at once greeted him in the field; and that his boon-companions sang them to welcome him at the alehouse? Something was certainly to be done in this way.

"On the other hand, what a pitiful figure is made by us Germans! Of our old songs—no less important than those of Scotland—how many lived among the people in the days of my youth? Herder and his successors first began to collect them and rescue them from oblivion; then they were at least printed in the libraries. Then, more lately, what songs have not Bürger and Voss composed! Who can say that they are more insignificant or less popular than those of the excellent Burns? but which of them so lives among us that it greets us from the mouth of the people?—they are written and printed, and they remain in the libraries, quite in accordance with the general fate of German poets. Of my own songs, how many live? Perhaps one or another of them may be sung by a pretty girl to the piano; but among the people, properly so called, they have no sound. With what sensations must I remember the time when passages from Tasso were sung to me by Italian fishermen!

"We Germans are of yesterday. We have indeed been properly cultivated for a century; but a few centuries more must still elapse before so much mind and elevated culture will become universal amongst our people that they will appreciate beauty like the Greeks, that they will be inspired by a beautiful song, and that it will be said of them, 'it is long since they were barbarians.'"

(Sup.) Friday, May 4, 1827.

A grand dinner at Goethe's, in honour of Ampère and his friend Stapfer. The conversation was loud, cheerful, and varied. Ampère told Goethe a great deal about Mérimée, Alfred de Vigny, and other talents of importance. A great deal also was said about Béranger, whose inimitable songs are daily in Goethe's thoughts. There was a discussion as to whether Béranger's cheerful amatory songs or his political ones merited the preference; whereupon Goethe expressed his opinion that, in general, a purely poetical subject is as superior to a political one as the pure everlasting truth of nature is to party spirit.

"However," continued he, "Beranger has, in his political poems, shown himself the benefactor of his nation. After the invasion of the allies, the French found in him the best organ for their suppressed feelings. He directed their attention by various recollections to the glory of their arms under the Emperor, whose memory still lives in every cottage, and whose great qualities the poet loved, without desiring a continuance of his despotic sway. Now, under the Bourbons, he does not seem too comfortable. They are, indeed, a degenerate race; and the Frenchman of the present day desires great qualities upon the throne, although he likes to take part in the government, and put in his own word."

After dinner the company dispersed in the garden, and Goethe beckoned me to take a drive round the wood, on the road to Tiefurt.

Whilst in the carriage he was very pleasant and affable. He was glad that he had formed so pleasant an intimacy with Ampère, promising himself, as a result, the fairest consequences with respect to the acknowledgment and diffusion of German literature in France.

"Ampère," continued he, "stands indeed so high in culture that the national prejudices, apprehensions, and narrow-mindedness of many of his countrymen lie far behind him; and in mind he is far more a citizen of the world than a citizen of Paris. But I see a time coming when there will be thousands in France who think like him."

(Sup.) Sunday, May 6, 1827.

A second dinner party at Goethe's, to which the same people came as the day before yesterday. Much was said about "Helena" and "Tasso." Goethe related to us that in the year 1797, he had formed the plan of treating the tradition concerning Tell as an epic poem in hexameters.

"In the same year," said he, "I visited the small cantons, and the lake of the four cantons, and this charming, magnificent, grand nature made once more such an impression upon me, that it induced me to represent in a poem the variety and richness of so incomparable a landscape. But, in order to throw more charm, interest, and life into my representation, I considered it good to people this highly-striking spot with equally striking human figures, for which purpose the tradition concerning Tell appeared to me admirably fitted.

"I pictured Tell to myself as a heroic man, possessed of native strength, but contented with himself, and in a state of childish unconsciousness. He traverses the canton as a carrier, and is everywhere known and beloved, everywhere ready with his assistance. He peacefully follows his calling, providing for his wife and child, and not troubling himself who is lord or who is serf.

"Gessler, on the contrary, I pictured to myself as a tyrant; but as one of the comfortable sort who occasionally does good when it suits him, and occasionally harm when it suits him, and to whom the people, with its weal and woe, is as totally indifferent as if it did not exist.

"The higher and better qualities of human nature, on the contrary, the love of native soil, the feeling of freedom and security under the protection of the laws of the country, the feeling, moreover, of the disgrace of being subjugated, and occasionally ill-treated, by a foreign debauchee, and lastly, strength of mind matured to a determination to throw off so obnoxious a yoke,—all these great and good qualities I had shared between the well-known noble-minded men, Walter Fürst, Stauffacher, Winkelried, and others; and these were my proper heroes, my higher powers, acting with consciousness, whilst Tell and Gessler, though occasionally brought into action, were, upon the whole, rather figures of a passive nature.

"I was quite full of this beautiful subject, and was already humming my hexameters. I saw the lake in the quiet moonlight, illuminated mists in the depth of the mountains. I then saw it in the light of the loveliest morning sun—a rejoicing and a life in wood and meadow. Then I described a storm,—a thunder-storm, which swept from the hollows over the lake. Neither was there any lack of the stillness of night, nor of secret meetings approached by bridges.

"I related all this to Schiller, in whose soul my landscapes and my acting figures formed themselves into a drama. And as I had other things to do, and the execution of my design was deferred more and more, I gave up my subject entirely to Schiller, who thereupon wrote his admirable play."

We were pleased with this communication, which was interesting to us all. I remarked that it appeared to me as if the splendid description of sunrise, in the first scene of the second act of "Faust," written in *terza rima*, was founded upon the recalled impressions of the lake of the four cantons.

"I will not deny," said Goethe, "that these contemplations proceed from that source; nay, without the fresh impressions of those wonderful scenes, I could never have conceived the subject of that *terza rima*. But that is all which I have coined from the gold of my Tell-localities. The rest I left to Schiller, who, as we know, made the most beautiful use of it."

The conversation now turned upon "Tasso," and the idea which Goethe had endeavoured to represent by it.

"Idea!" said Goethe, "as if I knew anything about it. I had the life of Tasso, I had my own life; and whilst I brought together two odd figures with their peculiarities, the image of Tasso arose in my mind, to which I opposed, as a prosaic contrast, that of Antonio, for whom also I did not lack models. The further particulars of court life and love affairs were at Weimar as they were in Ferrara; and I can truly say of my production, *it is bone of my bone, and flesh of my flesh.*

"The Germans are, certainly, strange people. By their deep thoughts and ideas, which they seek in everything and fix upon everything, they make life much more burdensome than is necessary. Only have the courage to give yourself up to your impressions, allow yourself to be delighted, moved, elevated, nay, instructed and inspired for something great; but do not imagine all is vanity, if it is not abstract thought and idea.

"Then they come and ask, 'What idea I meant to embody in my Faust?' as if I knew myself, and could inform them. *From heaven, through the world, to hell,* would indeed be something; but this is no idea, only a course of action. And further, that the devil loses the wager, and that a man, continually struggling from difficult errors towards something better, should be redeemed, is an effective, and to many, a good enlightening thought; but it is no idea which lies at the foundation of the whole, and of every individual scene. It would have been a fine thing, indeed, if I had strung so rich, varied, and highly diversified a life as I have brought to view in Faust upon the slender string of one pervading idea.

"It was, in short," continued Goethe, "not in my line, as a poet, to strive to embody anything *abstract*. I received in my mind impressions, and those of a sensual, animated, charming, varied, hundredfold kind, just as a lively imagination presented them ; and I had, as a poet, nothing more to do than artistically to round off and elaborate such views and impressions, and by means of a lively representation so to bring them forward that others might receive the same impression in hearing or reading my representation of them.

"If I still wished, as a poet, to represent any idea, I would do it in short poems, where a decided unity could prevail, and where a complete survey would be easy, as, for instance, in the Metamorphosis of Animals, that of the plants, the poem ' Bequest' (Vermächtniss), and many others. The only production of greater extent, in which I am conscious of having laboured to set forth a pervading idea, is probably my ' Wahlverwandtschaften.' This novel has thus become comprehensible to the understanding; but I will not say that it is therefore better. I am rather of the opinion, that the more incommensurable, and the more incomprehensible to the understanding, a poetic production is, so much the better it is."

(Sup.) Tuesday, May 15, 1827.

Herr von Holtey, from Paris, has been here for some time, and has been very well received everywhere, on account of his person and talent. A very friendly intimacy has also been formed between him and Goethe, and his family.

Goethe has for some days been drawn into his garden, where he is very happy with his quiet activity. I called upon him there to-day, with Herr von Holtey and Count Schulenburg, the former of whom took his leave, in order to go to Berlin with Ampere.

Wednesday, June 20, 1827.

The family table was covered for five; the rooms were vacant and cool, which was very pleasant, considering the great heat. I went into the spacious room next the dining-hall, where are the worked carpet and the colossal bust of Juno.

After I had walked up and down alone for a short time, Goethe soon came in from his work-room, and greeted me in his cordial manner. He seated himself on a chair by the window. "Take a chair too," said he, "and sit down by me; we will talk a little before the others arrive. I am glad that you have become acquainted with Count Sternberg at my house; he has departed, and I am now once more in my wonted state of activity and repose."

"The present appearance and manner of the Count," said I, "seemed to me very remarkable, as well as his great attainments. Whatever the conversation turned on, he was always at home, and talked about everything with the greatest ease, though with profundity and circumspection."

"Yes," said Goethe, "he is a highly remarkable man, and his influence and connections in Germany are very extensive. As a botanist, he is known throughout

Europe by his 'Flora Subterranea,' and he also stands high as a mineralogist. Do you know his history?"

"No," said I, "but I should like to hear something about him. I saw him as a Count and a man of the world, and also a person profoundly versed in various branches of science. This is a riddle I should like to see solved."

Goethe told me that the Count in his youth had been destined for the priesthood, and had commenced his studies at Rome; but that afterwards, when Austria had withdrawn certain favours he had gone to Naples. Goethe then proceeded, in the most profound and interesting manner, to set forth a remarkable life, which would have adorned the "Wanderjahre," but which I do not feel I can repeat here. I was delighted to listen to him, and thanked him with all my soul. The conversation now turned upon the Bohemian schools, and their great advantages, especially for a thorough æsthetic culture.

Frau von Goethe, young Goethe, and Fräulein Ulrica now came in, and we sat down to table. The conversation was gay and varied, the pietists of some cities in Northern Germany being a subject to which we often reverted. It was remarked that these pietistical separations had destroyed the harmony of whole families.

I was able to give an instance of the kind, having nearly lost an excellent friend because he could not convert me to his opinions. He, as I stated, was thoroughly convinced that good works and one's own merits are of no avail, and that man can only win favour with the divinity by the grace of Christ.

"A female friend," observed Frau von Goethe, "said something of the sort to me; but even now I scarcely know what is meant by grace and what by good works."

"According to the present course of the world, in conversing on all such topics," said Goethe, "there is nothing but a medley; and perhaps none of you know whence it comes. I will tell you. The doctrine of good works—namely, that man, by good actions, legacies, and beneficent institutions, can avoid the penalty of sin, and rise in the favour of God—is Catholic. But the reformers, out of opposition, rejected this doctrine, and declared, in lieu of it, that man must seek solely to recognise the merits of Christ, and become a partaker of his grace; which, indeed, leads to good works. But, nowadays, all this is mingled together, and nobody knows whence a thing comes."

I remarked, more in thought than openly, that difference of opinion in religious matters had always sown dissension among men, and made them enemies; nay, that the first murder had been caused by a difference in the mode of worshipping God. I said that I had lately been reading Byron's "Cain," and had been particularly struck by the third act, and the manner in which the murder is brought about.

"It is, indeed, admirable," said Goethe. "Its beauty is such as we shall not see a second time in the world."

"Cain," said I, "was at first prohibited in England; but now everybody reads it, and young English travellers usually carry a complete Byron with them."

"It was folly," said Goethe; "for, in fact, there is nothing in the whole of Cain which is not taught by the English bishops themselves."

The Chancellor was announced. He came in and sat down with us at table. Goethe's grandchildren, Walter and Wolfgang, also came in, jumping one after the other. Wolf pressed close to the Chancellor.

"Bring your album," said Goethe, "and show the Chancellor your princess, and what Count Sternberg wrote for you."

Wolf sprang up and brought the book. The Chancellor looked at the portrait of the princess, with the verses annexed by Goethe. Turning over the leaves, he came to Zelter's inscription, and read aloud, *Lerne gehorchen* ("Learn to obey").

"Those are the only rational words in the whole book," said Goethe, laughing; "as, indeed, Zelter is always majestic and to the point. I am now looking over his letters with Riemer; and they contain invaluable things. Those letters which he has written me on his travels are especially of worth; for he has, as a sound architect and musician, the advantage that he can never want interesting subjects for criticism. As soon as he enters a city, the buildings stand before him, and tell him their merits and their faults.

"Then the musical societies receive him at once, and show themselves to the master with their virtues and their defects. If a short-hand writer could but have recorded his conversations with his musical scholars, we should possess something quite unique in its way. In such matters is Zelter great and genial, and always hits the nail on the head."

Thursday, July 5, 1827.

Towards evening, I met Goethe in the Park, returning from a ride. As he passed he beckoned to me to come and see him. I went immediately to his house, where I found Coudray. Goethe alighted, and we went up the steps with him. We sat down to the round table in the so-called Juno-room, and had not talked long before the Chancellor came in and joined us. The conversation turned on political subjects—Wellington's embassy to St. Petersburg, and its probable consequences, Capo d'Istria, the delayed liberation of Greece, the restriction upon the Turks to Constantinople, and the like.

We talked, too, of Napoleon's times, especially about the Duke d'Enghien, whose incautious revolutionary conduct was much discussed.

We then came to more pacific topics, and Wieland's tomb at Osmannstedt was a fruitful subject of discourse. Coudray told us that he was engaged with an iron enclosure of the tomb. He gave us a clear notion of his intention by drawing the form of the iron-railing on a piece of paper.

When the Chancellor and Coudray departed, Goethe asked me to stay with him a little while. "For one who, like me, lives through ages," said he, "it always seems odd when I hear about statues and monuments. I can never think of a statue erected in honour of a distinguished man without already seeing it cast down and trampled upon by future warriors. Already I see Coudray's iron-railing about Wieland's grave forged into horse-shoes, and shining under the feet of future cavalry; and I may even say that I have witnessed such a case at Frankfort. Wieland's grave is, besides, much too near the Ilm; the stream in less than a hundred years will have so worn the shore by its sudden turn, that it will have reached the body."

We had some good-humoured jests about the terrible inconstancy of earthly things, and then, returning to Coudray's drawing, were delighted with the delicate and strong strokes of the English pencils, which are so obedient to the draughtsman, that the thought is conveyed immediately to the paper, without the slightest loss. This led the conversation to drawing, and Goethe showed me a fine one, by an Italian master, representing the boy Jesus in the temple with the doctors; he then showed me an engraving after the finished picture on this subject; and many remarks were made, all in favour of drawings.

"I have lately been so fortunate," said he, "as to buy, at a reasonable rate, many excellent drawings by celebrated masters. Such drawings are invaluable, not only because they give, in its purity, the mental intention of the artist, but because they bring immediately before us the mood of his mind at the moment of creation. In every stroke of this drawing of the boy Jesus in the temple, we perceive the great clearness, and quiet, serene resolution, in the mind of the artist; and this beneficial mood is extended to us while we contemplate the work. The arts of painting and sculpture have, moreover, the great advantage that they are purely objective, and attract us without violently exciting our feelings. Such a work either speaks to us not at all, or in a very decided manner. A poem, on the other hand, makes a far more vague impression, exciting in each hearer different emotions, according to his nature and capacity."

"I have," said I, "been lately reading Smollett's excellent novel of 'Roderick Random.' It gave me almost the same impression as a good drawing. It is a direct representation of the subject, without a trace of a leaning towards the sentimental; actual life stands before us as it is, often repulsive and detestable enough, yet, as a whole, giving a pleasant impression on account of the decided reality."

"I have often heard the praises of 'Roderick Random,' and believe what you say of it, but have never read it. Do you know Johnson's 'Rasselas?' Just read it, and tell me what you think of it."

I promised to do so.

"In Lord Byron," said I, "I frequently find passages which merely bring objects before us, without affecting our feelings otherwise than the drawing of a good painter. 'Don Juan' is, especially, rich in such passages."

"Yes," said Goethe, "here Lord Byron was great; his pictures have an air of reality, as lightly thrown off as if they were improvised. I know but little of 'Don Juan,' but I remember passages from his other poems, especially sea scenes, with a sail peeping out here and there, which are quite invaluable, for they make us seem to feel the sea-breeze blowing."

"In his 'Don Juan,'" said I, "I have particularly admired the representation of London, which his careless verses bring before our very eyes. He is not very scrupulous whether an object is poetical or not; but he seizes and uses all just as they come before him, down to the wigs in the haircutter's window, and the men who fill the street-lamps with oil."

"Our German æsthetical people," said Goethe, "are always talking about poetical and unpoetical objects; and, in one respect, they are not quite wrong; yet, at bottom, no real object is unpoetical, if the poet knows how to use it properly."

"True," said I; "and I wish this view were adopted as a general maxim."

We then spoke of the "Two Foscari," and I remarked that Byron drew excellent women.

"His women," said Goethe, "are good. Indeed, this is the only vase into which we moderns can pour our ideality; nothing can be done with the men. Homer has got all beforehand in Achilles and Ulysses, the bravest and the most prudent."

"There is something terrible in the 'Foscari,'" I continued, "on account of the frequent recurrence of the rack. One can hardly conceive how Lord Byron could dwell so long on this torturing subject, for the sake of the piece."

"That sort of thing," said Goethe, "was Byron's element; he was always a self-tormentor; and hence such subjects were his darling theme, as you see in all his works, scarce one of which has a cheerful subject. But the execution of the 'Foscari' is worthy of great praise—is it not?"

"Admirable!" said I; "every word is strong, significant, and subservient to the aim; indeed, generally speaking, I have hitherto found no weak lines in Byron. I always fancy I see him issuing from the sea-waves, fresh, and full of creative power. The more I read him, the more I admire the greatness of his talent; and I think you were quite right to present him with that immortal monument of love in 'Helena.'"

"I could not," said Goethe, "make use of any man as the representative of the modern poetical era except him, who undoubtedly is to be regarded as the greatest genius of our century. Again, Byron is neither antique nor romantic, but like the present day itself. This was the sort of man I required. Then he suited me on account of his unsatisfied nature and his warlike tendency, which led to his death at Missolonghi. A treatise upon Byron would be neither convenient nor advisable; but I shall not fail to pay him honour and to point him out at proper times."

Goethe spoke further of "Helena," now it had again become a subject of discourse. "I at first intended a very different close," said he. "I modified it in various ways, and once very well, but I will not tell you how. Then this conclusion with Lord Byron and Missolonghi was suggested to me by the events of the day, and I gave up all the rest. You have observed the character of the chorus is quite destroyed by the mourning song: until this time it has remained thoroughly antique, or has never belied its girlish nature; but here of a sudden it becomes nobly reflecting, and says things such as it has never thought or could think."

"Certainly," said I, "I remarked it; but, since I

have seen Rubens's landscape with the double shadow, and have got an insight into the idea of fiction, such things do not disturb me. These little inconsistencies are of no consequence, if by their means a higher degree of beauty is obtained. The song had to be sung, somehow or other; and as there was no other chorus present, the girls were forced to sing it."

"I wonder," said Goethe, laughing, "what the German critics will say? Will they have freedom and boldness enough to get over this? Understanding will be in the way of the French; they will not consider that the imagination has its own laws, to which the understanding cannot, and should not, penetrate.

"If imagination did not originate things which must ever be problems to the understanding, there would be but little for the imagination to do. It is this which separates poetry from prose; in which latter understanding always is, and always should be, at home."

I was pleased with this important remark, which I treasured up. I now took leave, for it was ten o'clock. We had been sitting without candles; the clear summer evening shining from the north over the Ettersberg.

Monday evening, July 9, 1827.

I found Goethe alone, examining the plaster casts which had been taken from the Stosch cabinet. "My Berlin friends," said he, "have had the kindness to send me this whole collection to look at. I am already acquainted with most of these fine things; but now I see them in the instructive arrangement of Winckelmann. I use his description, and consult him in cases where I myself am doubtful."

We had not long talked before the Chancellor came in and joined us. He told us the news from the public papers, and, among other things, the story of a keeper of a menagerie, who, out of a longing for lion's flesh, had killed a lion, and dressed a large piece of him.

"I wonder," said Goethe, " he did not rather try an ape ; that would have been a tender, relishing morsel."

We talked of the ugliness of these beasts, remarking that they were the more unpleasant the more they were like men.

"I do not understand," said the Chancellor, "how princes can keep these animals near them, and, indeed, take pleasure in them."

"Princes," said Goethe, "are so much tormented by disagreeable men, that they regard these more disagreeable animals as a means of balancing the other unpleasant impressions. We common people naturally dislike apes and the screaming of parrots, because we see them in circumstances for which they were not made. If we could ride upon elephants among palm-trees, we should there find apes and parroquets quite in their place, perhaps pleasant. But, as I said, princes are right to drive away one repulsive thing with something still more repulsive.

"On this point," said he, "a scrap of verse occurs to me, which perhaps you do not remember :—

> If men should ever beasts become,
> Bring only brutes into your room,
> And less disgust you 'll surely feel :
> We all are Adam's children still.*

The Chancellor turned the conversation on the pre-

* An anecdote which follows here is purposely omitted.—*Trans.*

sent state of the opposition, and the ministerial party at Paris, repeating, almost word for word, a powerful speech, which an extremely bold democrat had made against the minister, in defending himself before a court of justice. We had an opportunity once more to marvel at the happy memory of the Chancellor. There was much conversation upon this subject, and especially upon the censure of the press, between Goethe and the Chancellor; the theme proved fertile, Goethe showing himself, as usual, a mild aristocrat, and his friend, as usual, apparently taking his ground on the side of the people.

"I have no fears for the French," said Goethe; "they stand upon such a height from a world-historical point of view, that their mind cannot by any means be suppressed. The law restraining the press, can have only a beneficial effect, especially as its limitations concern nothing essential, but are only against personalities. An opposition which has no bounds is a flat affair, while limits sharpen its wits, and this is a great advantage. To speak out an opinion directly and coarsely is only excusable when one is perfectly right; but a party, for the very reason that it is a party, cannot be wholly in the right; therefore the indirect method in which the French have ever been great models is the best. I say to my servant plainly, 'Hans, pull off my boots,' and he understands; but if I am with a friend, and wish the service from him, I must not speak so bluntly, but must find some pleasant, friendly way, to ask him to perform this kind office. This necessity excites my mind; and, for the same reason as I have said, I like some restraint upon the press. The French have always had the reputation of being the most *spirituel* of nations, and they ought to preserve it. We Germans speak out our opinions without ceremony, and have not acquired much skill in the indirect mode.

"The parties at Paris would be still greater than they are, if they were more liberal and free, and understood each other better than they do. They stand upon a higher grade, from a world-historical point of view than the English; whose parliament consists of strong opposing powers, which paralyze one another, and where the great penetration of an individual has a difficulty in working its way, as we see by Canning, and the many annoyances which beset that great statesman."

We rose to go, but Goethe was so full of life that the conversation was continued a while standing. At last he bid us an affectionate farewell, and I accompanied the Chancellor home to his residence. It was a beautiful evening, and we talked much of Goethe as we went along, especially repeating his remark that an unlimited opposition becomes a flat affair.

Sunday, July 15, 1827.

I went at eight o'clock this evening to see Goethe, whom I found just returned from his garden.

"See what lies there?" said he; "a romance, in three volumes; and by whom, think you? by Manzoni."

I looked at the books, which were very handsomely bound, and inscribed to Goethe. "Manzoni is industrious," said I. "Yes, there is movement there," said Goethe.

"I know nothing of Manzoni," said I, "except his ode to Napoleon, which I lately read again in your translation, and have admired to a high degree. Each strophe is a picture."

"You are right," said Goethe, "the ode is excellent; but do you find any one who speaks of it in Germany? It might as well not have existed, although it is the best poem which has been made upon the subject."

Goethe continued reading the English newspapers, with which I had found him engaged when I came in. I took up that volume of Carlyle's translation of "German Romance" which contains Musæus and Fouqué. The Englishman, who is intimately acquainted with our literature, had prefixed to every translation a memoir and a criticism of the author. I read that upon Fouqué, and remarked with pleasure that the biography was written with much thought and profundity, and that the critical point of view, from which this favourite author was to be contemplated, was indicated with great understanding, and a tranquil, mild penetration into poetic merits. At one time, the clever Englishman compares Fouqué to the voice of a singer, which has no great compass, and but few notes, but those few are good and beautifully melodious. To illustrate his meaning further, he takes a simile from ecclesiastical polity, saying that Fouqué does not hold in the poetic church, the place of a bishop or dignitary of the first rank, but rather satisfies himself with the duties of a chaplain, and looks very well in this humble station.

While I was reading this, Goethe had gone into the

back chamber. He sent his servant, who invited me to come to him there.

"Sit down," said he, "and let us talk a while. A new translation of Sophocles has just arrived. It reads well, and seems to be excellent; I will compare it with Solger. Now, what say you to Carlyle?"

I told him what I had been reading upon Fouqué.

"Is not that very good?" said Goethe. "Ay, there are clever people over the sea, who know us and can appreciate us.

"In other departments," continued Goethe, "there is no lack of good heads even among us Germans. I have been reading in the Berlin Register, the criticism of an historian upon Schlosser, which is very great. It is signed by Heinrich Leo, a person of whom I never heard, but about whom we must inquire. He stands higher than the French, which, from an historical point of view, is saying something. They stick too much to the real, and cannot get the ideal into their heads; the German has this quite at his command. Leo has admirable views upon the castes of India. Much is said of aristocracy and democracy; but the whole affair is simply this: in youth, when we either possess nothing, or know not how to value tranquil possession, we are democrats; but, when in a long life we have acquired property, we wish not only to be secure of it ourselves, but also that our children and grandchildren shall be secure of inheriting it, and quietly enjoying it. Therefore, in old age, we are always aristocrats, to whatever opinions we may have been inclined in youth. Leo speaks with a great deal of thought upon this point.

"We are weakest in the æsthetic department, and may wait long before we meet such a man as Carlyle. It is pleasant to see that intercourse is now so close between the French, English, and Germans, that we shall be able to correct one another. This is the greatest use of a world-literature, which will show itself more and more.

"Carlyle has written a life of Schiller, and judged him as it would be difficult for a German to judge him. On the other hand, we are clear about Shakspeare and Byron, and can, perhaps, appreciate their merits better than the English themselves."

Wednesday, July 18, 1827.

"I must announce to you," was Goethe's first salutation at dinner, "that Manzoni's novel soars far above all that we know of the kind. I need say to you nothing more, except that the interior life—all that comes from the soul of the poet, is absolutely perfect; and that the outward—the delineation of localities, and the like, is in no way inferior. That is saying something." I was astonished and pleased to hear this. "The impression in reading," continued Goethe, "is such, that we are constantly passing from emotion to admiration, and again from admiration to emotion; so that we are always subject to one of those great influences; higher than this, I think, one cannot go. In this novel we have first seen what Manzoni is. Here his perfect interior is exhibited, which he had no opportunity to display in his dramatic works. I will now read the best novel by Sir Walter Scott,—perhaps Waverley, which I do not yet know,—and I shall see how

Manzoni will come out in comparison with this great English writer.

"Manzoni's internal culture here appears so high, that scarcely anything can approach it. It satisfies us like perfectly ripe fruit. Then, in his treatment and exhibition of details, he is as clear as the Italian sky itself."

"Has he any marks of sentimentality?" said I.

"None at all," replied Goethe; "he has sentiment, but is perfectly free from sentimentality; his feeling for every situation is manly and genuine; but I will say no more to-day. I am still in the first volume; soon you shall hear more."

Saturday, July 21, 1827.

When I came into Goethe's room this evening, I found him reading Manzoni's novel.

"I am in the third volume already," said he, as he laid aside the book, "and am thus getting many new thoughts. You know Aristotle says of tragedy, 'It must excite fear, if it is to be good.' This is true, not only of tragedy, but of many other sorts of poetry. You find it in my 'Gott und die Bayadere.' You find it in every good comedy, even in the 'Sieben Mädchen in Uniform' (Seven Girls in Uniform), as we do not know how the joke will turn out for the dear creatures.

"This fear may be of two sorts; it may exist in the shape of alarm (*Angst*), or in that of uneasiness (*Bangigkeit*). The latter feeling is awakened when we see a moral evil threatening, and gradually overshadowing, the personages, as, for instance, in the 'Elective Affinities;' but alarm is awakened, in reader or spectator, when the personages are threatened with physical danger, as, for instance, in the 'Galley Slave,' and in 'Der Freyschütz;'—nay, in the scene of the Wolf's-glen, not only alarm, but a sense of annihilation, is awakened in the spectators. Now, Manzoni makes use of this alarm with wonderful felicity, by resolving it into emotion, and thus leading us to admiration. The feeling of alarm is necessarily of a material character, and will be excited in every reader; but that of admiration is excited by a recognition of the writer's skill, and only the connoisseur will be blessed with this feeling. What say you to these æsthetics of mine? If I were younger, I would write something according to this theory, though perhaps not so extensive a work as this of Manzoni.

"I am now really curious to know what the gentlemen of the 'Globe' will say to this novel. They are clever enough to perceive its excellences; and the whole tendency of the work is so much grist to the mill of these liberals, although Manzoni has shown himself very moderate. Nevertheless, the French seldom receive a work with such pure kindliness as we; they cannot readily adapt themselves to the author's point of view, but, even in the best, always find something which is not to their mind, and which the author should have done otherwise."

Goethe then described to me some parts of the novel, in order to show me in what spirit it was written.

"There are four things," said he, "which have contributed especially to the excellence of Manzoni's works. First, he is an excellent historian, and, consequently, gives his inventions a depth and dignity which raise them far above what are commonly called novels. Secondly, the Catholic religion is favourable to him, giving him many poetical relations, which he could not have had as a Protestant. Thirdly, it is to the advantage of the book that the author has suffered much in revolutionary collisions, which, if they did not affect him, have wounded his friends, and sometimes ruined them. Fourthly, it is in favour of this novel that the scene is laid in the charming country near Lake Como, which has been stamped on the poet's mind, from youth upwards, and which he therefore knows by heart. Hence arises also that distinguishing merit of the work—its distinctness and wonderful accuracy in describing localities."

Monday, 23rd July, 1827.

When I asked for Goethe, about eight o'clock this evening, I heard that he had not yet returned from the garden. I therefore went to meet him, and found him in the park, sitting on a bench in the shade of the lindens; his grandson, Wolfgang, at his side. He seemed glad to see me, and motioned me to sit down by him. We had no sooner exchanged salutations, than the conversation again turned upon Manzoni.

"I told you lately," Goethe began, "that the historian had been of great use to the poet in this novel; but now, in the third volume, I find that the historian hurts the poet, for Signor Manzoni throws off at once the poet's mantle, and stands for some time as a naked historian. This happens in his descriptions of war, famine, and pestilence—things which are repulsive, and are now made insufferable by the circumstantial details of a dry chronicle.

"The German translator must seek to avoid this fault; he must get rid of a great part of the war and famine, and two-thirds of the plague, so as only to leave what is necessary to carry on the action. If Manzoni had had at his side a friendly adviser, he might easily have shunned this fault; but, as a historian, he had too great a respect for reality. This gives him trouble even in his dramatic works, where, however, he helps himself through by adding the superfluous historical matter in the shape of notes. Here, however, he could not get rid of his historical furniture in the same manner. This is very remarkable. Nevertheless, as soon as the persons of the romance reappear, the poet stands once more before us in all his glory, and compels us to our accustomed admiration."

We rose and directed our steps towards the house.

"You will hardly understand," said Goethe, "how a poet like Manzoni, capable of such admirable compositions, could even for a moment sin against poetry. Yet the cause is simple—it is this: Manzoni, like Schiller, was a born poet; but our times are so bad, that the poet can find no nature fit for his use in the human life which surrounds him. To build himself up, Schiller seized on two great subjects, philosophy and history; Manzoni, on history alone. Schiller's 'Wallenstein' is so great, that there is nothing else like it of the same sort; yet you will find that even these two powerful helpers—history and philosophy—have injured various parts of the work, and hinder a purely poetical success. And so Manzoni suffers from too great a load of history."

"Your excellency," said I, "speaks great things, and I am happy in hearing you."

"Manzoni," said Goethe, "helps us to good thoughts."

He was proceeding with his remarks, when the

Chancellor met us at the gate of Goethe's house-garden, and the conversation was then interrupted. He joined us as a welcome friend, and we accompanied Goethe up the little stairs, through the chamber of busts, into the long saloon, where the curtains were let down, and two lights were burning on the table near the window. We sat down by the table, and Goethe and the Chancellor talked upon subjects of another kind.

(Sup.) Wednesday, July 25, 1827.

Goethe has lately received a letter from Walter Scott, which has given him great pleasure. He shewed it to me to-day, and as the English handwriting was very illegible to him, he begged me to translate the contents to him. It appears that Goethe had first written to the renowned English poet, and that this letter was in reply.

"I feel myself highly honoured," writes Walter Scott, "that any of my productions should have been so fortunate as to attract the attention of Goethe, to the number of whose admirers I have belonged since the year 1798, when, notwithstanding my slight knowledge of the German language, I was bold enough to translate into English the ' Götz von Berlichingen.' In this youthful undertaking, I had quite forgotten that it is not enough to feel the beauty of a work of genius, but that one must also thoroughly understand the language in which it is written before one can succeed in making such beauty apparent to others. Nevertheless, I still set some value on that youthful effort, because it at least shows that I knew how to choose a subject which was worthy of admiration.

"I have often heard of you, through my son-in-law,

Lockhart, a young man of literary eminence, who, some years before he became connected with my family, had the honour of being introduced to the father of German literature. It is impossible that you should recollect every individual of the great number of those who feel themselves urged to pay you their respects; but I believe no one is more heartily devoted to you than that young member of my family.

"My friend Sir John Hope, of Pinkie, has lately had the honour of seeing you, and I hoped to write to you by him; I afterwards took this liberty through two of his relations, who designed to travel over Germany; but illness prevented them putting their project into execution, so that after two or three months my letter returned to me. I also, at an earlier period, dared to seek Goethe's acquaintance, and that before the flattering notice which he has been so kind as to take of me.

"It is highly gratifying to all admirers of genius to know that one of the greatest European models enjoys a fortunate and honourable retreat, at an age when he sees himself respected in so remarkable a manner. Poor Lord Byron's destiny did not grant him so fortunate a lot, since it carried him off in the prime of life, and cut short all that had been hoped and expected from him. He esteemed himself fortunate in the honour which you paid him, and felt how much he was indebted to a poet to whom all the writers of the present generation owe so much, that they feel themselves bound to look up to him with child-like veneration.

"I have taken the liberty of requesting MM. Treuttel and Würtz to send to you my attempt at a biography of that remarkable man who for so many years had so terrible an influence in the world which he governed. Besides, I do not know whether I am not under some obligation to him, inasmuch as he made me carry arms for twelve years, during which time I served in a corps of our militia, and, in spite of a long standing lameness, became a good horseman, huntsman, and shot. These good qualities have latterly a little forsaken me; rheumatism, that sad torment of our northern climate, having affected my limbs. However, I do not complain; for I see my sons join in the pleasures of the chase, since I have been obliged to give them up.

"My eldest son has a squadron of hussars, which is a great deal for a young man of five-and-twenty. My younger son has lately taken the degree of Bachelor of Arts at Oxford, and is now going to spend some months at home, before he enters into the world. As it has pleased God to take their mother from me, my youngest daughter manages my domestic affairs. My eldest daughter is married, and has a family of her own.

"This is the domestic condition of a man concerning whom you have so kindly inquired. For the rest, I possess enough to live quite as I wish, notwithstanding some very heavy losses. I inhabit a stately old mansion, where every friend of Goethe's will at all times be welcome. The hall is filled with armour, which would even have suited Jaxthausen; a large bloodhound guards the entrance.

"I have, however, forgotten him who contrived that people should not forget him while alive. I hope you will pardon the faults of the work, whilst you consider that the author was animated by the wish to treat the memory of this extraordinary man as sincerely as his island prejudices would allow.

"As this opportunity of writing to you has suddenly and accidentally been afforded me by a traveller, and admits of no delay, I have not time to say more, excepting that I wish you a continuance of good health and repose, and subscribe myself, with the most sincere and deepest esteem,

"WALTER SCOTT."

"Edinburgh, July 9, 1827."

Goethe was, as I said, delighted with this letter. He was, however, of opinion that it paid him so much respect that he must put a great deal to the account of the courtesy of a man of rank and refined cultivation.

He then mentioned the good and affectionate manner in which Walter Scott spoke of his family connections, which pleased him highly, as a sign of brotherly confidence.

"I am really quite impatient," continued he, "for his 'Life of Napoleon,' which he announces to me. I hear so many contradictions and vehement protestations concerning the book, that I am already certain it will, in any case, be very remarkable."

I asked about Lockhart, and whether he still recollected him.

"Perfectly well!" returned Goethe. "His personal appearance makes so decided an impression that one cannot easily forget him. From all I hear from Englishmen, and from my daughter-in-law, he must be a young man from whom great things in literature are to be expected.

"I almost wonder that Walter Scott does not say a word about Carlyle, who has so decided a German tendency that he must certainly be known to him.

"It is admirable in Carlyle that, in his judgment of our German authors, he has especially in view the mental and moral core as that which is really influential. Carlyle is a moral force of great importance. There is in him much for the future, and we cannot foresee what he will produce and effect."

Monday, September 24, 1827.

I went with Goethe to Berka. We drove off soon after eight o'clock; the morning was very beautiful. The road is up-hill at first, and, as there was nothing in the scenery worth looking at, Goethe talked on literary subjects. A well-known German poet had lately passed through Weimar, and shown Goethe his album.

"You cannot imagine what stuff it contains," said Goethe. "All the poets write as if they were ill, and the whole world were a lazaretto. They all speak of the woe and the misery of this earth, and of the joys of a hereafter; all are discontented, and one draws the other into a state of still greater discontent. This is a real abuse of poetry, which was given to us to hide the little discords of life, and to make man contented with the world and his condition. But the present generation is afraid of all such strength, and only feels poetical when it has weakness to deal with.

"I have hit on a good word," continued Goethe, "to tease these gentlemen. I will call their poetry 'Lazaretto-poetry,' and I will give the name of Tyrtæan-poetry to that which not only sings war-songs, but also arms men with courage to undergo the conflicts of life."

Goethe's words received my full assent.

At the bottom of the carriage lay a basket made of

rushes, with two handles, which attracted my attention. "I brought it with me from Marienbad," said Goethe, "where there are baskets of the sort of every variety of size, and I am so accustomed to it that I cannot travel without it. You see when it is empty it folds up, and occupies but little room, but when it is full it stretches out very wide, and holds more than you would imagine. It is soft and pliant, and, at the same time, so tough and strong that the heaviest things can be carried in it."

"It has a very picturesque and even an antique appearance," said I.

"You are right," said Goethe; "it does approach the antique character, since it is not only as fit for its purpose as possible; but it has the simplest and most pleasing form, so that we may say it stands on the highest point of perfection. During my mineralogical excursions in the Bohemian mountains, I have found it especially serviceable; now, it contains our breakfast. If I had a hammer, I should not lack an opportunity to-day to knock off a piece here and there, and bring home the basket full of stones."

We had now reached the heights, and had a free prospect towards the hills behind which Berka lies. A little to the left we saw into the valley which leads to Hetschburg, and where, on the other side of the Ilm, is a hill, which now turned towards us its shadowy side, and, on account of the vapours of the valley which hovered before it, seemed blue to my eye. I looked at the same spot through my glass, and the blue was obviously diminished. I observed this to Goethe. "Thus you see," said I, "what a great part the subject plays with these purely objective colours; a weak eye increases the density, while a sharpened one drives it away, or, at any rate, makes it diminish."

"Your remark is perfectly just," said Goethe; "a good telescope dispels the blue tint of the most distant mountains. The subject is, in all the phenomena, far more important than is supposed. Even Wieland knew this very well, for he was wont to say, 'One could easily amuse people, if they were only amusable.'"

We laughed at the pleasant meaning of these words. We had, in the mean while, descended the little valley where the road passes over a roofed wooden bridge, under which the rain-torrents, which flow down to Hetschburg, had made a channel, which was now dry. Highway labourers were employed in setting up against the bridge some reddish sandstones, which attracted Goethe's attention. At about a stone's throw over the bridge, where the road goes gradually up the hill which separates the traveller from Berka, Goethe bade the coachman stop.

"We will get out here," said he, "and see whether we shall not relish a little breakfast in the open air."

We got out and looked about us. The servant spread a napkin upon a four-cornered pile of stones, such as usually lie by the road-side, and brought the osier basket from the carriage, out of which he took roast partridges, new wheaten rolls, and pickled cucumbers. Goethe cut a partridge, and gave me half; I ate, standing up and walking about. Goethe had seated himself on the corner of a heap of stones. The coldness of the stones, on which the night-dew was still resting, must hurt him, I thought, and I expressed my anxiety. Goethe, however, assured me it would not hurt him at all, and then I felt quite tranquil, regarding it as a new token of the inward strength he must feel. In the mean while, the servant had brought a bottle of wine from the carriage, and filled for us.

"Our friend Schütze," said Goethe, "is quite right to fly to the country every week; we will take pattern by him, and if this fine weather continues for a while, this shall not be our last excursion."

I was rejoiced by this assurance.

I passed, afterwards, with Goethe, a most interesting day, partly in Berka, partly in Tonndorf. He was inexhaustible in intellectual communications, and talked much of the second part of "Faust," on which he was just beginning to work in earnest; I therefore lament so much the more, that nothing is noted down in my journal beyond this introduction.

END OF VOL. I.

London: Printed by STEWART & MURRAY, Old Bailey.